DEVELOPING OUTCOMES-BASED ASSESSMENT FOR LEARNER-CENTERED EDUCATION

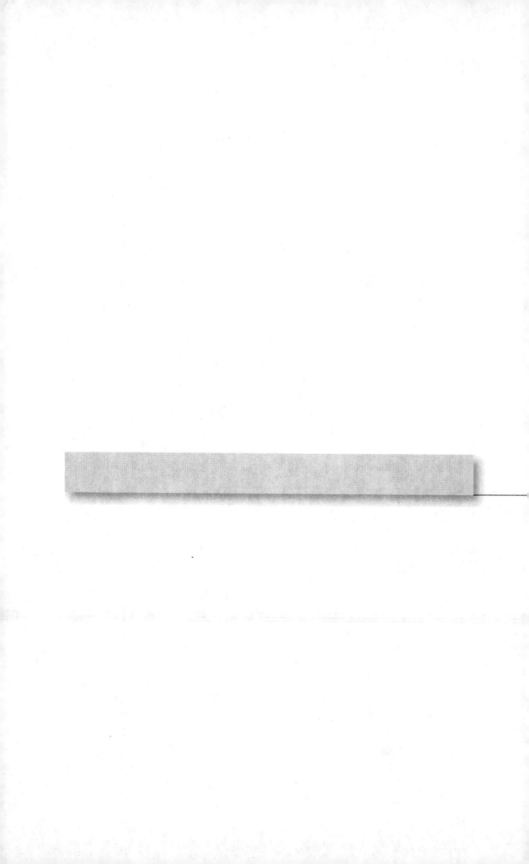

DEVELOPING OUTCOMES-BASED ASSESSMENT FOR LEARNER-CENTERED EDUCATION

A Faculty Introduction

Amy Driscoll and Swarup Wood

STERLING, VIRGINIA

Sty/us

COPYRIGHT © 2007 BY
STYLUS PUBLISHING, LLC.

Published by Stylus Publishing, LLC
22883 Quicksilver Drive
Sterling, Virginia 20166-2102

Library of Congress Cataloging-in-Publication-Data
Driscoll, Amy.
Developing outcomes-based assessment for learner-centered
education : a faculty introduction / Amy Driscoll and
Swarup Wood.—1st ed.
p.   cm.
ISBN 1-57922-194-7 (cloth : alk. paper)—ISBN 1-57922-195-
5 (pbk. : alk. paper)
1. Educational tests and measurements—United States. 2.
Competency-based education—United States. I. Wood,
Swarup, 1962- II. Title.
LB3051.D665 2007
378.1'664—dc22   2006031890

ISBN: 978 1 57922 194 2 (Cloth)
ISBN: 978 1 57922 195 9 (Paper)

Printed in Canada

All first editions printed on acid-free paper
that meets the American National Standards Institute
Z39-48 Standard.

Bulk Purchases

Quantity discounts are available for use in workshops
and for staff development.
Call 1-800-232-0223

First Edition, 2007

10   9   8   7   6   5   4   3   2

This book of stories, insights, and shared expertise is dedicated to our faculty colleagues at California State University Monterey Bay. Together we learned about and experimented with outcomes-based education and its dynamic assessment model. These faculty colleagues, whose work we describe and share in the pages that follow, inspired our commitment to learner-centered education. Consistently they asked the most important questions:

What does this mean for students?
How will this improve student learning?
How can students have a voice in this?
What will this contribute to the student learning process?

The successes that we describe in this book are their successes. We honor and appreciate their excellent pedagogy and curriculum. And we urge their continued dedication to the processes that we describe and to those innovations that faculty create in future years.

This book is also dedicated to our families and friends. *From Swarup*: To Chris, Erin, and Madeleine, you are the extraordinary teachers of my life's richest lessons. *From Amy*: To Rich for your gentle and loving encouragement.

We both acknowledge and appreciate the enthusiasm of our publisher John von Knorring, who provided wonderful encouragement with his attention to this book; the contributions of Stacey Malone for the accuracy of this book; and the help of Holly Fairbank, our copyeditor, and Judy Coughlin, our production manager.

CONTENTS

WHY DEVELOP OUTCOMES FOR ASSESSMENT AND LEARNING?

Why Not?

Story: Difficult Beginnings

In the beginning . . . a group of faculty leaders met with the provost and expressed the need for help with a new model—outcomes-based education (OBE)—perhaps a director of some type. "We need someone who can help us understand how this outcomes-based model works. . . . We're going round and round and have too much else to do." The campus was new, and everything including the curriculum was being created from scratch. A director of teaching, learning, and assessment was found and hired and even supported with a million-dollar grant (yes, $1,000,000) for assessment work. A building was identified, the new Teaching, Learning, and Assessment Center; a staff person was provided; and materials and resources were made abundantly available.

For a year after the director's arrival, a puzzling but not surprising phenomenon occurred. Faculty members were friendly and welcoming, interested in workshops and information on teaching and learning, but their interactions went flat and they backed away when assessment came up. Puzzled and frustrated as the year went on, the director tried a number of strategies to entice faculty to work on assessment, always with offers of money in a grant or a project to compensate for their time. After all, there was a commitment to being an outcomes-based institution, and the grant was there for the spending.

The isolation and loneliness continued. One day, as a large group of faculty attended a seminar on technology-assisted instruction, a young faculty member approached the director. This faculty member was casually dressed—Hawaiian shirt and shorts—and admitted to being a part-time chemistry instructor.

"I am starting to understand teaching and learning better, and I recently got a glimpse of how assessment could affect my teaching. I honestly don't know anything about assessment but I think that it could teach me about my teaching," he said. He then continued, "I would like to work with you."

As the director, I was temporarily speechless but soon accepted with boundless enthusiasm and encouragement, adding, "We have plenty of money to support you."

I wasn't about to lose this one interested participant.

This story sounds like fiction—all that money, resources, a building, even a stated commitment of the institution. It's not fiction, and the reality was that all of those factors didn't make a dent in faculty resistance and distance. The literature on assessment would have predicted faculty members' likely disengagement and should have alerted me to the reality that they are motivated by intrinsic factors, not extrinsic or monetary factors. In this story, the faculty had been struggling with course and program planning and related assessment for three years prior to my arrival but were understandably reluctant to share their progress out of defensiveness or lack of confidence. When asked about support or resources for their early efforts, they described occasional workshops on outcomes-based assessment amid the exhaustive work of opening a new university with almost no advance planning. It was not surprising that my new colleagues were hesitant to question their assessment strategies, to permit a review of their outcomes, or to acknowledge what that one lone faculty member had admitted: "I don't know anything about assessment."

Our Approach to This Book and Outcomes-Based Assessment

The previous events took place at California State University Monterey Bay (CSUMB) 10 years ago. This book on outcomes-based assessment is written by that director, Amy Driscoll (also the author of this chapter), and the lone faculty member, Swarup Wood, now a tenured chemistry professor and chair of the General Education Faculty Learning Communities. Our approach in this book is unique in that we discuss the topic of outcomes-based assessment from those two perspectives: an administrative standpoint with the entire campus as context, provided by Amy; and a faculty standpoint with individual courses as context, provided by Swarup. The pages represent a synthesis of our memories, our awakenings, our mistakes, our reflections, and our advice. This straightforward book addresses the essential question of "how to." It is not an "Assessment for Dummies" book. It is complicated and comprehensive—addressing two themes for outcomes-based assessment. The first theme addresses that intrinsic motivation of faculty as it focuses on student-centered learning and improvement of curriculum and pedagogy through outcomes-based assessment. The second theme continues with an approach that promotes faculty trust through constructive dialogue and collaboration.

One final admission about how we are writing this book is appropriate here. Like Parker Palmer (1998) in *The Courage to Teach,* we believe in putting ourselves in that "dangerous intersection of personal and public life" (p. 17) when we talk about our professional work, especially teaching, learning, and assessment. We begin by abandoning traditional academic writing style and by ignoring a long-held bias against subjectivity, especially in work about assessment. We embrace "I" and "we" and reveal our passions, our biases, and ourselves. We want our writing to both teach and mentor our readers. We ask you not to notice just the knowledge, the practices, and the ideas that we bring to the teaching/mentoring role, but to be aware of yourself as you read. Parker Palmer urges us to attend even more closely to "the truths and the heart that you reclaim, or discover or reveal" (p. 21), We urge you to do the same as you join us in this book.

A First Question: Why Now?

Our observations of faculty responses to assessment initiatives on all kinds of campuses have directed our writing efforts. We have reached a point when we can step back from the intense labors of implementing outcomes-based assessment. This is also a time when we are able to analyze those labors and reflect on the learning process of our work. It is a time when most campuses around the country are asking the questions that structure our chapters. We have reflected on, questioned, and challenged our practices to the extent that we think our insights are clear enough to be shared.

We begin by recognizing that most faculty members have been pressured about being student centered and swear that they are student centered in their practices. Most faculty swear differently about the pressure for assessment and the demands on their time and expertise. It's probably safe to say that few faculty members are easily convinced that assessment, specifically outcomes-based assessment, can be achieved in ways that actually promote a student-centered educational program. That's the heart of this book—making a case for developing and achieving outcomes-based assessment to provide student-centered education while simultaneously sharing related insights about pedagogy and learning.

The Big Picture of Outcomes-Based Education

Before getting directly into outcomes-based assessment, we will create a context for this book, the big picture of outcomes-based education (OBE). It's not a new movement, by the way. You may not know this, but outcomes-based approaches have been around in some form or another almost as long I have been involved professionally—at least 30 years. The OBE model just never went very far, probably because its early interpretation and implementation with rigid formats and lack of teacher involvement turned people off, causing it to disappear for periods of time. That explains some of the resistance that exists. We address and honor that resistance later in this chapter, but, first, a definition of OBE is in order.

With a current interpretation, we describe OBE as an educational model in which curriculum and pedagogy and assessment are all focused on student learning outcomes. It's an educational process that fosters continuous attention to student learning and promotes institutional accountability based on student learning. Simply put, OBE emphasizes student learning. Some of the "promising practices" of good assessment describe well the outcomes-based model:

- Faculty publicly articulate assessment information in advance of instruction.
- Students are able to direct their learning efforts to clear expectations.
- Student progress and completion of learning outcomes are determined by achievement of learning outcomes (Larkin, 1998).

What these statements do not acknowledge is the dynamic role that learning outcomes play in the structuring and development of curriculum.

At the risk of offending our colleagues, I must say that I believe that the curriculum development processes of higher education are often driven by the individual faculty member's disciplinary knowledge and expertise, experiences, preferences, schedules, successes, and class size. I have heard students attest to this, and I am sure that my courses were often developed similarly. The problem with such development processes occurs when we look at the big picture of student learning. When departments or programs or an institution design program descriptions or articulate the baccalaureate intentions, the end result is usually a curricular framework that is achieved by a set of prescribed courses. However, once the curriculum is developed, the individual courses are left to the wishes of the instructors. This is where learning outcomes come in. They provide a common framework for individual courses, programs, and an overall baccalaureate degree. They do not specify teaching strategies, learning activities, assignments, readings and resources, or assessment, so you will not be limited in your course planning. Outcomes do not interfere with faculty creativity. That said, one does need to pay attention to learning outcomes and assess whether the course components are aligned with those outcomes. Said differently, an outcomes-based course is designed so that students are supported in meeting the learning outcomes. In chapters 7 and 8, which discuss syllabi and course alignment, respectively, we specifically address what outcomes mean for planning and course design.

Defining Learning Outcomes

The key component of OBE is *outcomes*. In our simplest definition, an outcome is a stated expectation. A *learning outcome* is a stated expectation of what someone will have learned. As we stated previously, learning outcomes inform curriculum, teaching, and assessment. Today's outcomes are being designed to promote more effective learning at all levels from kindergarten through higher education. At some levels, the outcomes originate from outside the educational setting, and at other levels, the outcomes originate from within. For very important reasons, which we will elaborate throughout this book, faculty are the most appropriate source of learning outcomes for their students. Our commitment to you is to provide the understandings and practices that will empower you to seek and maintain ownership of assessment, specifically to articulate the learning outcomes and specify the evidence to be produced.

Current assessment leaders have offered more detailed and informative definitions of learning outcomes for our use today:

- "A learning outcome statement describes what students should be able to demonstrate, represent, or produce based on their learning histories" (Maki, 2004, p. 60).
- "Learning outcomes describe our intentions about what students should know, understand, and be able to do with their knowledge when they graduate" (Huba & Freed, 2000, pp. 9–10).

There are more definitions and we will share them in chapter 3, but it's apparent that there is a common understanding about what an outcome is. Another way of describing an outcome is one that I use when working with faculty members who have not previously experienced outcomes-based approaches. I ask them to focus on what will happen after students finish their class or complete their program or graduate from the university or college. I pose the question, "What do you want the learners to do, to understand, to be when they finish your course or complete the program?" Our tendency is to focus on what learners do while they are with us—in classes, in a major program of courses, or on the campus. That tendency keeps our focus on our pedagogy (teaching and learning approaches) and keeps us in the teaching paradigm. Instead, authentic outcomes push us to think differently, to describe those departure skills, understandings, and so on, and then to focus our planning on how to promote them during our time with the learners. That keeps us in the learning paradigm. Those paradigms or models begin to lay a foundation or rationale for outcomes-based assessment. They respond to the "why?"

Outcomes-Based Assessment—Why?

At CSUMB, there was a commitment to being learner centered or student learning centered, and that commitment filtered many of the major institutional decisions. It took visible form in the kinds of teaching, learning, and assessment approaches that faculty designed for their courses. Such attention to student learning really begins to make the shift "from teaching to learning" that Barr and Tagg (1995, p. 13) urged for American higher education.

Many of us who were already acknowledging that the traditional paradigm of large lecture formats sprinkled with an occasional question and answer was ineffective enthusiastically received their message.

Shifting to a Learning Paradigm

Barr and Tagg (1995) described their "learning paradigm" as one in which the goal is for our institutions to operate like learners, continuously learning how to produce more learning. They described the learning approaches for their paradigm with descriptive qualities such as "holistic," "environments ready for students," "student discovery and construction of knowledge," and "active learning" (pp. 16–18). There weren't many specific "how tos" in their urges to change our practices. There was, however, one exception. There was specificity in terms of assessment—with language such as "learning and student-success outcomes," "quantity and quality of outcomes," "specified learning results," and "degree equals demonstrated knowledge and skills" (pp. 16–18). With compelling arguments, they asserted that "the learning paradigm necessarily incorporates the perspectives of the assessment movement" and acknowledged that "few colleges across the country systematically assess student learning outcomes" (p. 16).

Support and Objections

You may be thinking to yourself that outcomes seem fairly basic and that they make sense. If this is the case, why haven't they remained prominent all this time? Why have they surfaced, disappeared, and resurfaced over the last 30 years? Each time they have reappeared, there have been both widespread support and strong objections. At present, it looks like outcomes may be here to stay, especially with accreditation requirements, state mandates, and plenty of learning theory and research as a foundation. Nevertheless, both strong support and passionate objections continue to emerge from our own educational community. It would be so easy for us to wow you with the reasons to embrace outcomes-based approaches, to convince you with quotes from famous educators, and to tug at your emotions with statements about enhancing student learning. And we will. But we will also share the sentiments of those faculty and administrators and even some students who resent and resist outcomes-based approaches. These sentiments address the question, "Why not?"

Outcomes-Based Assessment—Why Not?

Now that we have answered the question "Why Develop Outcomes for Assessment and Learning?" let's find the answer to the question "Why not?" To do so, we will address both the misconceptions and the legitimate concerns about outcomes-based assessment.

Concerns and Objections

Remember when as the director of teaching, learning, and assessment I felt so isolated from faculty and realized that they were avoiding assessment? Well, when they finally began to talk about that "A" word (assessment), they expressed abundant worries and determined avoidances. I heard comments such as these:

- "It's inflexible, mechanistic, and reductionistic."
- "It privileges lower-order measurable knowledge and skills."
- "It's unresponsive to multiple intelligences and diverse learning styles."

These concerns were important to hear and to consider in the work ahead. Early unofficial documents of the campus reinforced some of the faculty members' concerns with a set of "key hazards" (the actual language) of outcomes-based assessment:

- The potential to force potentially harmful "normalization" of learning
- A tendency to be highly prescriptive, for both learners and educators, thereby inhibiting creativity and flexibility

The group of faculty who continued to resist any direct involvement with outcomes-based assessment were clear:

We are committed to education that is constructivist, cumulative, situated, and collaborative, and we hope to improve campuswide curricular development and instructional practice. Outcomes-based assessment does not appear to be a good fit for those intentions. We don't see it having the potential to address our commitments.

In addition to those negative connotations generated from within the campus, we encountered critical reactions from our peers nationally. For some, the term *outcomes* "gives the image of a factory model in which something is produced rather than developed" (Braskamp & Braskamp, 1997, p. 8). The unique 21st-century vision of the university appeared to be a poor fit for an educational approach that has been characterized as "dehumanizing" and "unconnected to lifelong learning and development" (p. 8). For many educators, outcomes-based assessment triggers an image of rigid rubrics, behavioral objectives, tightly contained curricula, and reduction to quantitative measures. My memory of OBE in some of its earlier forms could rightly be characterized with those descriptions.

Outcomes-based assessment additionally suffers from problems with measurement in general. There are those who argue that "true education cannot be measured" (Barr & Tagg, 1995, p. 18). Furthermore, there are specific disciplines, especially in the arts, in which developing outcomes appears to be at odds with the philosophy of the discipline: "I don't think that we could possibly state the learning outcomes that we want our art majors to achieve. . . . It's so individual. . . . Creativity cannot be analyzed that way. . . ."

Important Faculty Dialogue: Starting Points

While those obstacles and criticisms of outcomes-based approaches may sound discouraging, it is important to discuss and listen to such worries as well as to check misconceptions. A faculty dialogue about concerns and objections is a critical first step in the institutionalization of outcomes-based assessment. It's a dialogue that begins to ensure its connection to student-centered learning. Just as we ask students at the beginning of a course what they already know about our topic(s), we need to ask ourselves what we've heard or experienced or wonder about outcomes-based approaches.

Recently I traveled to a small state university in Kansas to work with the faculty on outcomes-based assessment. The day's schedule was limited by faculty availability, class schedules, and meetings, so I spent most of the day giving talks and workshops about outcomes-based assessment. At the end of the day, an open session was scheduled in which faculty could ask questions, express concerns, and so forth. It's a session that I should have insisted on first thing in the morning so that I could respond to and accommodate their queries in my presentations and learning activities. Instead, I spent an intense hour "backpedaling" with faculty to clear up misconceptions and respond to concerns, which appeared to have blocked how they heard my messages in the earlier sessions. Thus, I recommend to faculty readers that you discuss outcomes-based assessment with your colleagues. Bring up hearsay, experiences, readings, and concerns about new approaches or changes well before even considering any development of assessment. However, be mindful that gathering our concerns and criticisms as a starting point is not intended to be used for debate. That will push us further away from each other and interfere with the kind of collaboration that supports outcomes-based assessment and student-centered learning.

Some of those early conversations will begin to build a community—the kind of supportive context that we describe in the next chapter. You may have a kind of informal community in your hallway or department, or you may be part of a more formal faculty learning community, which is also described in the next chapter. Some kind of community context will promote ongoing conversations and connections as you struggle with assessment.

As a director of teaching, learning, and assessment, I realized early in my dialogues with faculty that the role of director was not the right one for supporting faculty. I embraced a facilitator role as I encouraged the faculty sharing sessions, listening carefully and noting any concerns. My intent was to avoid characteristics and terminology that colleagues perceived negatively. Accepting the legitimacy of concerns and experiences is a positive starting point for working together. It is also important to acknowledge that the process of understanding and accepting takes time. Even when Barr and Tagg's (1995) work (with its great appeal to the CSUMB campus) assured that "measures of outcomes could provide genuine information about learning" (p. 18), it was some time before my colleagues were convinced.

It was important to store the information from my faculty conversations to review later when development was happening. At points in the implementation, it was helpful to use the concerns as a sensitivity check to ensure that our worries were being addressed: "Remember when we first talked about outcomes-based assessment and we worried that it would be prescriptive and might limit our creativity? Let's check what we have developed so far and assess whether it sounds prescriptive. If we use those outcomes to plan a course, would they limit our creativity?"

Once we begin to talk about the possibility of outcomes-based assessment, it is the ideal time to make connections between assessment and what we know about learning. Again, a conversation about student learning feels safe, important, and relevant to our faculty work. It's another collaborative learning opportunity, another community-building opportunity, as our peers share their insights and, it is hoped, their questions about learning. Helpful literature about learning is growing, providing the opportunity for you to create study groups, book clubs, and seminars, thereby enabling you to pursue your interest in a more formal way, if desired. These avenues of learning may also help to build a learning community with your colleagues.

Significant Connections: Learning Theory and Research

In the midst of conversations expressing negative impressions about outcomes-based assessment, one of the positive spins on those conversations is that someone always mentions student learning in the midst of his or her concerns. The conversations begin to form a culture with such focus. As our CSUMB faculty colleagues criticized outcomes-based assessment, their dialogue typically included what was important to student learning. It is not difficult to move those conversations to a consideration of what we know about learning. It is an ideal time to investigate current learning theory and related research.

The Nature of Learning: Supporting Outcomes-Based Assessment

Starting with what faculty know about learning provides a strong foundation for our outcomes-based assessment. Peter Ewell's (1997) summary of our efforts to organize higher education for learning identifies a major handicap keeping us from success. Many of the reforms efforts, including assessment, "have been implemented without a deep understanding of what learning really means and the specific circumstances and strategies that are likely to promote it" (p. 3). Ewell encourages us to use the emerging research on human learning to guide our efforts. He urges us to develop a collective understanding of the nature of learning to help us reach the goals that we work so intently to achieve in higher education.

Most of us are ill prepared to discuss human learning when we have been taught to be experts in our disciplines with little or no preparation for or study of teaching, student development, learning theory, or how learning occurs. Yet, faculty have much wisdom about learning, probably because they have been and will continue to be learners for a very long time. Any time we ask faculty about learning, they provide insights such as the following:

- Learning happens differently for individual learners.
- Learning is accelerated when students are motivated and have a reason to learn.
- Learning occurs best in a supportive environment.
- Learning builds over time—it is cumulative.
- Learning is a social process, enhanced when learners talk and interact.
- Students have very different learning strengths.
- Students who feel confident about their learning are the most successful.

What would your list look like? If yours was like the one presented here, I would feel comfortable challenging you with the question, "If outcomes-based assessment could promote or support all of those conditions, could you go along with it?" I can't imagine that you would say no to such a request. It would be like asking if you would use an approach that supports student learning. There would be hesitation, but few of us would be willing to refuse.

A leader in the movement to study and use the "science of learning" is Diane Halpern. She teases her peers for teaching in ways that contradict what we know about learning, and we laugh uncomfortably. She provides extensive insights about the science of learning for faculty study, analysis, curriculum development, and course design. One of her principles of learning that is especially relevant for outcomes-based assessment is the following: Less is more, especially when considering long-term retention and transfer.

Halpern and her colleague Milton Hakel (2003) comment on the difficulty faced in our information age with prioritizing what information we teach or what concepts we develop or how to limit the broad expanse of curricular content. She urges us to emphasize deep understanding of a few topics rather than to cover a broad range or a cursory knowledge of topics. Outcomes-based approaches support such emphasis in our curriculum and prioritization in our teaching. Such prioritizing allows several processes to occur:

- More effort can be put into learning.
- Students can focus on applying their new learning.
- Students remember more and are able to transfer new learning to new situations (Halpern & Hakel, 2003, p. 41).

This brief list is quite compelling if outcomes-based approaches can help us achieve those processes. Another compelling reason to pursue outcomes-based approaches is the potential for "deep learning."

Outcomes Support "Deep Learning" for Students

One of the most important conclusions about the effect of outcomes on student learning comes from the studies of John Biggs. Biggs (1999) found that students achieve "deep learning" when they have outcomes on which to focus. It's similar to the principles that Halpern and Hakel propose, and it makes sense. If you don't know what is important to focus on in your studying and assignments, you try to cover all the information, so you skim, you cram, and you stay on the surface. If you have a priority or focus, you are able to dig, to expand, and to achieve depth of understanding. Noel Entwistle (1998, 2000) compares the idea of "surface learning" to "deep learning" in terms of the learning context. When you review the differences, you and most of your colleagues would agree that the qualities of "deep learning" are what we intend in our teaching (see table 1.1).

An important conversation to have with faculty is one about the kind of learning that we expect from students. Most of us can discuss with ease the kind of learning that really excites us. For example, one might have this to say about a student: "The learner dug into the ideas, came up with original examples, made connections with ideas from other classes, and took a stand on the issues using support from the literature." At the same time, we express consistent disappointment with the student who simply "summarizes the information" or "applies it only in the course context" or "paraphrases the readings and lectures." Without calling it deep learning, most of us yearn for the depth of learning in the first description and experience ongoing disappointment with the results of our teaching when depth is not there. That

TABLE 1.1
Comparison of Surface Learning and Deep Learning

Surface Learning	*Deep Learning*
Unrelated bits of knowledge	Relationships
Memorization, formulas, following directions	Patterns, principles, integration
Difficulty "making sense"	Logic, evidence, conclusions
Study without reflection or strategy	Understanding, metacognition
External motivation	Internal motivation
Little meaning, value course, tasks	Active interest, engagement
Feelings of pressure, worry, anger, uncertainty	Pleasure, satisfaction, self-assessment

Source: Adapted from *Achieving "Deep Learning,"* by N. J. Entwistle, 2000, paper presented at the annual meeting of the American Association of Higher Education, Chicago.

yearning is a good motivation for reviewing practices that support deep learning.

When the insights about producing deep learning are summarized, the following set of practices emerges:

- Overarching goals and outcomes, generative topics, and clear expectations are provided.
- Teaching is done in a way that clarifies meaning and arouses interest.
- Formative assessments are designed to develop more understanding.
- Curriculum content is organized in personally meaningful and academically appropriate ways (Angelo, 1995, p. 12).
- High but realistic expectations are set and maintained.
- Teachers and students ask for, provide, and make use of regular, timely, and specific feedback.
- Teachers and students look for and experiment with real-world applications of what is being learned in the classroom (Angelo, 1995, p. 12).

Outcomes-based assessment will not make this list of teaching practices happen but it will support them. The bottom line is that most faculty members believe their mission is to help students learn, and that's the starting point. Once we begin designing learning outcomes, our conversations will stay focused on learning. In fact, we will specifically begin to address the learning that students need to live and thrive in society. These conversations are happening on individual campuses and at a national level. The reports from national organizations and study groups, accreditation agencies, and federal/state research together with conversations held at institutions of higher learning provide dynamic foundations for our own interactions that must precede the work of articulating institutional outcomes. I must pause here to emphasize an important theme of this book: we do not encourage adoption of a ready-made outcomes-based approach. As Peter Ewell (2001a) so aptly puts it, "Any innovation or new practice must flow from the institutional mission." We've learned that lesson from other advances in higher education, such as civic engagement. So our message is to browse national reports or review the outcomes of another institution, not to use them as models, but to provide possibilities or to prompt a discussion with colleagues. An occasional outcome or two from another institution or a national report might even be a good fit for your campus and will save you time. Otherwise, you will want to be your own designer of outcomes and maintain ownership of the process.

External Pressures for Outcomes-Based Assessment

Positive Perspectives

The topic of national reports brings us to the strong possibility that outcomes-based assessment may be a requirement for your institution. It may be expected by an accreditation association, the state, or the federal government. Presidents, provosts, and deans are under pressure to provide evidence that students are learning, and that in itself is a difficult task. It is especially challenging when the learning outcomes have not been specified. In this case, the institutional leadership, often in collaboration with an institutional research director, typically turns to faculty for their assistance. Although this may be an unpopular stance, I insist that these individuals are the right ones to turn to for such information. I cannot imagine any faculty member feeling comfortable with someone else designing the learning outcomes and assessment for his or her courses and programs. Yes, this process does mean a lot of work—years' worth of work—but it is an integral part of the faculty teaching role. It also has such great potential for enhancing that role and making it more satisfying in terms of results.

We are trying to show you here that an unpleasant or unwelcome situation can be turned into a positive one. This can be demonstrated by the fact that once we get familiar with those outside the institution who pressure us, we often find that their values are consistent with ours, or simply said, they care about the same goals as we do. Take a look at the *Policy on Institutional Effectiveness* from the Northeast Association of Schools and Colleges (2005):

> While assessment is an overall concern, as reflected in the various standards for accreditation, its primary focus is the teaching-learning experience. To the greatest extent possible, therefore, the institution should describe explicit achievements expected of its students and adopt reliable procedures for assessing those achievements. (p. 1)

These statements are symbolic of the changes in thinking and priorities of our accreditation associations. I cannot imagine any of us having a disagreement with the philosophy expressed in this policy.

External pressures aren't usually met by any of us with enthusiasm, but if they are motivated by a concern for student learning, we all need to meet them more than halfway and listen to them. If your institution is under pressure to produce, then there are bound to be resources to help you achieve this goal. Resources to support faculty work that focuses on student learning are usually available and appreciated on most campuses. This is especially true when one considers the alternative—focusing the resources and data gathering on the usual, which is institutional inputs such as how many courses are offered, facilities and equipment, decision-making policies, and financial arrangements.

Building a Learning Community

The demands from accreditation agencies and others make way for a public inquiry about learning. I cannot think of anything more appropriate for a university or college. In the process, and you will have to trust me on this, there will be support for careful study of student learning and the opportunity to make recommendations for its outcomes in ways that enhance and strengthen teaching and student learning. Peggy Maki's (2004) description of assessment is convincing: "Assessment promotes sustained institutional dialogue about teaching and learning. . . . Building a collective commitment to assessing student learning also involves establishing new and different relationships and opportunities for dialogue" (p. 3). As I have listened to faculty over the years, I have often heard a yearning for such relationships with colleagues and a thirst for critical conversations about the priorities of the faculty role. Our experiences at CSUMB affirm Maki's described potential for "transforming working relationships that already exist" (p. 3) in the context of a culture of inquiry. In my continuing role as facilitator, I learned to support the inquiry processes that are described in chapter 2. I also learned that I couldn't rush the process, that some of the questions had to emerge naturally as faculty engaged in assessment work. Swarup and I experienced that culture of inquiry, and you will hear from him that the culture stimulated exciting and meaningful conversations and thinking for faculty.

It is important to recognize that assessment and the consequent improvement in teaching and learning must remain in the hands of faculty instructors rather than administrators or outside testing agencies. There's that plea for ownership again. The same is true of the data gathering, analysis and interpretation, and recommendations that achieve much more effective improvement when initiated by the user (faculty instructors) than by external entities (e.g., administrators, accreditors). I will continue to repeat this appeal—that faculty take and maintain ownership of assessment. We are writing this book at a time when there are suggestions, possibly rumors, that assessment of higher education may be attended to by those outside of education. Trudy Banta (2005) describes a "push by some policy makers to require faculty to use standardized tests to assess student learning" (p. 35). A few years earlier, Peter Ewell (2001b) warned that there had been "a significant increase in the number of states seriously—or actively—piloting standardized testing as a deliberate element of higher education policy" (p. 21). The seriousness of this situation makes it compelling for you, as a faculty member, in collaboration with administrators, students, community, and accreditation agencies, to take and maintain stewardship of the process of determining the learning outcomes and assessing their achievement.

So far, we've got possible resources, administrative support and facilitation, dialogue and relationships, and ownership as positive reasons for you to respond to external demands for learning outcomes and related assessment. One additional reason leads to the next section of this chapter. Involvement by faculty in assessment, specifically involvement in articulating outcomes, developing and analyzing evidence, and setting criteria and standards, enables them to have "academic currency."

Developing Academic Currency: Another Role for Outcomes-Based Assessment

Academic currency is not a well-used or popular term but I do think it captures well the idea of what outcomes can provide. Simply said, academic currency means that our grades and credit hours have a commonly agreed-upon meaning and, ultimately, credibility. As early as 1870, courses became a standardized unit of instruction of a certain length and the "credit hour became accepted as a way to measure and account for student progress" (Edgerton, 2002, p. 1). That credit-based system was satisfactory for many years, but the multitude of changes (new technologies, student demographics and attendance patterns, distributed learning, and so on) in higher education has raised questions and challenges about the system. The question of credibility is further complicated by the uncertain value of grades mixed with the credit-hour system. With the additional concerns and accusations of grade inflation that stirred in the 1980s, "credits backed by faculty-awarded grades came to have less value as a portable academic currency, and the overall integrity of the baccalaureate degree was increasingly questioned by the academic community" (Johnstone, Ewell, & Paulson, 2002, p. 5). Those questions are now raised from within and from outside the academic community, and the consensus is that at present we do not have "academic currency."

My favorite example about the lack of currency is a scenario in which three sections of Sociology 101 are offered regularly, and in a very short time, students are aware of and share the information about the differences:

> If you want an easy A, take the section taught by _____.
> If you take the section taught by _____, you will work hard for your A.
> The instructor of section _____ teaches very intriguing material from his experiences, and it's quite entertaining and not hard to make an A.

In addition to the grading differences, if you were to look at the syllabi for the three sections in this example, you would wonder how they could be the same course. It is important to be clear here that we do not advocate that the courses look the same in terms of the teaching and learning activities or even the assessment processes, but Sociology 101 or any course and all of its sections need to be directed to some common outcomes in terms of knowledge and understandings, skills, and even attitudes and values. And there need to be common criteria for how well the students must meet those outcomes in order to receive an A. Once these requirements are met, we can applaud the variety of approaches that faculty might take—the course with collaborative learning dominating the class sessions and a group project for the final assessment, the course with a weekly reflection paper and structured discussions within class, or even the lecture course with regular quizzes and a final paper (if those are aligned with the outcomes). Our bias may not hide well, but we do support exams and quizzes in many cases in which they are the appropriate evidence for students to demonstrate their achievement of outcomes. We will discuss this further in chapter 4, which focuses on student evidence.

In the previous paragraph, I casually referred to "common outcomes" and "common criteria." It is important to understand that establishing these requires extensive discussion, debate, reflection, and decision making on your part. In chapter 6, Swarup describes those processes in depth and also shares faculty members' responses to their collaborations. These responses are compelling and make a good case for "academic currency." Even if you don't see much value in that currency, an undeniable responsibility is being raised for such agreement. It ultimately results in improved learning for students as well as for faculty—and that's hard to resist.

A Conversation With Swarup

Before ending this chapter, I'd like to share this conversation I had with Swarup about his perspectives and memories regarding the ideas of this chapter. I began by asking him to dig back into his early career before he became involved in assessment.

What did you think when you came to a university that claimed to be an outcomes-based educational campus? What did you hear about it? What did you think it meant?

When I came to CSU Monterey Bay, I knew nothing about outcomes-based education or assessment. Not what it meant! Nothing! In my interview, the person who hired me said that the university was outcomes based and that I'd have to develop outcomes for my courses. He gave me a brief book describing OBE, but being a non–book learner, I found that it did not help. At that point, it did register with me that this was a different approach to education, and I remember thinking, "Hmmm, actually telling students what we expect from them, rather than just expecting them to get it, really sounds different." At the same time, it felt so vague and undefined that it did not have much impact on my first year of teaching at the university.

Can you reach back further and remember how you designed courses and assessment before coming to CSU Monterey Bay?

This is funny. No, it is embarrassing, as I now consider my former teaching . . . feels like a rather pathetic waste of time. I think it's what's been called "banking." I generally repeated what had been done to me during my education. I taught and they learned (not very well). I remember being very discouraged about my students and their learning. What's interesting to me as I remember this is that I was getting bored with teaching and I could see that my students were bored also. I know that I graded "on the fly," never rubrics (didn't even know what that meant). I clearly never used assessment as a teaching tool—never thought of the concept. I'm really stunned thinking about this now.

Author's note: Swarup received the outstanding faculty teaching award from students four years ago—quite a contrast to his memory of early teaching. Another good story!

A Promise to Our Readers (Learners)

With all of the previews of the chapters to come, you're probably feeling impatient to get on with it. Throughout this chapter, I had to hold myself back because I wanted to help you understand more about outcomes-based assessment, how to write outcomes, how to analyze student work, and what kind of improvements you can expect, so I, too, am feeling impatient and ready to get on with the book. But before moving on to chapter 2, which elaborates on and honors faculty resistance to outcomes-based assessment, suggests resources, and addresses more of the realities associated with assessment, Swarup Wood and I wish to make a promise to you, our readers (and, it is hoped, our learners and mentees). We promise that we will respect our faculty colleagues throughout this book. We will do so with the integrity of our information, with an understanding of the complexity and stresses of faculty lives, and with recognition of the commitment that most faculty members have to students and their learning. We begin each chapter with real stories of real faculty and students, from CSUMB and from campuses around the country. We end each chapter with a conversation between us to maintain that dual perspective we promised early in this chapter. We fill the chapters with examples from different colleges and universities and we stay in touch with reality. We have asked a few of our colleagues to describe "hands-on" ways that they use outcomes-based assessment as learning activities in their classes, and their ideas will be useful for your courses. Finally, we promise that we will be available to you if you need to talk about the content of any of the chapters, to ask more questions, or to work through a new dilemma, and to help clarify anything that we have discussed in this book that may be confusing to you. We will always continue to learn from you.

References

Angelo, T. (1995). Improving classroom assessment to improve learning: Guidelines from research and practice. *Assessment Update, 7*(6), 12–13.

Banta, T. W. (2005, September/October). How much have we learned? *BizEd*, 35–38.

Barr, R. B., & Tagg, J. (1995). From teaching to learning—A new paradigm for undergraduate education. *Change, 12*(6), 13–25.

Biggs, J. B. (1999). *Teaching for quality learning at university*. Buckingham, Great Britain: Open University Press.

Braskamp, L. A., & Braskamp, D. C. (1997, July). The pendulum swing of standards and evidence. *CHEA Chronicle*, 8–11.

Edgerton R. (2002). *Our present approach*. Unpublished paper from the Pew Forum. Washington, DC: Pew Foundation.

Entwistle, N. J. (1998). Improving teaching through research on student learning. In J. Forest (Ed.), *University teaching: International perspectives* (pp. 73–112). New York: Garland.

Entwistle, N. J. (2000). *Achieving "deep learning."* Paper presented at the annual meeting of the American Association of Higher Education, Chicago.

Ewell, P. (1997). Organizing for learning. *AAHE Bulletin, 50*(4), 3–6.

Ewell, P. (2001a). *Assessment "inside–out."* Paper presented at the International Assessment Conference, Glasgow, Scotland.

Ewell, P. (2001b). Statewide testing in higher education. *Change, 33*(2), 21–27.

Halpern, D. F., & Hakel, M. D. (2003). Applying the science of learning to the university and beyond: Teaching for long-term retention and transfer. *Change, 35*(4), 37–41.

Huba, M. E., & Freed, J. E. (2000). *Learner-centered assessment on college campuses.* Boston: Allyn & Bacon.

Johnstone, S. M., Ewell, P., & Paulson, K. (2002). *Student learning as academic currency.* Washington, DC: American Council on Education, Center for Policy Analysis.

Larkin, J. (1998). *Workshop materials: CSUMB outcomes-based education.* Seaside, CA: CSUMB.

Maki, P. L. (2004). *Assessing for learning: Building a sustainable commitment across the institution.* Sterling, VA: Stylus.

Northeast Association of Schools and Colleges, Commission on Institutions of Higher Education. (2005). *Policy on institutional effectiveness.* Bedford, MA: Author.

Palmer, P. J. (1998). *The courage to teach: Exploring the inner landscape of a teacher's life.* San Francisco: Jossey-Bass.

2

A CULTURE FOR FACULTY LEARNING ABOUT OUTCOMES-BASED ASSESSMENT

Honoring and Addressing the Realities

Story: Evidence of Trust

S everal California State University Monterey Bay (CSUMB) faculty members are sitting around a conference table describing issues about their learning outcomes for the general education goal of ethics. There's a big veggie pizza in the center of the table (this is California), and it's getting a lot of attention at 12:45 P.M.

These faculty members are continuing to struggle with descriptions of the ethical behaviors and understandings that they would like students to demonstrate as they leave the university. They have actually been meeting for almost three years, and for much of that time, they operated like a study group. "We had much to learn because most of us began without any expertise in ethics studies, didn't really know about ethics theory, curriculum, or pedagogy." This faculty group represents diverse disciplines: business, environmental science, communication, health, social work, and theater. If you were to listen, you would be impressed by what they have in common: a passion for ethics and a commitment to developing high-quality outcomes and curriculum. They have been continual learners together.

As we listen, they sound stuck. "I think that it sounds right to say that we want students to use varied ethical frameworks to make decisions, but do we know what we are talking about?" one faculty member asks. A silence surrounds the table, and in time, Ron admits, "I'm not sure that I'm familiar with many ethical frameworks." Others nod their heads in agreement. One of the group members, Liliana, ventures, "I know quite a bit about ethics theory but I am probably not as up to date as I should be." She laughs, then admits that she's been too busy helping to open a university (in just three years) to read her disciplinary literature very consistently. After a brief discussion and with much relief, the members of the group agree that they need to pause in their outcome development and study and learn more about ethics.

Within weeks, the group has identified a national conference focused on teaching ethics and a number of literature references to share. The director of teaching, learning, and assessment agrees to support their conference attendance (funds for travel and registration), never mentioning the word *assessment,* of course. The faculty members are visibly energized about their learning adventure. It's easy to predict the kind of intense reflection, discussion, and study processes that will occur while they are away from campus. Their history of working together and the trust that has emerged in their years of interactions have prepared them well for the conference experience. It's not surprising that when they return, they are refreshed, brimming with new ideas and thinking, and ready to work on those ethics outcomes.

A Culture for Faculty Learning and Empowerment

If you reread the story carefully, you will note a phenomenon that is still rare in higher education. There is a lot of trust within that faculty group. Can you imagine a faculty member admitting that he doesn't know much about the topic of his curriculum? It's just not something we do at universities. The academy, with its policies and practices, has not fostered such trust or intimate sharing among its members. In such a culture, the pressure not to ever admit that you do not know something comes in all forms.

If you were sitting at the table with the ethics faculty, you would notice another quality within the interactions. There's an intense kind of learning context surrounding this work group, a readiness and support for new ideas, information, and so on. The dynamics of the ethics faculty group demonstrate two important contextual qualities required for change in our institutions of higher education: trust and openness for learning. The enthusiasm that these individuals expressed for attending the conference to learn or to share ideas about their pedagogy demonstrates that openness. Other qualities include inquiry, communication and collaboration, commitment, and reflection—all of which are essential for achieving an outcomes-based assessment on an institutional level.

These qualities are the focus of this chapter, and I describe strategies and processes to develop such elements as trust and openness (not easy). The strategies presented in this chapter are consistently designed to honor faculty—their expertise, experience, commitments, and realities. As we expand our expectations of your faculty role, we must stay aware of what those expansions do to your work life. Although assessment is integral to the teaching role, it is often seen as an "add on" in terms of work or responsibility, even in a group as committed as the ethics faculty group. It will take some time and some learning before it is truly integral to other responsibilities. Consequently, some of the realities of assessment may place time demands on you, require new kinds of collaboration (also time-consuming), and demand quite a bit of unlearning. As we promised in the previous chapter, we will be sensitive to those realities.

The theme of faculty ownership was introduced in chapter 1. In this chapter, I (Amy Driscoll) urge you to expand on that role as I extend the discussion to empowerment of faculty. As promised in the first chapter, this one will also be vigilant to the theme of student-centered learning. There is much to glean from research and practice focused on student learning as we plan for and support faculty learning. One such practice that has been studied extensively is the use of learning communities, and there are insights *from* student communities *for* the development and enhancement of faculty communities.

A Look at Faculty Learning Communities

The group of faculty you met at the beginning of this chapter is actually known as the Ethics Learning Community. Its three-year history has been filled with debate, frustration, transitions, and relationship building—not a smooth road. Its members look and sound quite different than they did the first year. This group is a good example of the kind of faculty learning communities (FLCs) that are experiencing success in institutions all over the country. You may be asking, "What exactly are those communities?"

FLCs have been defined in different ways:

- "We define a faculty learning community as a cross-disciplinary faculty and staff group of six to fifteen members who engage in an active, collaborative yearlong program with a curriculum about enhancing teaching and learning, and with frequent seminars and activities that provide learning, development, the scholarship of teaching, and community building" (Cox, 2004, p. 8).
- "Faculty learning communities are a continuous process of learning and reflection, supported by colleagues, with an intention of getting things done" (McGill & Beaty, 2001, p. 11).
- "Learning communities work collaboratively toward shared significant goals, in environments in which competition is de-emphasized. Everyone has the opportunity and the responsibility to learn from and help teach everyone else" (Angelo, 1996, p. 1).

Angelo's (1996) definition is general for all kinds of learning communities, but it is a good fit for the kind of community that we have been urging you to begin developing. At Miami University, FLCs offer membership and provide opportunities for learning across all faculty ranks. Those involved in the FLCs see multidisciplinarity and community as the elements that make them successful. Other descriptions of effectiveness include voluntary membership, designated meeting times, environments conducive to learning, empathy among members, operation by consensus, and holistic approaches. The faculty group we watched and listened to earlier had developed its own culture, openness, and trust over time. We saw its members energized and empowered in their work. It was substantive work, complex and meaningful for their faculty roles, and they had experimented, made mistakes, and reflected deeply on their impact on student learning. Parker Palmer (1998) describes their pursuits and commitments well:

> Involvement in a community of pedagogical discourse is more than a voluntary option for individuals who seek support and opportunities for growth. It is a professional obligation that educational institutions should expect of those who teach—for privatization of teaching not only keeps individuals from growing in their craft but fosters institutional incompetence as well. By privatizing teaching, we make it hard for educational institutions to become more adept at fulfilling their mission. . . . The growth

of any craft depends on shared practice and honest dialogue among the people who do it. We grow by trial and error, to be sure—but our willingness to try, and fail, as individuals is severely limited when we are not supported by a community that encourages such risks. (p. 144)

The ethics FLC did provide support to its members: Ron was able to admit his lack of knowledge. What we saw was a kind of internal support. That is, within the group, there was respect, trust, collaborative behaviors, and the "esprit de corps" described for the sense of community in an FLC (Cox, 2004, p. 18). We witnessed the safety its members felt with each other when we heard more than one faculty member admit "not knowing." There was also the essential institutional support, external to the FLC, with money for their conference travel and attendance, payments to part-time faculty to participate, rewards for FLC contributions in the promotion and tenure process, and public valuing and recognition of the achievements of FLC members. CSUMB not only expected a community of discourse, but it supported and rewarded it as well. Figure 2.1 summarizes those internal and external supports and other qualities necessary for community in FLCs (Cox & Richlin, 2004, pp. 18, 19).

The qualities and kinds of interaction described in figure 2.1 take time to develop in any type of community. FLCs are just one example of a structure that fosters a culture for faculty learning. It is not the only way, but the set of qualities described for them is essential for any type of community that will foster learning, be it students or faculty. It will also be important to foster trust and openness in a climate that values questions and not knowing. Again, it's new for us in higher education—we have always needed to know. However, achieving change means unlearning and not knowing and leads to a climate of inquiry.

A Climate of Inquiry

Peggy Maki (2002) writes about the attraction of most faculty members to their work as "intellectual curiosity" (p. 18) and calls it the connecting thread between their commitment to their work and the commitment of the institution. She describes this thread with descriptors such as the following:

- The disposition to question, deliberate, and craft well-reasoned arguments

FIGURE 2.1
Qualities Necessary for Community in FLCs and
Examples of Supportive Statements

1. Safety and trust

   "It's good that we can come to terms with our lack of information—it helps to know that many of us are uncomfortable with moving forward without learning more."

2. Openness

   "That's such an unusual approach for our assessment. I've never thought of it but I'd like to hear more of your ideas so I can understand them better."

3. Respect (internal and external)

   "I appreciate that you've done some research about multicultural issues related to ethics and want us to set aside more time to hear about and discuss those ideas." (internal)

   "I feel much less anxious about the time commitment for this community and the extra work we've planned now that we know that this outcomes-based assessment development is described in our promotion and tenure policies." (external)

4. Responsiveness

   "Some of you have expressed an interest in pursuing more reading on this topic and I have a new chapter for you. I think that the ideas will guide our next outcome."

5. Collaboration

   "We have two major agenda items and not enough time. Any ideas of how to handle them?" Members suggest strategies for achieving both items.

   "Great, half of our group will work on student petitions, while the other half will continue to process the criteria and standards. Next time we meet, we can share our work results with the other half of the group."

6. Relevance

   "Even when I am not teaching ethics, I think about how we planned this assessment and align my curriculum so much better than I ever did."

7. Challenge

   "As we complete this assessment for ethics, I encourage us to submit it for review by colleagues around the country. I think that there's an ethics center at Duke University, isn't there? It would be great to have their feedback and critique."

8. Enjoyment
   "I still remember our first tries at these outcomes!" Laughter and humorous examples of outcomes are offered. "Remember when we listed song lyrics as a form of assessment—we were trying so hard to have varied and creative forms of evidence. What would we have done if a student wrote a song?"

9. Esprit de corps
   "We've been asked to prepare a poster session on Ethics outcomes and evidence for the big Faculty Day. We'll get someone from the technology support group to prepare a professional looking poster. Who wants to work with them? How about handouts and examples?"

10. Empowerment
   "My department has asked me to help facilitate the outcomes development for our major next semester. Some of my colleagues saw our poster session and were impressed."

Source: Building faculty learning communities (pp. 18–19), by M. D. Cox and L. Richlin, 2004, San Francisco: Jossey-Bass.

- The tendency to look at an issue from multiple perspectives
- The determination to seek more information before rushing to judgment (p. 1)

When faculty are able to apply their "intellectual curiosity" to questions regarding student learning, they end up posing questions that call for assessment in order to provide answers. When their assessment work begins with inquiry about learning and about their teaching, that work has the potential to become scholarly—an avenue of research that advances pedagogy and broadens and challenges what we know about "what and how students learn" (Maki, 2002, p. 1), and the beginning of a willingness to "seek out and examine the assumptions that underlie our current teaching practices" (Huba & Freed, 2000, p. 272). Each of those descriptions is relevant to a culture of inquiry.

Starting With Your Questions

Think about questions that you would like answered about your teaching, about a particular class, about the graduates of your institution. Questions about what triggers a student's motivation to learn, about why a particular learning activity sometimes works and sometimes does not, and so on. One of the best ways to begin to work toward a culture of inquiry is to get together with a group of faculty colleagues and brainstorm a list of questions that are of interest. In figure 2.2, Maki (2002) provides some major questions that might extend that intellectual curiosity we described earlier to move toward inquiry. They are ideal for triggering thoughts about outcomes-based assessment, for either individual faculty members, faculty groups, or an entire campus.

I'll stop with those four questions because they are complex and comprehensive—not easy to answer. Of course, there are many more questions to be answered, but for now focusing on those complex and comprehensive ones provided by Maki is a good start. New questions will inevitably arise in the process of answering her questions. Such inquiry will engage you and your colleagues for a significant amount of time. It will also build trust. Gradually, it will become acceptable and even promising to not know—to question, to be puzzled, to be curious.

Building Communities of Inquiry

Some institutions ask that first question in figure 2.2 of all faculty members and encourage response in writing or by e-mail in order to begin developing

FIGURE 2.2
Questions Extending Faculty Intellectual Curiosity into Inquiry about Student Learning

"What kinds of understandings, abilities, dispositions, habits of mind, ways of thinking, and problem solving do you believe students should achieve by the time they graduate?"

"What evidence would document students' progress toward those expectations and how could that evidence be captured so that you could learn about patterns of students' achievement to inform pedagogy and curriculum?"

What evidence is there that our curriculum designs and teaching strategies result in desired student learning and development?

"Given the diversity of students in higher education, including their experiences and learning histories, which students benefit from which teaching strategies, educational experiences, and educational processes believed to be responsible for contributing to expected student learning and development?"

Source: Quoted material from "Moving from Paperwork to Pedagogy," by P. L. Maki, 2002, *AAHE Bulletin,* p. 2.

a campus composite. When the faculty at St. Mary's in San Antonio, Texas, engaged in this process, they listed more than 150 kinds of learning. It was an overwhelming but exciting starting point that promoted campuswide involvement and inquiry and provided a foundation for the outcomes work that followed. At other institutions, a campuswide committee engaged in that first level of inquiry by identifying the essential kinds of learning for all students. From there, committee members engaged their colleagues from all over campus to respond to their draft list. At Portland State University, town hall meetings were scheduled at varied times to promote the highest level of response from the faculty. Note that in all of these scenarios the conversations were focused on student learning. The learning paradigm was, in effect, not the teaching paradigm.

At Alverno College, faculty work in a "community of inquiry" (Rogers, 2003). Their conversations about learning are a distinct form of inquiry. They use synthesizers to extend their conversations over time and across disciplines as well as to foster institutional memory. Rogers describes some key ingredients for creating such communities of inquiry:

- Structures and support for both time and space for sustained conversations
- A commitment to focus on student learning
- A broad perspective on teaching, learning, and assessment
- Roles and skills in collaborative inquiry (p. 17)

Throughout this book, you will be encouraged to consider a range of questions, a continuous inquiry process, in order to be truly student centered as you develop outcomes-based assessment. Much of the work will involve high-quality communication with supportive channels, collaborative structures, and multiple forms of dialogue. The focus of such communication will always be teaching and learning at its core. A dialogue that focuses on teaching and learning is a sign that the assessment process is developing and maturing (Maki, 2004, p. 15).

Communication and Collaboration: Honoring and Addressing the Realities

Before describing or suggesting communication and collaboration approaches, I wish to acknowledge some of the realities of the relationship between faculty and outcomes-based assessment. In chapter 1, we described some of the "Why nots?" expressed by faculty at CSUMB—worries, concerns, and reasons not to support outcomes-based assessment. In the bigger picture of faculty resistance to assessment in general, especially when it is imposed from the outside or by administration, there are legitimate fears and reasons for resisting. A not often expressed fear is that assessment will be used against us as faculty. Student learning assessment will be used to judge, to rate, or to differentially reward faculty. This is a legitimate fear. Such concern opens up an entire dilemma—a dilemma that is central to the unresolved issues of how to evaluate faculty teaching. Many of us fear the use of standardized tests and the pressure to teach to the test. This fear is not so hard to admit and is expressed publicly and often. However, a third fear stays fairly private. It is a fear related to our lack of expertise when it comes to assessment. Some years ago, a colleague and I, both with doctorates in education, were writing a book on teaching strategies. When it came time to write the chapter on assessment, we had to admit to each other that neither of us knew much about assessment, even with our advanced degrees and study of education. We finally resorted to a coin toss, and the loser had to learn about assessment quickly so that the book could be finished. Yes, you're probably wondering how it turned out—I lost. Knowing that may comfort you about your lack of assessment expertise.

I begin to respond to (or address) the first two fears and suggest some institutional processes for getting started on outcomes-based assessment—processes that ease those fears and build confidence. The first process is one in which groups of faculty and ultimately all faculty have a voice in the purpose of assessment and in the description of assessment. That faculty voice eases the fear of assessment being used against us and the fear of standardized tests.

Continuous Communication in Multiple Forms

When Trudy Banta (Banta & Associates, 2002) recommends the characteristics of effective outcomes-based assessment, she urges "continuous communication with constituents" (p. 274). She encourages public communication (catalogs, Web sites), collaborative analysis of assessment findings and implications, celebration of successes, sharing of individual projects, open forums for concerns, and dialogue about published reports (p. 274). The list of communication formats could go on for pages, because there is no limit to the forms with which we communicate about assessment. There are particular guidelines for the way that we communicate and the collaboration that follows. Angelo (2002 p. 185) recommends the following guidelines, which I echo in my role as facilitator:

Guidelines for Communicating about Assessment	Examples of Facilitated Communication
Keep the focus on the main purposes, improving student learning.	"When we look at these forms of evidence we've planned, let's ask ourselves if they will enhance students' learning."
Start with the familiar and make connections.	"All of us have used essay exams in the past, so we will look at some examples to analyze for use with our new outcomes."
Provide scaffolding for novice and intermediate practitioners.	"In each of your work groups are two new faculty members and two experienced members. New faculty are encouraged to stop the process often, asking, '*Why* are we doing this?' and '*How* will this help student learning?' Experienced faculty will provide explanations and examples. If you get stuck as a group, write your question and we will all address it at a break."

Angelo also guides us to develop and sustain social supports for practitioners, much like the FLCs or other ongoing collaborations. And in chorus with other assessment experts, he recommends that we share information on efforts, findings, and successes widely.

Communicating Our Purposes

At several universities with which we have worked, there has been deliberate work on developing a mission for assessment. It's an important process requiring communication and collaboration as well as the involvement of expanding numbers of faculty. Decisions about the purposes and mission of assessment in general have the potential to address some of the legitimate fears introduced earlier. A good beginning is a consideration of institutional materials from other campuses and a review of the literature to see what others say. Even the most basic assessment texts provide reasons for assessment, and as Brown and Glasner (1999) suggest, there is a wide range of rationales. They suggest that we may wish to assess student learning in order to

- Provide feedback to students.
- Classify or grade student achievement.
- Enable students to correct errors and improve learning.
- Motivate students and focus on their sense of achievement.
- Consolidate and summarize student learning.
- Help students to apply abstract principles to practical contexts.
- Estimate students' potential to progress to other levels or courses.
- Guide selection or option choices for other courses or units.
- Give us feedback on how effective we are at promoting learning.
- Provide data for internal and external accountability (p. 6).

As you read this list, you may immediately shake your head in disagreement with some of the reasons, and that's an important response. Now get a group of faculty colleagues together to review the list as well. Ask them to eliminate those reasons that contradict their philosophy of teaching, and to expand the list with reasons that "fit" their thinking and the mission of the institution. From this discussion, faculty can move to the development of a mission statement for assessment. In doing so, faculty might consider Tom Angelo's and Peggy Maki's thoughts on assessment in order to enhance the discussion. Angelo (2002) says that "assessment should be first and foremost about improving student learning" (p. 185). Peggy Maki (2004) provides a broad look: "Assessment becomes an institution's means to examine its educational intentions on its own terms within the complex ways that humans learn and within the populations an institution serves" (p. 15). Individual faculty members could transform that definition into "assessment becomes a means for an individual faculty member to examine his or her educational intentions on his or her own terms. . . ."

Qualities and Principles of Assessing Learning

Huba and Freed (2000) describe some intentions of "learner-centered assessment" in ways that will appeal to all of us:

1. Learner-centered assessment promotes high expectations.
2. Learner-centered assessment respects diverse talents and learning styles.
3. Learner-centered assessment promotes coherence in learning.
4. Learner-centered assessment involves students in learning and promotes adequate time on task.
5. Learner-centered assessment provides prompt feedback to students.
6. Learner-centered assessment fosters collaboration (pp. 22–24).

These intentions begin to articulate qualities and principles of assessing learning. Some institutional examples will help make those qualities and principles even clearer.

Institutional Examples of Qualities and Principles of Assessing Learning

The example that follows comes from DePaul University, School for New Learning. It is followed in the school's statement by a comprehensive set of principles derived from current practices and guidelines for improvement. It is evident that the faculty who developed those principles really studied assessment for its best practices.

> Assessment links teaching, advising, and evaluating with learning; it is a process that provides information about a variety of aspects of learning to the learner. As such, it is a multilevel, multiparticipant process that involves faculty, students, administrators, and often people from the extracollegial community. The School for New Learning (1994) advocates assessment strategies and practices oriented to learning goals and contexts of adult learners and integrated with relevant academic standards both within and outside of DePaul University.

At CSUMB (2000), an assessment advisory council composed of representatives from across campus studied examples such as the ones from DePaul and literature sources and developed the following statement, which put a lot of fears to rest: "Assessment is a dynamic pedagogy that enhances, extends, supports, and expands student learning."

That statement is really a philosophy of assessment as well as a mission statement. What helped the faculty at CSUMB was the "fit" with the way they think about teaching and learning. The language of the statement eased their fears of rigid exams when it limited assessment to only those forms that contribute to student learning. Pause a moment here and think about the assessments that you have experienced throughout your learning processes. Ask yourself if any of them really "enhanced, extended, supported, or expanded" your learning. What were they like? What kind of assessments were they? This is a useful and insightful exercise to do as we begin talking about and listening to each other's ideas of assessment. Note that the statement is really a criterion for assessment that maintains a student-centered focus. Being clear about the purpose of assessment does not completely ameliorate fears and resistance, but the clarity may ease your fears and garner support from your faculty colleagues (Wildey, Vanek, & Trevisan, 2003, p. 7). In addition to leading to the formation of purpose statements or missions for assessment of any kind, conversations will enhance the process if you can surface diverse perspectives from a campuswide group.

Gathering Perspectives: Building Community

Another process of communication is one in which your task force, or learning community, begins by listing all of the unofficial leaders on campus. Clearly this is a strategy that follows your involvement of others in the inquiry and development processes. It's an insight-producing strategy. Among those unofficial leaders are individuals without a title but with such respect that everyone listens to their ideas. With that list—and it's not difficult to come up with those names—set up an interview schedule to visit and listen to those campus leaders. The goal is not to convince them of an agenda but, rather, to hear their thoughts. There will be great value in those interviews if there is a mix of resistant leaders and supportive leaders. At Portland State University, when we used this process, we learned so much from those leaders who opposed changes, and it broadened our own thinking about our work (S. Davidson & D. Lieberman, personal communication, March, 1996).

In his guidelines for promoting, supporting, and sustaining the scholarship of assessment (or other innovations) to improve learning, Tom Angelo (2002) recommends that we engage and involve opinion leaders right from the beginning. He suggests that we select the less obvious participants as well as make strategic selections such as department chairs and elected leaders (e.g., faculty senate chair, curriculum committee chair).

Many of the ideas provided in the next section are equally significant for communication. The two "C" processes go hand in hand and require the same kind of context, supports, and commitments.

Collaboration: Involving Our Colleagues

In the previous discussion of communication, we demonstrated that trust and collaboration are essential. Trust requires continual effort, vigilance, and many different processes over time. There is no easy answer. Collaboration also has no universal model that fits higher education or all colleges or universities. Rather, it relies on the culture of the institution and the kind of processes that have evolved or are embedded in the culture (Maki, 2004, p. 4). From our perspective and experiences, Maki's description of a "series of nested discussions, decisions, and actions" (p. 4) captures what needs to happen for the development of outcomes-based assessment. That series begins with the kind of dialogue about concerns and worries that we encouraged in chapter 1 and begs for an extensive time frame (years), ongoing work sessions, resources to support the participants, and preparatory dialogue (e.g., reasons for assessment, mission), as you read in the previous chapter. The particular kind of collaboration needed here requires that you and your colleagues consistently find value in your participation—preferably value tied to your teaching role, so that your intrinsic motivation is nurtured. The collaboration must build on your intellectual curiosity, be scholarly and fulfilling, and be extended from the culture of inquiry that we described previously. Let's look at an example. Adrianna Kezar (2005) recently completed a study of four institutions described as having collaborations with unusual depth and quality compared to other institutions. She found several features that helped these institutions organize for collaboration:

- A mission that respects and encourages collaboration
- Already developed relationships, networks, or coalitions fostered by the institution with incentives, support, and connections
- Integrating structures such as technology systems, a central unit for fostering collaboration, and cross-campus representation
- Rewards and incentives for collaboration
- A sense of priority and support from upper-level administrators

- Pressures from external groups such as accrediting agencies, disciplinary societies, and foundations
- Learning from peers, colleague-to-colleague information sharing, and conversation as motivator (pp. 53–56)

Kezar thinks that the lessons from her four target campuses are timely considering the current reduction of resources, demands for reform, and the need for new approaches to institutional operations. She predicts a real payoff for such collaboration, especially for our capacity to achieve the collective mission of our institutions. From my (Amy Driscoll's) perspective, for an institution without collaboration and the organizational features that support such a process, achieving outcomes-based assessment is an impossibility. There is also the reality of traditional isolation for faculty that must be addressed if collaboration is to be achieved.

From Privacy to Collaboration

Prior to much of the assessment work that we have described thus far, assessment was a very private activity. Palmer (1998, p. 142) talks about faculty closing the door when it is time to teach, and assessment is probably the most private activity of all of our pedagogy. Most of us have maintained the privacy of information provided by assessment in our individual courses. Only when it is translated into grades or pass/fail does it become public data, and as we described in chapter 1, those data may not have much meaning. Thus, I approach you with renewed sensitivity when I ask you to suddenly shift another paradigm, moving assessment from a private to a collaborative focus. Be encouraged, however, because the minute you begin discussing assessment processes or results, you will find yourself focusing on student learning and possibly on how to improve that learning. That can add a level of comfort for you as you consider going public with assessment.

When you do start talking about assessment, you will probably find that a number of your colleagues have been working solo on outcomes-based assessment. As with many reforms in higher education, many individuals pursue their philosophical beliefs about learning and maintain teaching approaches that are at odds with the traditional culture of their institutions. They often work harder, feel isolated, and lack support because they are alone. We have often heard faculty describe such experiences when they join a learning community. They are usually quite relieved to find kindred colleagues and revel in their collaboration. That is our wish for you.

Already in these first two chapters, we have urged you to make a number of shifts. I wish to introduce one more shift or, better described, a transformation to be encouraged once you become comfortable with assessment being public. Many leaders in higher education have called for a transformation that brings the institutional constituencies (administrators, staff, faculty, students) into a common focus that allows them to operate as a whole. Again, this shift means the abandonment of traditional isolation, or "working independently," and an emphasis on the individual or even "academic freedom." What does this transformation mean in operational examples?

- It means that all of the members become part of "a system with interdependent parts" (Huba & Freed, 2000, p. 274).
- It means that faculty and everybody else in the institution are unambiguously committed to each student's success (Barr & Tagg, 1995, p. 23).
- It means that everyone is responsible for student learning (Driscoll & Wood, 2006).
- It means that the typical division between academic affairs and student affairs is no longer relevant (Driscoll & Wood, 2006).
- It means that the reward systems, the hiring processes, and the resource allocation must reflect a common purpose—student learning (Driscoll & Wood, 2006).

Finally, this transformation means that we need to learn how to collaborate if we are to achieve all of these shifts. Most of us will spend a lifetime learning how to collaborate, but for now, we urge you to become aware of examples of effective collaboration in your environment. Approach your observations with the understanding that collaboration begins with an acknowledgment or public sharing of the resources and assets of each member, an agreement to respect the ideas and contributions of all members, and a commitment to a shared or common agenda. This requires enormous effort on the part of the participants as well as of an effective facilitator. Throughout all of our discussion about communication and now our introduction to collaboration, we feel compelled to urge the hiring or selection of a facilitator. Another idea would be to find a director who chooses the facilitator role rather than a director role. This may sound contradictory to the notion of collaboration, but most of us have learned that a skilled facilitator is essential. As Kuh, Kinzie, Schuh, and Whitt (2005) urge in their lessons from high-performing colleges and universities, "Put someone in charge, but make it collaborative" (p. 49).

Facilitating Collaboration (and Communication) Effectively

We have learned a lot from FLCs about the role of an effective facilitator and the effect of skilled facilitation on community building or collaboration. If outcomes-based assessment is going to be part of an institutional approach, then extensive planning, implementation, and evaluation for improvement processes must have leadership. I use leadership here but not with a traditional definition. Petrone and Ortquist-Ahrens (2004, p. 64) suggest that there are three essential roles for the facilitator of FLCs: champion, coordinator, and energizer. Within those roles is the critical dimension of building relationships, trust, and so forth, often not part of a leadership role. Our experience at CSUMB demonstrated that a facilitator with some status as leader was necessary for change, development, commitment, and resources. Banta (Banta & Associates, 2002) calls for a "knowledgeable, effective leadership" (p. 262) for the systematic work of becoming an outcomes-based institution. Once you have finished this book and reviewed the processes and steps for planning, implementation, and improvement of effective outcomes assessment, you will be convinced of the critical need for a manager, an organizer, a motivator, a teacher, a communicator, a partner and collaborator, an evaluator, a designer, and a writer. You will also have learned that the individual who fulfills these roles must have expertise in the theories of learning, assessment strategies, human relations, goal setting, organizational effectiveness, and community building. Finally, you will have learned that this individual must be above all a quick learner, flexible, and patient.

After that extensive description of an effective facilitator/leader, I hesitate to add more to this discussion. However, my firsthand experience tells me that this is a most important conversation for institutions and for the faculty who teach there. I therefore add the following guidelines to be used whether you take on that facilitation role or participate in a process facilitated by another:

- Know when to let the conversation continue in its new direction.
- Know when to clarify the direction.
- Know when and how to quiet the dominant voice so that others can contribute.
- Know when and how to get the discussion on track to completion.
- Know when and how to check in with the group members to determine comfort, clarity, and presence of issues or concerns.
- Know how and when to motivate a lagging conversation.

These facilitation behaviors are useful in all parts of life to improve and extend communication and to initiate and support collaboration. Collaboration, when all is said and done, is complex and requires extensive preparation, maintenance, and encouragement, and even probably assessment, to ensure that everything is working toward a common end. As Adrianna Kezar (2005) reminds us, it has huge benefits in terms of achieving change or an end as comprehensive as institutionalized outcomes-based assessment. Effective communication and collaboration are essential to the next and final set of qualities for an authentic learning community.

Commitment through Ownership and Empowerment

Ownership and empowerment are a lot like communication and collaboration—difficult to separate and impossible without their mutual support. With all of the previous discussion, it must be said that this aspect of faculty learning is the most critical for "honoring and addressing the realities" (the subtitle of this chapter). It is also the most ineffable in terms of describing faculty development. You know when you have achieved ownership and empowerment because everyone is working together, motivated, and committed to long-term efforts. I will approach ownership and empowerment from two perspectives—one theoretical and one practical—both of which are required to achieve these qualities.

Constructivist Faculty Development

Yes, this is the theoretical part. The advice regarding this approach came from months of reflection about faculty development for outcomes-based assessment at CSUMB. One day, one of those illuminating moments occurred. Swarup and I became quite animated and excited as we realized that much of the success of the faculty ownership and empowerment that we observed came from the fact that we had engaged faculty in a constructivist model of learning. Let me start by admitting that I gave only one workshop on assessment in my six years as director of teaching, learning, and assessment. In the first month, the administrators who hired me requested that I conduct a campuswide workshop on the basics of assessment, a kind of Assessment 101. I did and it was satisfying and feedback was positive, but the year that followed was an isolated time when faculty avoided assessment. Enough said.

Discouraged, I began to offer projects and group work sessions (general education learning communities, departmental groups) to actually *do* things. I began with an individual project, the course alignment project (see chapter 8), which faculty members did in private to assess their own courses. It was completely nonthreatening. As we describe in chapter 8, faculty found value in the project and began to "mess around" with assessment. A tiny bit of trust was established. From there I sponsored group activities such as developing outcomes and criteria (see chapters 3 and 4). Participation began to build. Years later, I read a description of what we were doing:

> Knowledge-building communities such as a college evolve particularly effectively through collaborative activities that include not just the exchange of information, but the co-construction and design of something meaningful to participants. . . . The goal is not for participants to assume clearly defined and separate roles but rather to re-imagine generative ways to co-construct knowledge. (Resnick, 1996)

When we had our revelation about why this was successful, we realized that the campus was committed to a constructivist approach to student learning, so it made sense that faculty would respond to it so eagerly. Constructivism is a philosophical view of education in which learners construct their own knowledge. Faculty were "making meaning from their own interactions and experiences" (Driscoll & Wood, 2004, p. 12). Constructivism is a direct contrast to the delivery model of education, or as Friere (1990) describes it, a "banking model." Just as the CSUMB faculty were not depositing information into the minds of their students, I was not depositing information into the minds of faculty and staff. We were all teachers and learners. When you read Swarup's descriptions in chapters 6 and 10 of what faculty learned from our major development processes, you will realize that one person could not possibly teach that many insights. Each of our faculty members created an enormous foundation about teaching and learning from doing assessment work. The assessment work was focused on creating a set of outcomes from which to design assessment so that the ensuing conversations and learning would remain student centered, as you will read later in this book.

The more faculty created their assessment designs, or protocols, as we called them later, the more they acknowledged what they were learning. And, best of all, they claimed ownership of their assessment designs. I was no longer the only facilitator or expert. Faculty gradually began to facilitate, provide direction, change agendas, and raise questions. Their quotes in chapter 7 demonstrate the growing empowerment that was occurring. Late in the process, I casually said that we wouldn't have to repeat some of our processes after a year or so, and David, a serious, usually quiet faculty member, had to restrain himself from shouting when he said, "No way—we have to continue this so that I can improve my teaching on a regular basis." Faculty like David were clearly taking over and felt empowered to make decisions about the assessment processes. Later, when we describe processes for analyzing student work, you will learn that faculty voted unanimously to conduct such analysis processes every other year.

Practical Guides for Achieving Ownership

I would be remiss if I did not acknowledge that I had funding to support all of those faculty work sessions. I am not sure that I could have enticed faculty to come to work half days before they had a taste of "ownership and empowerment." Angelo (2002) discourages payments for assessment projects, saying, "Don't pay participants to do what should become part of routine practice" (p. 185). I believe that to some extent, but the practical and sensitive part of me paid attention to the overwhelming workload of starting a new university, the ever-increasing demands on faculty, and the extensive time required of outcomes-based assessment. I considered our early payments as "seed money" and often used the funds to support travel, book and media purchases, and other professional development uses. I also made certain that the work processes yielded valuable insights about teaching and learning so that when the money ran out, faculty would continue to participate.

Willard, Dearing, and Belair (2004) list the following incentives that they incorporated into their assessment system:

- Release time for tenured faculty
- Support and guidance from the Office of Assessment
- Monetary support for internal and external assessment training
- Advice and feedback from the institutional research office (p. 11)

I must admit that my funding paid for lots of attendance at American Association for Higher Education assessment conferences, state and CSU systemwide assessment conferences, visits to Alverno College, and the annual assessment conference at Indiana University–Purdue University, Indianapolis. There was clearly public support from the upper level of administration for the assessment work: kudos, recognition for the scholarship, grants, and e-mail notes of appreciation to individual faculty members.

And of course, there was attention to those "creature comforts": food, lots of coffee and tea, cozy surroundings, a big round table with surrounding sofas. That building that I was fortunate enough to have provided isolation from faculty offices and work deadlines, enabling participants to let go of other concerns and focus on assessment. That's not to say that I never worked within the departments—the business department had a similarly cozy room that we used every Friday for about four months—circled around pizza or long submarine sandwiches, and laughing a lot. It was a group of faculty members who had not worked together well for a few years. In fact, there was much concern about the dynamics of the department, and a consultant had been called in to support the chair. Something about assessment put everyone on equal ground and we began slowly. I still remember a lot of enjoyment, both humor and intense dialogue, and, ultimately, a well-developed set of outcomes for the faculty's program. As we finished, there was a visible sense of pride and recognition. Notes of congratulations from the president and provost expanded the good feelings.

As I said at the beginning, much of ownership and empowerment must be experienced for understanding to occur. Throughout the remainder of this book, all of our strategies will continue to attend to faculty empowerment and ownership because they are essential to faculty learning. They pave the way for an entire institution to be outcomes based and student centered.

A Conversation With Swarup

I could not wait to ask questions of Swarup, to probe his faculty perspective of what I describe in this chapter, to hear his responses and memories of his participation. This was especially nerve-wracking for me as this chapter's author, because I wished to report his answers as authentically as possible. "What if he describes insights that conflict with mine?" I thought. Well, we did promise you, our readers, reality. Here is our discussion:

Describe your early experiences in one or more general education faculty learning communities to which you belonged (as a lecturer)—what were the pluses and minuses?

I have always enjoyed the learning community meetings and have participated substantially in both the science and community participation communities. For the most part, the meetings were a great venue for talking about pedagogy and important aspects of a discipline. In the community participation community, the focus varied greatly because faculty represented diverse disciplines and the issues of its curriculum were tricky to teach. It is a curriculum area in which what students frequently know is usually factually incorrect, so there is a challenge of teaching issues that are contrary to what students believe to be true. In the science community, I remember some excellent discussions on teaching about evolution. Once again, the issue is not what students know but what they misunderstand.

The tone of these meetings has always been intensely collaborative and I can remember feeling many times how wonderful it was to work on an issue with five or six different faculty colleagues. I can also remember being impressed by a particular perspective and thinking, "I never would have thought of something that way." I would say that diversity of perspective is truly the heart of peer collaboration and has been the most valuable aspect of those communities.

Compare the experience of developing assessment in the departmental community.

Historically, my department developed its major learning outcomes before we had a center for teaching, learning, and assessment. Many of the faculty were confused and resistant. There was a different kind of diversity among the departmental participants—faculty who were committed to grants and research and not very involved in teaching, faculty with real pedagogical expertise and dedicated to the scholarship of teaching, and faculty who were learning as they taught. It was an uneven kind of participation, not at all a collaboration. The leadership saw the assessment design process as something to finish and then get on with our work. We worked hard but never had the rich experiences of the general education FLCs. When the department focused on the capstone experience (senior-level, graduation requirement), our outcomes went through an intense review and revision, primarily by one faculty member. I can't honestly say that there was or is much ownership within the department.

Talk about reality! Swarup's answers really demonstrate the challenges of sustaining communication and collaboration, of building trust and openness, and of supporting ownership and empowerment. I see examples and nonexamples as great teaching tools, and there is much to be gleaned from the comparisons in Swarup's answers. Those contrasting realities can probably be found in entire institutions across the country as outcomes-based assessment is designed and implemented. What's difficult to observe and hear in Swarup's second scenario is that so much effort is directed to a development with untouched potential for faculty learning. Throughout this chapter, I worked to promote an awareness that extensive effort is required just to build a context for faculty learning, and yet, we see that the benefits in a context that honors and addresses the realities are compelling. We hope that you are convinced to begin developing a culture for faculty learning, specifically about outcomes-based assessment.

References

Angelo, T. A. (1996). Seven shifts and seven levers: Developing more productive learning communities. *The National Teaching and Learning Forum, 6*(1), 1–4.

Angelo, T. A. (2002). Engaging and supporting faculty in the scholarship of assessment: Guidelines from research and best practice. In T. W. Banta & Associates (Eds.), *Building a scholarship of assessment* (pp. 185–200). San Francisco: Jossey-Bass.

Banta, T. W., & Associates (Eds.). (2002). *Building a scholarship of assessment.* San Francisco: Jossey-Bass.

Barr, R. B., & Tagg, J. (1995). From teaching to learning—A new paradigm for undergraduate education. *Change, 12*(6), 13–25.

Brown, S., & Glasner, A. (1999). *Assessment matters in higher education: Choosing and using diverse approaches.* Suffolk, Great Britain: The Society for Research into Higher Education & Open University Press.

California State University Monterey Bay. (2000). *Assessment mission and purposes.* Seaside, CA: Author

Cox, M. D. (2004). Introduction to faculty learning communities. In M. D. Cox & L. Richlin (Eds.), *Building faculty learning communities* (pp. 5–23). San Francisco: Jossey-Bass.

Cox, M. D., & Richlin, L. (Eds.). (2004). *Building faculty learning communities.* San Francisco: Jossey Bass.

Driscoll, A., & Wood, S. (2004). Creating learner-centered assessment: A faculty-driven process. *Peer Review, 7*(1), 12–15.

Driscoll, A., & Wood, S. (2006). *Fostering student-centered educational programs through outcomes-based assessment.* Paper presented at the Annual Meeting of the Western Association of Schools and Colleges, Irvine, CA.

Friere, P. (1990). *Pedagogy of the oppressed.* New York: The Continuum Publishing Company.

Huba, M. E., & Freed, J. E. (2000). *Learner-centered assessment on college campuses.* Boston: Allyn & Bacon.

Kezar, A. (2005). Moving from I to we: Reorganizing for collaboration in higher education. *Change, 37*(6), 50–57.

Kuh, G. D., Kinzie, J., Schuh, J., & Whitt, E. (2005). Never let it rest: Lessons about success from high-performing colleges and universities. *Change, 37*(4), 44–51.

Maki, P. L. (2002). Moving from paperwork to pedagogy. *AAHE Bulletin,* http://aahebulletin.com/public/archive/paperwork.asp.

Maki, P. L. (2004). *Assessing for learning: Building a sustainable commitment across the institution.* Sterling, VA: Stylus.

McGill, I., & Beaty, L. (2001). *Action learning* (2nd Rev. ed.). Sterling, VA: Stylus.

Palmer, P. J. (1998). *The courage to teach: Exploring the inner landscape of a teacher's life.* San Francisco: Jossey-Bass.

Petrone, M. C., & Ortquist-Ahrens, L. (2004). Facilitating faculty learning communities: A compact guide to creating change and inspiring community. In M. D. Cox & L. Richlin (Eds.), *Building faculty learning communities* (pp. 63–69). San Francisco: Jossey-Bass.

Resnick, M. (1996). *Distributed constructionism.* Paper presented at the International Conference on Learning Sciences, Association of Computing in Education, Northwestern University, Chicago.

Rogers, G. (2003). *Alverno College: Integrated liberal arts and professions program.* Paper presented at the seventh annual CSU Fullerton Assessment Conference, Fullerton, CA.

School for New Learning. (1994). *Qualities and principles for assessing learning at SNL.* Chicago: De Paul University.

Wildey, A. R., Vanek, G. T., & Trevisan, M. S. (2003). Assessment coordinators: Professional characteristics and institutional support. *Assessment Update, 15*(3), 6–7.

Willard, W. A., Dearing, F., & Belair, S. J. (2004). Community college strategies: Facilitating assessment through faculty ownership. *Assessment Update, 16*(3), 11–13.

3

OUTCOMES

Articulating Our Learning Expectations

Story: What Am I Supposed to Be Doing in This Class?

I t's a large class—42 students, mostly sophomores fulfilling a general education requirement—and it's bustling with conversations in Spanish. The course instructor is Dr. Ray Gonzales, who has had at least four illustrious careers. One of the best features of the course, according to the students, are the stories, anecdotes, and examples that Ray brings to his teaching. He holds student interest with vivid tales of his mother's cooking, child rearing, and social life in Mexico. Students chuckle with him as he recounts his rich, colorful memories and illustrates the historical and cultural traditions associated with the language he is teaching. He also tells eye-opening tales of his days in the Foreign Service in South America.

The other side of this story is that Dr. Gonzales often loses track of the class's learning intentions. He will tell you himself that he is a storyteller and loves an audience, and he will sheepishly add that he can "get carried away." On the day that we watch his class, he begins reveling in one of his adventures in the Foreign Service. His storytelling begins as he provides an example of vocabulary used incorrectly by a student, and soon the story takes over. Today's class, according to the syllabus, is supposed to be focused on a set of verbs and their conjugation, but it's difficult to tell if you listen to Ray. His excitement is contagious and we join in it as he takes us to Latin America and its sounds and sights. We all listen with eager expressions and are captured by Ray's tales of intrigue and danger.

After a rich extended description of those days in Latin America, Ray pauses and notices a student with a raised hand. "Dominic, do you have a question?" The student replies in a most respectful tone, "Well, yes, Dr. Gonzales, I'm wondering what outcome we are working on right now." Ray stops and laughs, with just a touch of discomfort, and the students join him with quiet humor and chatter. A minute later, students are conjugating verbs in pairs, and Ray moves about the room providing feedback on pronunciation and accuracy of tense.

Ray Gonzales tells this story unabashedly and uses it to describe how outcomes have helped his teaching and, ultimately, student learning. There is nothing worse than a group of students leaving a class session scratching their heads, shrugging their shoulders, and wondering with much frustration, "What was that class about?" This story is a true account of a situation that repeated itself at California State University Monterey Bay (CSUMB) many times in 2000. Faculty and students had committed to studying the alignment of course outcomes with their weekly class meetings, and, therefore, awareness of outcomes was heightened. There are more of these stories, and you will read them in chapter 8 as we describe the Course Alignment Project that was designed to promote awareness in students like Dominic and in faculty members like Ray Gonzales.

This chapter begins with a return to definitions of outcomes. We wish to extend our description of what outcomes can do for student learning in case you need to convince a colleague. The work of developing outcomes has rich meaning for your work and significant implications for your institution's accountability. These two positive benefits are not usually talked about in the same sentence, but with outcomes-based assessment, they integrate naturally and with enhanced mutual effectiveness. This chapter also describes qualities of effective outcomes and provides examples of each quality from campuses all over the country—and we think it is just fine to use already developed examples that "fit" your program or course or graduation requirements. We share teaching strategies; we share instructional materials; we even share syllabi. Why not share outcomes? Ten years ago, faculty at CSUMB were forced to create learning outcomes "from scratch" because so few were available to even study as examples. That is not true anymore, and we urge our readers to tap into the Web sites on pages 263–264 as resources for various kinds of outcomes.

Outcomes—What and Why?

We begin by illustrating outcomes and have written several learning outcomes for you as a learner to achieve by the end of this chapter:

1. Develop and critique learning outcomes.
2. Describe the impact of using outcomes on student and faculty learning.
3. Explain how learning outcomes direct curriculum development, planning of pedagogy, and program or institutional accountability.

These outcomes describe implicitly what we want you to be able to do when you finish reading and thinking with us. When you read these learning outcomes, what happens to your thinking? How will you read this chapter? What will you need to achieve these outcomes? By the way, these are appropriate questions to use with your students at the beginning of a course or class session. Your answers and those of your students will indicate the sense of direction for reading and studying that outcomes supply. That sense of direction is one of the best advantages of using learning outcomes to promote learning. Before expanding on those advantages, we will define learning outcomes one more time.

Defining Learning Outcomes—Again!

It is our hope that the examples we have provided begin to communicate the idea that learning outcomes describe specifically what we want you to be able to do when you finish this chapter. They can describe the same for the completion of a class session, a course, a major program of study, and a baccalaureate or masters' degree:

> "At the end of today's class, you will be able to describe the main steps of collaborative problem solving and evaluate the importance of each step for the success of the process."
> "At the end of this course, you will be able to describe and use the inquiry practices of the disciplines of social sciences" (Association of American Colleges and Universities, 2004).
> "All graduates of the major in health and human services will be able to articulate the values and ethics that are the foundation for health and

human services practice, to recognize areas of conflict between the professional values and each graduate's own, and to clarify conflicting values in the delivery of health and human services" (Department of Health and Human Services, CSU Monterey Bay, 2006).

"All graduates of this university will be able to evaluate their role as agents of long-term, sustainable, and systemic change" (Clayton, 2005).

I am convinced of the power of examples as teachers, so I will continue to supply as many examples as I can fit in this chapter. A few more definitions will help elaborate what learning outcomes are. For example, according to Huba and Freed (2000), "Learning outcomes are statements describing our intentions about what students should know, understand, and be able to do with their knowledge when they have graduated" (pp. 9–10). They expand their definition with a reminder that those statements are learner centered. Taken as a whole, those statements enable us to describe what graduates of a major know, understand, and are able to do, and to do the same in the broader context of the institution for those who graduate.

Here are some other definitions of learning outcomes:

- Brown and Glaser (1999) talk about learning outcomes as describing "the intended purposes of higher education" (p. 7).
- Maki (2004) talks about learning outcomes as statements that "define what students should be able to demonstrate or represent at the end" of a course, a class session, and so on (p. 72).
- Palomba and Banta (1999) talk about learning outcomes as descriptions of the intended results of educational activities. They say that learning outcomes tell us specifically what needs to be assessed (p. 26).

When you start categorizing outcomes into types or dimensions, they will become more familiar and easier to develop.

Dimensions of Learning Outcomes

If we were to look at the universe of learning outcomes, we would probably see four familiar dimensions of learning outcomes in undergraduate education:

1. *Knowledge outcomes* (cognitive content, a common core of concepts, principles of inquiry, a broad history, core questions, and varied disciplinary techniques)
   EXAMPLE: Students will describe how oppression, racism, discrimination, and stereotyping affect all people, including those with a history of oppression by the dominant culture and those with internalized oppression (California State University Monterey Bay, 2006).
2. *Skills outcomes* (application, basic skills, higher-order cognitive skills, knowledge-building skills, and skills for effective practice in particular professions or occupations)
   EXAMPLE: Psychology students should be able to frame a question, define the relevant evidence that will answer it, analyze that evidence, and draw a conclusion (Bernstein, 2005, p. 38).
3. *Attitudes and values outcomes* (affective outcomes, personal/professional/social values, ethical principles)
   EXAMPLE: Students appreciate the language, art, religion, philosophy, and material of different cultures (American Council on Education, 2006).
4. *Behavioral outcomes* (a manifestation of the knowledge, skills, and attitudes; performance and contributions)
   EXAMPLE: Students will challenge the assumptions, stereotypes, and biases of others (Department of Health and Human Services, CSU Monterey Bay, 2006).

As you encounter examples of learning outcomes in the remainder of this chapter, stop and identify the dimension(s) of each outcome. It is a useful analysis in that you typically want a balance of outcome dimensions when you plan a course or program. We often emphasize knowledge outcomes and neglect the others. The experience of identifying the dimension of outcomes you encounter will also continue to support your readiness to meet the outcomes of this chapter.

We hope that all of the definitions, dimensions, and examples that we have presented have given you some confidence about learning outcomes. You may, however, be wondering how faculty or students or others come up with those statements. Our next topic responds to that curiosity and continues your learning process to meet the first outcome of this chapter: developing learning outcomes.

Sources of Learning Outcomes

We intend to satisfy your curiosity or concern about the sources of learning outcomes in this section, and we describe a broad range of sources for your consideration and use. Let's begin with the most prevalent source, goals.

Goals: Translating to Learning Outcomes

Banta (2005) encourages us to begin by articulating our goals and outcomes, and translating goals to outcomes is the first step in the development of learning outcomes. I think visually of goals as umbrellas with a set of outcomes hanging from their frame points. So I start with goals—broad, non-specific categories of learning, such as critical thinking, communication, ethics, multicultural understandings, and science literacy. Critical thinking and communication are quite meaningful in providing a context for our curriculum or teaching, or even student learning, but impossible to assess or measure without taking them apart into smaller specific learning outcomes. Start with the goal of critical thinking and think like a student for a minute. What would you plan to do to learn what you need to achieve that goal? Or how would you demonstrate that you have met that goal? Now think like a faculty teacher. What pedagogy will you use to support students to achieve that goal? What evidence will you need to ensure you that students have met that goal? You should be able to come up with some answers to these questions because goals do begin to direct your thinking as student and as faculty member.

So we take a goal like critical thinking and translate it for students into a set of learning expectations—outcomes—so that they can be clear and directed in their learning efforts. We do the same for teachers. Outcomes provide specific directions for what kind of pedagogy we plan and for the curricular content we teach. For example, critical thinking is analyzed into learning outcomes such as the following:

- Students will approach an issue or problem from multiple perspectives.
- Students will make claims or arguments based on evidence, information, or research.
- Students will compare and contrast academic materials and concepts (from reading assignments) with their community experiences and explain the reasons for the differences (Clayton, 2005).

Now, ask yourself the same questions you asked earlier. Begin as a student. What would you plan to do to learn what you need to achieve these outcomes? How would you demonstrate that you have met these outcomes? Now think like a faculty teacher. What pedagogy will you use to support students to achieve these outcomes. What evidence will you need to ensure you that students have met these outcomes? I hope that you will compare your answers for the outcomes to those same questions when applied to just goals; they should illustrate how helpful learning outcomes are for your work and for that of students.

Now that we have identified goals as a source of outcomes, you may be wondering, "How do institutions and faculty and students come up with goals?" We explore this next.

The Influence of Context on Goals to Outcomes—Institutional Missions and Values

Articulating goals and translating them into relevant learning outcomes is an opportunity for you as a faculty member to support the mission and values of your institution, or the promises (check your brochures) of your program, or even to direct your individual expertise or passion for particular content into curriculum. Almost every institution in the United States claims the goal of critical thinking, but each college or university translates it into different sets of learning outcomes. The previously given set of three critical thinking outcomes illustrates a range of contextual translations. At CSUMB, multiculturalism is an important value, so the first outcome regarding multiple perspectives is a high priority. At North Carolina State University, critical thinking is a focus for students' engagement in community, so the third outcome is a priority at that institution. As faculty, you can exercise control and creativity in the development of learning outcomes for your students' learning and for your teaching. With colleagues, you can expand and enrich student learning experiences by designing relevant and meaningful learning outcomes.

Professional and Disciplinary Associations

An important source of learning outcomes are the professional and disciplinary associations such as the American Association of Health Education, the American Council of Teachers of Foreign Language, or the National

Communication Association. These sources are not to be ignored in the process of setting learning outcomes. There are very practical reasons for attending to and using their already established goals and outcomes. First, the outcomes have been developed by groups of experts in the discipline who typically undertake their development with serious and dedicated long-term study. Second, for accreditation purposes, those learning outcomes should be reflected in institutional curriculum and assessment. You can look at the learning outcomes (sometimes called competencies) already developed for your use either positively or negatively. On the positive side, they can save you extensive development time; on the negative side, you have little ownership in them and less motivation to implement them.

My experience with groups of faculty who must work with disciplinary or professional outcomes is that they have been able to put their energy and creativity into the criteria for assessment or into designing student evidence that integrates local mission with professional association outcomes. For example, the Master of Public Health in Community Health Education Program (2006) at San Francisco State University must address the competencies from the American Association of Public Health in the context of its mission to "promote health and social justice in urban communities" (p. 1). Students achieve the learning outcomes or competencies of "selecting methods and media best suited to implement program plans for diverse populations" and "critically analyzing technologies, methods, and media for their acceptability to diverse groups" (p. 1) in the urban setting of San Francisco with attention to both health and social justice issues.

Community Sources

Future employers and community partners are another related source of learning goals and outcomes. Faculty at many institutions have creatively involved future employers in assessment design. At Colorado State University, business faculty used a combination of surveys and focus groups of employers of their graduates to identify learning outcomes for their program (Kretovics & McCambridge, 1999). What they learned from those employers motivated them to make curriculum changes, revise introductory courses, and design new assignments and other learning activities. The findings from their surveys and focus groups also motivated students to achieve the learning outcomes recommended by future employers.

The members of one of CSUMB's departments, Health and Human Services, used some of those same sources early in their work to develop learning goals and outcomes in collaborative processes with their community partners, and again later when they had developed some skill and confidence in their development work. Listen to Brian Simmons (2006) as he recounts their history:

> Like most of the early CSUMB faculty, CHHS's first professors had little understanding of what an "outcomes-based approach to education" meant and the implications for curriculum-building, pedagogy, and assessment. Rather, the faculty simply knew that they were assigned to build an outcomes-based program. To establish the first set of learning outcomes for the major, the first department chair conducted an informal survey of the . . . agencies of the tri-county area served by CSUMB. The thrust of the survey's questions was very basic: What did they want a recently graduated, entry-level employee to know and know how to do? The survey was included in a newsletter that went out to local agencies on a mailing list. No formal records were kept regarding the number of surveys distributed or the number returned. That notwithstanding, based on the responses and the professional judgment of the faculty, a list of learning outcomes and their corresponding definitions was generated. (p. 172)

Several years later, Simmons (2006) described their process for community input to their learning outcomes:

> The program faculty, with the support of a grant from the Stuart Foundation, and using a common Delphi process, surveyed health and human service agencies in the local area; 75 agencies were part of the initial response group and formed the core of the remaining Delphi cycles. In the first cycle, the respondents were provided with each of the current MLOs and were asked to suggest additional learning outcomes. Department staff from those responses generated an aggregate list of possible learning outcomes. In the second cycle, respondents were asked to rank the relative importance of the potential learning outcomes. (In a third cycle, respondents then identified which MLOs they believed they could offer [for] field-based instruction to the students. This information would serve later to enhance the program's capacity to assist students who wanted to increase their knowledge and skills in specific areas with the identification of field placement sites that were able to address their needs). . . . The Delphi process affirmed the 11 MLOs that existed at that time. While a few respondents made some suggestions for additions, there was either no systematic

pattern to the responses that warranted adding an additional learning outcome, or the CHHS faculty deemed. . .the suggestions. . .covered by existing MLOs. (pp. 174–175)

This process may seem overwhelming to you, but it would not be appropriate as a start-up process. The first process was simple, communicated well
to the community, and provided good information even though it was conducted with little organization. Note that the community input was blended
with the professional expertise of the faculty members.

Faculty and Students

Faculty and students are important but often neglected sources of learning
outcomes. Faculty members are the most appropriate leaders of the interpretation process in which the mission and values of the institution are translated into learning goals. They also have the best insights for analyzing those
goals into learning outcomes, because they know their disciplinary content,
their students, and the expectations of graduates in their field. A primary
reason that faculty are hesitant about learning outcomes is that they are concerned that their disciplinary leadership and pedagogical expertise will be ignored. And that probably has been true on occasion. However, when you
and your faculty colleagues work collaboratively, are empowered and respected sources of learning outcomes, the institution ends up with a rich,
diverse, and broadly conceived set of learning outcomes. Ensuring that
role and ownership requires that you be an active participant in designing
assessment, and that you do so with the public support and recognition of
administration.

We have held a naive traditional belief for many years that students need
us to direct their learning and, therefore, have seldom asked students about
what kind of learning outcomes are important for their studies. We recently
attended a seminar on graduate education, and the graduate student atten-
dees described the most important process to improve graduate education as
"being listened to in terms of their own goals and purposes for graduate
studies." We think that students of all ages have important ideas about their
own learning and are essential sources of learning outcomes.

At CSUMB we involved students at varied levels of developing outcomes, criteria, and standards. If we look at the work of Richard Light
(2002), we see that students can provide credible and useful information

about the strengths and weaknesses of courses and programs. In the process, students learn and gain experience in communication, understanding of others' perspectives, and assessment. When students at CSUMB learned about outcomes in their first year seminars and were held accountable for designing and using learning outcomes, they became supportive of the outcome-based assessment in their courses and programs. In one of the vignettes at the end of this book, Natasha Oehlman describes her first year seminar course in which her students meet learning outcomes that help them understand what outcomes are and use outcomes in their learning about outcomes. She also describes the pedagogy and assessment she uses to support their understandings.

Ensuring High-Quality Learning Outcomes

Designing quality learning outcomes requires us to consider and use sources with care. We encourage multiple sources and perspectives.

Multiple Sources and Perspectives

The very first assurance in designing quality learning outcomes is that all of the sources we have just described are considered and used with care. Each source is relevant for varying kinds of outcomes, however, and should be considered accordingly. For example, it would be negligible to develop learning outcomes for mathematics without consulting and using the national outcomes from the National Committee of Teachers of Mathematics. Or to develop learning outcomes for language instruction without consulting the American Council of Teachers of Foreign Language. Or to develop learning outcomes for business or social work without consulting the future employers and related community agencies and businesses. Or to develop communication outcomes and ignore the faculty member who has just published a book on cooperative argumentation. Or to develop the more difficult learning outcomes associated with the goals of self-discipline or lifelong learning or confidence without involving the thinking and input of students.

Another critical consideration for high-quality learning outcomes is clarity, which we discuss next.

Clarity as a Beginning Foundation

Clarity is of utmost importance, simply in terms of usefulness. If outcomes are not clear, neither faculty nor students will use them. In the process of trying to understand and use outcomes, both faculty and students will become turned off or reject learning outcomes that do not make sense or are fuzzy. It is important to stop here and acknowledge that clarity may be interpreted differently by these two groups. Therefore, we will address clarity for each of these users.

Clarity for Faculty

Faculty tend to use technical and disciplinary jargon that is typically but not always understood by their peers. We found in interviews with faculty that clarity is not necessarily achieved even when groups of faculty develop the actual learning outcomes (chapter 6). Thus, we recommend that faculty have common understandings and agreement about the meanings, intentions, and scope of their learning outcomes. Angelo (2005) urges faculty to "build a shared language" starting with common terms such as *learning, assessment,* and *improvement* (p. 2). Once you practice and have success at establishing common meanings for such generic terms, you can then work together on outcome language. It is often useful to begin with some generic outcomes from an outside source and discuss their meanings. You might approach your colleagues with a scenario like this:

> "We have been asked to implement this set of learning outcomes by a national organization—to integrate them with our own outcomes and weave them into the curriculum. Before we can make a decision about doing that, let's look at them and see what they mean to us. If you received this first outcome and were asked to achieve it in your classes, how would you interpret it?"
>
> *Learning Outcome. Students will summarize and critique the policies related to environmental protection of wetlands.*

Have a peer take notes using large sheets on a flip chart or white board to capture the collection of interpretations. It will be readily apparent that individual faculty members interpret the same words quite differently. Even if there are only two of you, the differences will be illustrative of the challenge of outcome clarity. An important follow-up question will stimulate the process of understanding the variation of meanings. For example:

> "Why do you think I came up with this meaning but you came up with that one?"

"What is it about this term that caused so much confusion?"

"How could we word this to help us agree on the meaning of the outcome?"

The understanding gained in the process just described will support future collaboration and agreements about common meaning of learning outcomes when you and your colleagues design sets of outcomes. You could use a similar process with a group of students when you are ready to address clarity for students.

Clarity for Students

Although clarity sounds simple, our experiences tell us that it is a quality that is illusive and demanding of guided discussion to achieve mutual understanding. Once clarity for faculty has been achieved, it will be important to ask, "Will students be able to understand this learning outcome?" Of course, students are the best source for answers to that question, but faculty can go a long way to achieving such clarity by simply reading the outcome from a student's perspective.

Faculty members at Alverno College found that they themselves had a clear sense of what they wanted their students to learn but that the process of explicitly identifying learning outcomes was not so simple. Somehow, faculty could make informed statements about course or program goals, but "articulating learning outcomes in ways that are clear, appropriate, and meaningful for students is another matter" (Student Learning Initiative, 2000, p. 5). Faculty at CSUMB commiserated with the Alverno dilemma in that they struggled with both articulating learning outcomes clearly and making them meaningful in their courses. Just as the faculty became fully engaged in their use of learning outcomes, they experienced swift disillusionment as students skipped the outcomes in their course syllabi and asked the age-old questions, "Is it going to be on the test?" and "What do I need to do to pass?" After a semester of such experiences, faculty groups gathered and brainstormed ways to make the learning outcomes meaningful.

Eric Tao, chair of technology, media, and communication at CSUMB, experimented in the first class session of his courses by asking students to rate the learning outcomes (at the front of his syllabus) with "I" for interesting, "D" for dreading, "U" for unclear, "A" for anticipation, "E" for essential, "F" for fuzzy, and so on. The actual ratings were not so important.

What was important was that he was able to get his students to think about and reflect on those learning outcomes early in their learning processes. The student ratings did, however, provide Eric with some information for his future class sessions and for clarifying the outcomes that students indicated were fuzzy.

Other faculty members used the learning outcomes as a pre-post self-assessment with students, or as a progress check midway throughout their courses. One faculty member had her students identify the learning outcomes they worked toward each time they read an article or a chapter, watched a video, or used a Web site. Two of our colleagues, David Reichard and Laura Lee Lienk, both describe their strategies to integrate their learning outcomes into meaningful and relevant pedagogy in the vignettes at the end of this book. All of these strategies for faculty are effective if the learning outcomes are clear to students to begin with, so your ultimate challenge is to ensure that clarity.

There are no easy answers to the issue of clarity for students, but it is critical to begin with an awareness of its importance. After developing student-learning outcomes, ask yourself, "Will these outcomes help students to learn?" or "Will students be clear of my learning expectations with these outcomes?" Such questions will remind you that learning outcomes are meant to support student learning, not to confuse or misguide it. If you are vigilant in asking yourself these kinds of questions, you will likely avoid fuzzy outcomes.

A Final Consideration: Is It the Right Outcome?

This last consideration is difficult to describe. We have used words such as *rigor, appropriate, fit,* and *enough,* but they are not quite adequate descriptions. When a group of faculty members from a disciplinary major or a faculty learning community (FLC) working on one general education goal finishes articulating a set of learning outcomes for its students, there is usually a quiet sense of uncertainty. We have often heard questions such as, "How do we know that these are the right outcomes?" "Are these outcomes enough?" "Is there enough rigor in these outcomes?" and "Is anything missing?" These are very important questions, but where do we turn for answers?

A significant starting point is the use of national standards or disciplinary goals/outcomes for alignment. We usually suggest that faculty send their learning outcomes out for review to colleagues in programs at other institutions—programs similar to their own program of studies—especially to those colleagues whom they highly regard. We also encourage returning to those future employers or community professionals in related fields for feedback. Alumni are another source of feedback on the adequacy of learning outcomes. We highly recommend that all three groups be contacted for review and critique when a set of learning outcomes is ready to use.

This is probably a good time to remind our readers that learning outcomes are never completely finished; disciplines change, information expands, and new skills are required, prompting revision of our learning outcomes. We are quite certain that you will not need that reminder. As a professional, you will be aware of those advances and changes and be ready to integrate them into your program starting with learning outcomes. When the Documenting Effective Educational Practices Project studied colleges and universities that had higher than predicted graduation rates and higher than predicted scores on the National Survey of Student Engagement, one of its findings was "an improvement-oriented ethos" (Kuh, Kinzie, Schuh, & Whitt, 2005, p. 46). It found a "positive restlessness" among faculty and administrators who were never quite satisfied with their performance. CSUMB was one of those institutions, and its ongoing revision of learning outcomes is evidence of that restlessness and an intense desire to improve what the institution is providing for students.

This chapter probably feels a little backward to you. We have not yet described how to develop outcomes, but we have described with great detail what they need to look like. After much reflection on this sequence, we determined that it would be helpful for you to have those qualities in mind as you begin your development work. We now move to that process of developing outcomes and describe it as a learning process with powerful dialogue.

Developing Outcomes: A Faculty Dialogue and Learning Process

This is the difficult part of the book—trying to describe for you how to write learning outcomes. I will say up front that there is no recipe or formula for articulating outcomes. It is sometimes a long drawn-out process of thinking and discussing what we want students to be able to do with their learning. And although that sounds time-consuming, it is the most important part of the process. In chapter 2, I talked about a culture of inquiry and the importance of spending time with *big* questions, such as "What do we want our graduates to be able to do and be?" or "What do we expect students who major in history to be able to do and be?" Our research backgrounds should send us to the literature at this point to study current thinking and practices in our disciplines, in general education, or in whatever our focus is. There you will find supports and resources to help you articulate learning outcomes.

Taxonomies: Support for Development

Once you begin to articulate some of the answers to the big questions, there is help for your work of developing outcomes. Since 1956 educators have used a taxonomy of cognitive levels and learning outcomes, and the taxonomy continues to be relevant for our work. Benjamin Bloom and his colleagues (Bloom, Englehart, Furst, Hill, & Krathwohl, 1956) initiated the taxonomy, which begins with simple cognitive processes and then moves to complex processes. Figure 3.1 describes each level of the taxonomy. These descriptions will assist you in thinking through what you really want students to be able to do and will help you to write outcomes. Figure 3.2 is an excellent resource with verbs for each level, making your outcome development an easier task.

Almost a decade after the taxonomy of cognitive domains was developed, another taxonomy was designed—that of the affective domain (Krathwohl, Bloom, & Masia, 1964). It is quite useful to describe some of those more difficult learning outcomes that we care about but find difficult to put into words. The affective levels also begin with simple behaviors and move to complex behaviors. The affective domain taxonomy is ideal for helping you to develop goals of diversity, ethics, responsibility, and lifelong learning. Figure 3.3 describes each of the domain's levels and provides verbs for your use.

Finally, there is a set of levels for the psychomotor domain, which is useful for determining some of the skills we expect students to demonstrate in varied disciplinary areas (Harlow, 1972).

FIGURE 3.1
Levels of the Cognitive Domain

Cognitive Domain. The cognitive domain includes thinking outcomes that range from simple to complex cognitive processes:

1. *Knowledge,* the lowest level, asks learners to remember previously learned material or to make a factual observation. When you want learners to tell when, how many, who, or where, they are using knowledge.
2. *Comprehension* asks learners to grasp the meaning of information, to interpret ideas, and to predict using knowledge. Learners are asked to translate knowledge into their own words. When asked why, to explain, or to summarize, they are using comprehension.
3. *Application* asks learners to use previously learned knowledge in new and concrete situations, to use information, and to do something with knowledge.
4. *Analysis* requires learners to break something into its constituent parts. They are asked to organize, to clarify, to conclude, or to make inferences. The process of analysis helps learners understand "big ideas" and the relationship of parts.
5. *Evaluation* requires a judgment. Learners must give defensible opinions with criteria for their judgment. They may be judging accuracy, consistency, logic of information, or argumentation. They may also be using selected criteria.
6. *Synthesis (Create)* requires the putting together of elements and parts to form a whole. Learners arrange and combine the elements in such a way as to create a pattern or structure not clearly seen before (Bloom et al., 1956).

Prioritizing Curriculum Content

The taxonomies take care of some of the mechanics of writing learning outcomes. They help you articulate what you want students to be able to do with the content of your curriculum. That content draws upon your disciplinary expertise, your graduate studies, current literature, and recommendations of your professional association. You will probably end up with more content than you can fit in one class and sometimes in one program. This is when your ability to prioritize will be essential. The cognitive levels from Bloom's taxonomy will help because there is some information that will require low levels of attention: *defining, describing,* and *summarizing.* There is also information that requires high levels of attention because of its importance, complexity, and centrality to the discipline. This is the content that you will want your students to *evaluate, analyze,* and *synthesize.*

Another way to prioritize the information or content that will become part of your learning outcomes is to create a web of that information, with

FIGURE 3.2
Verbs for Each Level of the Cognitive Domain

Cognitive Domain Levels and Learner Outcomes

Knowledge	defines, repeats, lists, names, labels, asks, observes, memorizes, records, recalls, fills in, listens, identifies, matches, recites, selects, draws
Comprehension	restates, describes, explains, tells, identifies, discusses, recognizes, reviews, expresses, locates, reports, estimates, distinguishes, paraphrases, documents, defends, generalizes
Application	changes, computes, demonstrates, shows, operates, uses, solves, sequences, tests, classifies, translates, employs, constructs, dramatizes, illustrates, draws, interprets, manipulates, writes
Analysis	dissects, distinguishes, differentiates, calculates, tests, contrasts, debates, solves, surveys, appraises, experiments, diagrams, inventories, relates, maps, categorizes, subdivides, defends
Evaluation	compares, concludes, contracts, criticizes, justifies, supports, states, appraises, discriminates, summarizes, recommends, rates, decides, selects
Synthesis	creates, composes, proposes, formulates, sets up, assembles, constructs, manages, invents, produces, hypothesizes, plans, designs, creates, organizes, prepares, speculates

FIGURE 3.3
Levels of the Affective Domain

Affective Domain. This domain is also arranged in a hierarchy from a simple level to a complex level:

1. *Receiving* requires learners simply to attend—to listen, to notice, to observe—in order to receive.
2. *Responding* asks learners to discuss, argue, or agree/disagree in response to what is heard or observed.
3. *Valuing* requires learners to consider what was received, to use it to make decisions about its importance, to regard it as priority, and to place a value on it.
4. *Organizing* requires learners to place values in relationship to other values, to organize judgments and choices, and to be influenced by the value.
5. *Characterizing,* the highest level, requires learners to organize their values to the point that they are internalized or become a part of the learners' lives.

the big ideas in central boxes and the less important ideas in appendages branching off the main ideas. If you haven't used webbing before, you might wish to look at the web of learning outcomes that we created in chapter 7 to get an idea of what a web looks like. Webbing will help identify the central ideas as well as the connections between the ideas or information.

Brainstorming all of the possible content for a course or program, preferably with a peer or group of colleagues, is another way to prioritize curriculum content. A great way to do this is to write ideas on large sheets of paper, providing a helpful visual effect. The information can then be color coded using underlines. The most important ideas, "the ideas without which the course could not be complete or acceptable," can be coded in red. The information that is "important but not as essential" can be coded in blue, and the information that is "interesting but could be skipped" can be coded in green. Once you have prioritized the content, you will be ready to use the taxonomy to create your outcomes.

Final Reminders for Articulating Learning Outcomes

I wish to add a few more suggestions to complete our discussion of how to develop learning outcomes First, you need to continue reviewing samples and examples of learning outcomes from multiple sources. Second, collaboration is essential to this process; it provides the richness and depth to the end result—learning outcomes. Even if you wish to sit down quietly and develop outcomes for one of your courses, at the least you should have one colleague review them or a group of students (seniors or those ready to graduate or a former student) assess their clarity and usefulness. Finally, you need to ask yourself, "What do I want students to be able to do or be *after* they finish my course, our program, and the baccalaureate degree?" Once you are satisfied with your answers—those student learning outcomes—you are ready to think about teaching and learning, curriculum, and assessment.

Using Outcomes to Plan Teaching and Learning, Curriculum, and Assessment

Learning outcomes are really the heart of planning for teaching and learning; curriculum; and, of course, assessment. Based on my experiences over the last 10 years, I must admit that it seems impossible to design any of these processes without learning outcomes. However, thinking back to my early teaching experiences, I find it difficult trying to explain how I designed curriculum or planned my teaching and learning without having outcomes as a compass or guide. Many of us who have been teaching for a long time have only vague answers.

Outcomes as the Focus

The work of designing and articulating learning outcomes is intensified by the insecurity that faculty often experience upon completion. That insecurity comes from the knowledge that so much importance is placed on each outcome, and so much planning of pedagogy, resources, and assessment is focused on each outcome. Some of that uncertainty is addressed by the considerations previously reviewed: clarity, multiple sources, feedback, etc. Another process that assured us that our intentions were communicated well by the learning outcomes was a process of analyzing them for curricular and pedagogical implications.

Using Learning Outcomes as a Centerpiece

Learning outcomes should be used as a centerpiece for all of your design work, whether it is a program, a course, or a degree. Be sure that you can say, "When students finish our major, they will . . ." or "When students finish my course, they will . . ." or "Our graduates will . . ." From there, your responsibility is to plan curriculum and teaching and learning that supports students in achieving those outcomes. As you plan program components and descriptions, ask yourself and your colleagues, "How will this support students to achieve our programmatic outcomes?" Or as you plan your course and design the syllabus with readings, activities in class, assignments for outside of class, and so forth, ask, "How will each of these support students to achieve the learning outcomes of this course?" We recommend that you do as much of this inquiry and planning with colleagues. The end result will be richer and more meaningful and will benefit from multiple perspectives.

One of my and Swarup's favorite faculty learning activities is to post a learning outcome and describe the following scenario:

> You have just been hired to teach a course in _____ [any discipline], and you are informed that your students have to achieve the posted

learning outcome. Brainstorm all of the resources, information, teaching and learning strategies, and environmental considerations you would pull together to plan your course.

For now, we will leave that course generic and work with the following learning outcome to demonstrate the kind of thinking we have heard from faculty instructors on many campuses:

> Students will analyze real-world ethical problems or dilemmas and identify those affected by the dilemma.

That outcome came from the ethics FLC that you met in chapter 2, and it's a beginning-level outcome that could be addressed in a variety of courses or disciplines (e.g., business, environmental science, history, art, health and human services, teaching). With that outcome in mind, we came up with the following considerations for teaching the course assigned to us:

Use of newspapers	*Reflective writing*
Definition of ethical problems or dilemmas	*Guest speakers*
Sensitivity for troubling issues that may arise	*Readings in the disciplinary area*
Practice with analysis processes	*Class culture of support*
Collaborative group work for intensive discussion	*Movies, videos, art, theater, and literature*
Role play or simulation	*Identifying "real world" cases*
Ethical frameworks for analysis	*Readings in ethics*
Criteria for determining whether a problem is an ethical dilemma	*Local as well as global issues*

That's a beginning. Keep in mind that the outcome is probably one of a set of five or six outcomes for a course, so our list is not comprehensive for planning the teaching and learning and curriculum. Again, it is an enriching and expanding process when conducted with a group of faculty colleagues. Now, we want to take it a step further and conduct the same kind of brainstorming in a different scenario:

You are a student who is required to take a course in which the outcome ("Students will analyze real-world ethical problems or dilemmas and identify those affected by the dilemma") is listed in the syllabus. When you read it, what concerns, hopes, expectations, and interests are piqued by the learning outcome?

Here is what we came up with:

I'm nervous about possible issues.	*Will my values agree with those of the faculty?*
What are ethical dilemmas?	*Do I know how to analyze?*
We could get into some tricky stuff.	*Are there right answers?*
Why do I need ethics?	*Will it be safe to talk about my ideas?*
I hope we work on some of the local happenings.	*How will I use this in my career?*
How do you know when it is an ethical dilemma?	*Does this apply to my personal life?*

Again, this is not a comprehensive list but you should get the idea. We have often put these types of lists side by side to see if we are attending to student perspectives in our planning. It's a good awareness activity. The second activity really attends to being student centered in our use of outcomes for course or program planning.

Checking Your Readiness for the Learning Outcomes

It is important that you attend to the verbs in your learning outcomes. If you are asking students to analyze or synthesize, first make sure that you know how to use those processes well yourself. You may be offended by that advice, but we recently sat with a group of faculty members who were critiquing student work because there was no synthesis (as required in the learning outcome). Fortunately, there was that quality of trust in this faculty community, and one member quietly said, "I don't know how to teach students to synthesize; in fact, I'm not sure that I know how to synthesize myself." Some of those high-level processes in Bloom's taxonomy do require sophisticated thinking and skills, so start with yourself. From there, it's still a strenuous task to figure out how to help students gain that sophistication. A major teaching strategy for most of the processes is modeling the process yourself. As you do so, be sure to "think aloud" with the students. For example, "I'm analyzing the assignment you are taking home tonight to determine what skills or steps you will need to take to be successful. Break it down with me. What is your first step? Why do we need to start there?" Then you could continue with, "We have just analyzed the homework assignment into its required steps. If you had to define analysis, what would you tell someone that analysis means?" It will also help learners if you note whenever a student uses the process. For example, "Notice that Lawrence just synthesized our situation in Afghanistan. What did he do?" Or, "Did you notice that Melba conducted a quick analysis of why that community project did not work? What are the advantages of analysis?" Examples are a wonderful teaching tool, but don't forget the power of nonexamples too. For example, "Did you listen to Hiram's analysis? What was missing? Why was it ineffective?"

Some of our colleagues from CSUMB share their teaching and learning strategies in vignettes at the end of the book. They have each used their outcomes and criteria as a form of pedagogy, much like Swarup describes in the following section.

A Conversation With Swarup

I don't have the advantage of working directly with students anymore, so I am very curious about how they respond to learning outcomes. I asked Swarup:

What do students say about outcomes?
   I work primarily with first-year students and learning outcomes are still new to them. Once they get used to them, my students value them and talk about how they help. I have heard students criticize faculty privately for not providing outcomes, which certainly impressed me.

At the end of this book, we include the graduation speech of a former student who framed her talk around the importance of outcomes. She is quite articulate about her development from resistance to valuing, and what outcomes meant for her studies and for her life. From my conversations with faculty, I know how challenging it is to get students to the point of valuing and understanding learning outcomes. I had to ask Swarup the next question:

How do you use outcomes in your courses besides putting them in the syllabus?
   I now require students to do an extensive reflective exercise on my course learning outcomes for their first homework assignment. In this assignment,

students are asked to reflect on the meaning of each outcome, their current level of mastery, and to discuss the kind of evidence that they would bring to demonstrate how they would meet the outcome at their current level of competence. I have them do the same assignment at the end of the course as their final homework assignments as they prepare for the final exam. I constantly focus students' attention on learning outcomes by having the outcomes we are working for that class session visible on the board in front of all of us. That is, I use them to visually frame most everyday activities.

In closing, we urge you to patiently remain on this course with us. Learning outcomes do not stand alone. Thus, the work is not complete when you finish articulating learning outcomes, but you will feel quite accomplished. We are going to proceed to designing evidence, criteria, and standards to accompany learning outcomes. Those assessment packages or protocols will be important for extending this conversation about using outcomes to plan curriculum teaching and learning, and assessment.

References

American Council on Education. (2006). *International learning outcomes.* Washington, DC: American Council on Education/FIPSE Planning Grant.

Angelo, T. (2005). *Doing assessment as if learning matters most.* Materials for the Annual Assessment Institute Conference, September, Indianapolis.

Association of American Colleges and Universities. (2004). *Our students' best work: A framework for accountability worthy of our mission.* Washington, DC: Author.

Banta, T. W. (2005). *Developing assessment methods at classroom, unit, and university-wide levels.* Paper presented at the Assessment Institute, Indianapolis.

Bernstein, D. (2005). Disciplining the minds of students. *Change, 37*(2), 36–43.

Bloom, B., Englehart, M., Furst, E., Hill, W., & Krathwohl, D. R. (1956). *Taxonomy of educational objectives: The classification of educational goals, Handbook I, Cognitive domain.* New York: McKay.

Brown, S., & Glaser, A. (1999). *Assessment matters in higher education.* Philadelphia: The Society for Research in Higher Education.

California State University Monterey Bay. (2006). *General education outcomes* (University Learning Requirements). Seaside, CA: Author.

Clayton, P. H. (2005). *Critical thinking by design: An integrated approach to assessment.* Presentation at the Assessment Institute, Indianapolis.

Department of Health, Human Services and Public Policy. (2006). *Major learning outcomes.* Seaside, CA: Author.

Harlow, A. (1972). *Taxonomy of the psychomotor domain.* New York: McKay.

Huba, M. E., & Freed, J. E. (2000). *Learner-centered assessment on college campuses.* Boston: Allyn & Bacon.

Krathwohl, D. R., Bloom, B., & Masia, B. (1964). *Taxonomy of educational objectives: The classification of educational goals, Handbook II, Affective domain.* New York: McKay.

Kretovics, M. A., & McCambridge, M., Jr. (1999). A seven-step approach to developing an outcomes assessment program. *Assessment Update, 1*(12), 10–11.

Kuh, G., Kinzie, J., Schuh, J., & Whitt, E. (2005). Never let it rest: Lessons about student success from high-performing colleges and universities. *Change, 37*(4), 44–51.

Light, R. J. (2002). *Making the most of college: Students speak their minds.* Cambridge, MA: Harvard University Press.

Maki, P. L. (2004). *Assessing for learning: Building a sustainable commitment across the institution.* Sterling, VA: Stylus.

Master of Public Health in Community Health Education Program. (2006). *Program mission and description brochure.* San Francisco: Master of Public Health in Community Health Education Program, San Francisco State University.

Palomba, C. A., & Banta, T. W. (1999). *Assessment essentials: Planning, implementing, and improving assessment in higher education.* San Francisco: Jossey-Bass.

Simmons, B. (2006). One department's assessment story: Processes and lessons. In A. Driscoll & D. Cordero de Noriega (Eds.), *Taking ownership of accreditation* (pp. 171–203). Sterling, VA: Stylus.

Student Learning Initiative. (2000). *Creating a framework for making student learning the central focus of institutions of higher education.* Milwaukee, WI: Alverno College Institute.

4

STUDENT EVIDENCE

Designing Assignments and Assessments for Diverse Learners

Stories: Student Interpretations of Our Assignments and Assessments

I n our first of two vignettes, it is the end of a long day of reviewing students' final papers in a general education course that focused on culture and equity issues. Most of the faculty members around the table are enthusiastic about the quality of student writing and extensive descriptions in their papers. But they unanimously agree that there is little, if any, analysis in most of the work. The students had been directed to demonstrate the following outcome:

> Students will describe and analyze issues of equity and power and privilege in a cultural context.

We are all quite puzzled and Juan, the faculty member whose students' work has been reviewed, is crestfallen. One of the faculty learning community (FLC) members tries to provide assurance, saying, "I have trouble getting students to analyze material too." However, Juan is not comforted and replies: "I've really worked on the process of analysis this semester, modeled it every chance I could, and I was feeling quite pleased with the class progress." Upon careful examination of his syllabus, specifically the directions for the final paper, someone notes that the phrase "and analyze" was omitted from the outcome. So students had described at great length, following directions, thinking that description was the requirement. Quite a hubbub occurs after that discovery and Juan jokes, "I guess I should feel good that students followed my information so closely." He then sighs as he vows to "check my assignments and assessments very closely in the future."

In our second vignette, a faculty work group is reviewing Spanish assignments written in response to a film. The intention was for students to demonstrate two outcomes. The first outcome was related to their understanding and ability to communicate in Spanish. The second outcome was to demonstrate their understanding of the cultural issues and traditions that were integrated in the movie and to relate personally to those issues and traditions. After reading a small sample of the reflective papers, most of the faculty participants look unenthusiastic. Rina expresses the consensus of the group when she pronounces, "These are not reflections—they are merely summaries with no analysis of the cultural context." She then continues, "I had to search to find any personal response."

The director, in her facilitator role, listens as faculty take turns commenting but reinforcing Rina's assessment. When the discussion begins to dwindle, she asks the faculty members to examine the directions for the reflective paper. Everyone skims the syllabus to find the directions and quickly note that they are minimal. The directions merely ask students to discuss the film with no mention of personal reflection or analysis of the cultural context.

In an instant, faculty begin talking about the directions and their importance. One faculty member suggests that they spend a few minutes practicing—writing a set of directions for the paper that would communicate their expectations to students. The learning is extended when the director asks, "What kind of directions would you give if you wanted the students to compare the film with a previously read short story, or if you wanted students to analyze a cultural conflict in the film?" The session becomes a powerful learning experience for all, and the work ends on a high note with serious resolutions about writing directions for students to be successful.

The preceding vignettes illustrate the following concepts. This chapter follows the discussion of outcomes in chapter 3 by describing the kind of evidence (student work) that demonstrates that students have achieved the outcome. The theme of the vignettes is that the design of and directions for student evidence are critical in terms of students being able to demonstrate outcomes successfully.

Designing Student Evidence: Support for Student Learning

For us, the content of this chapter is critical to being a learner-centered teacher, to providing learner-centered programs, and to assessing in ways that support student learning. If we had continued those vignettes until faculty finished all of their review processes, you would have gained deeper insight about this practice of our profession. Each time faculty reviewed student work, there were papers from savvy students who consistently achieve straight As. In the second vignette, those students put themselves in the film review and compared their cultural traditions with those of the characters. No matter what the directions or criteria or descriptions the faculty teacher provides, such students will always add more to their papers or other assignments. It's as if they can read our minds even when we are not aware of our own expectations. Their work makes us smile and feel a little better about our teaching, but they are the exception.

In contrast to their peers who follow directions, thinking that it is the right way to go, these students intuitively know enough to expand their answers even when the directions call for minimal depth or detail. When teachers provide a set of directions with clear, detailed information that is well matched to their expectations, they "level the playing field," giving all students a fair chance to achieve well. The practice of providing such directions is a student-centered practice.

Qualities of Student-Centered Assignments or Assessments

We will return to directions at the end of this chapter, but for now, we describe how student work provides evidence of achieving outcomes and how to design those student work assignments or assessments so that our diverse student populations are able to demonstrate their learning. Let's take a look at a list of characteristics of a quality undergraduate education:

- High expectations
- Respect for diverse talents and learning styles
- Coherence in learning

- Synthesis of experiences
- Ongoing practice of learned skills
- Integration of education and experience (Education Commission of the States, 1996).

This insightful list provides a prescriptive framework for this chapter's focus: designing assignments and assessments to provide evidence of learning for diverse students. When we can achieve this list of features with our assessment, we can call it authentic assessment, and it's a practice that fits our learner-centered education model. Later in the chapter, I want to get you thinking about fair assessment practices, that is, giving students equitable opportunities to demonstrate their achievement of outcomes.

Moving Toward Authentic Assessment

The years of multiple choice and true/false exams to demonstrate learning have given way to what educators at all levels are calling authentic assessment. Dissatisfaction with measures that did not provide "evidence of analytical skills, creativity, resourcefulness, empathy, and abilities to apply knowledge and transfer skills from one environment to another" (Association of American Colleges and Universities, 2002, p. 13) directed efforts to developing an alternative kind of evidence. "Conventional test questions, be they from national tests or the teacher down the hall, do not replicate the kinds of challenges that adults face in the workplace, in civic affairs, or in their personal lives" challenged Grant Wiggins (1989, p. 703; Wiggins & McTighe, 1998) along with both educators and students. Many of the more current initiatives to describe the goals and outcomes of a well-educated graduate describe qualities and capabilities that cannot be assessed with traditional approaches.

The concept of authentic assessment that has evolved from the dissatisfaction with traditional assessment calls for processes that are embedded in relevant and real-world activities for professionals in the disciplines. Authentic assessment provides students with opportunities to respond to the kinds of challenges Wiggins (1989) described and to questions and problems that are meaningful and engaging. Furthermore, authentic assessment provides students with opportunities to integrate their personal experiences with their academic learning. Remember back in chapter 2 we described the philosophy of assessment derived by faculty at CSU Monterey Bay (CSUMB) as follows: "Assessment . . . enriches, extends, and expands learning." When we design evidence for students to demonstrate their achievement of learning outcomes in ways that are relevant, engaging, integrating of experience, and representative of life's challenges, assessment achieves those ends well.

I have been providing extensive descriptions here, so some examples will expand your understanding of those qualities of authentic assessment. Start with a learning outcome:

> "Students who complete the requirements for a Bachelor of Science degree in Psychology will engage in informed, critical, intellectual discussion of questions of human behavior" (St. Mary's College, 2006).

Traditional assessment would have asked those students (prior to graduation) to respond to a particular question of human behavior in an essay exam. More authentic assessment could take the following forms:

- Role plays of a discussion about a question of human behavior
- Debates about a question of human behavior
- Letters to the editor about a current event or an issue that represents a question of human behavior
- An interview of a public figure about a question of human behavior accompanied by an analysis of the interview data
- Multimedia or other visual forms of presentation to illustrate a question of human behavior and multiple answers
- Autobiographical descriptions of personal examples of human behavior with reflections based on theory and research of human behavior

Each of these examples could provide evidence that students achieved the outcome, and almost as important, each form of assessment would engage learners, address real-world issues, and challenge learners on a personal level. The examples are also well aligned with the learning outcome. If we were to use CSUMB's criteria for assessment—that assessment must extend or enrich the learning—every one of these examples would work as well. When students are able to choose their own form of evidence, for example, choose among role plays, debates, or multimedia forms of evidence, we begin to address the diversity of our learners. Figure 4.1 provides an example from

FIGURE 4.1
Sample Syllabus with Evidence

Outcome 1A

1) Describe the essential attributes of the scientific way of knowing and compare and contrast the scientific and popular meanings of "hypotheses" and "theories."

Selected Examples of Evidence

Quiz	Exam	Interview
Worksheet	Debate	Paper
Popular press review	Role play	Written story that explains the difference

Outcome 1B

2) Use the scientific method of inquiry and standard scientific techniques to answer questions about physical, biological, or social processes.

Selected Examples of Evidence

Research project	Poster	Demonstration
Diagram	Video	Critical review
Term paper	Web page	Examination
Community problem solving		

Outcome 1C

3) Explain how peer review contributes to the reliability of scientific knowledge.

Selected Examples of Evidence

Essay examination	Debate of the pros and cons of peer review
Experiment	Lesson plan incorporating peer review
Story about the peer review process	Poster presenting a model of the peer review process

Source: From *Syllabus example for VPA 320, Museum Studies,* by L. Staples, 2006, Seaside, CA: Department of Visual and Public Arts, CSUMB. Reprinted with permission.

one of our colleagues at CSUMB that illustrates a syllabus strategy that achieves authentic assessment, gives students a choice, and demonstrates the alignment of assignments with each outcome.

Tim Riordan (2005) provides another example of authentic assessment, one inspired by his students. The students tape-recorded their small-group discussions as they responded to Tim's questions about Dewey's pragmatism—on a day when Tim had to miss class as the result of illness. The tape recordings were their idea, and when he listened to them, he realized that his students were using the kind of philosophical thinking described in his learning outcomes and demonstrating the skills they practiced in his class. Soon after, Tim rethought the essay exam he had planned for their final assessment and scheduled that same kind of taped discussion in small groups (without his input) as an assessment format. He describes his thinking as follows: "I realized that the interactive situation was closer to how they would actually be using my discipline in their lives" (p. 53). That quality of being closer to use in their lives is a key to authentic assessment.

Tim realized that it was likely that some of his students would be better able to demonstrate their philosophical thinking processes in a writing assignment, so he also assigned a brief reflective essay. That consideration of student diversity is the next consideration in designing assignments and assessments for students to demonstrate their achievement of learning outcomes.

Designing for Diversity

One of the major challenges we face and one of the most exciting resources available to us is the increasing diversity of learners. With that increase come questions of the relevancy and effectiveness of our curriculum, our modes of instruction, and even the "fit" of our learning environments. Almost 10 years ago, Schilling and Schilling (1998) reminded us of the extreme differences between faculty members' own learning experiences and current students' approaches to learning. Within today's challenges, assessment is seen as being in need of complete revision or redesign. At the same time, it is seen as having potential to help us diversify instruction to meet the needs of our diverse populations.

Within the concept of diversity of learning are two theories that are useful for thinking about learning and how to support learners: Gardner's theory of multiple intelligences, and Kolb's learning styles. These theories have important implications for designing student work. In addition, there is extensive research on the effects of socioeconomic factors and cultural differences on learning, and those effects also have implications for designing student assignments and assessments. We discuss all three to expand your thinking about student evidence and to encourage you to broaden the possibilities when asking students to demonstrate that learning outcomes have been met.

Gardner's Multiple Intelligences

Gardner's (1983) theory of multiple intelligences and the research that followed (Gardner & Hatch, 1989; Krechevsky & Gardner, 1990) have had a significant impact on our thinking about intelligence. Our traditional overreliance on narrow measures of achievement becomes immediately problematic when we consider Gardner's seven intelligences. Gardner's seven forms of thinking include the most traditionally emphasized and valued intelligences: logical-mathematical and linguistic. Beyond these, he expands intelligence to musical abilities, spatial capabilities, bodily-kinesthetic abilities, and interpersonal and intrapersonal intelligences. Our challenge is to find ways to value and enable the many types of intelligence that diverse students bring to our classes.

When it comes to assessment, it is especially critical that our forms of evidence be inclusive as well as engaging for students to use to demonstrate their learning. When members of the ethics FLC began designing evidence for their outcomes, they were especially tuned in to multiple intelligences and included the following forms of evidence in their first draft of assessment:

- A written account
- A multimedia presentation
- A display board
- A role play or dramatization
- Lyrics and a musical score
- An audiotape

In the seven years since they designed the list of evidence, not one student ever came up with the lyrics of a musical score. Nonetheless, these faculty members were committed to that possibility being available. We had many conversations about how to evaluate such evidence, but the members of the group decided that they would "cross that bridge" when they came to it. I feel quite certain that they would. Along with theories of multiple intelligences, learning styles create a foundation for innovative pedagogy and assessment.

Kolb's Learning Styles

Kolb (1976, 1985) used a four-stage learning process to suggest a typology of learning that includes experiential learning. His thinking has been quite useful to the service learning movement as well as to internships and studies abroad. Kolb's idea is that learners have preferences for learning that include concrete experiences, reflective observations, active experimentation, and abstract conceptualization. The theory begins to separate the thinkers and doers. The learning styles have been capsulated into four groups:

1. *Convergers* are comfortable with abstract concepts and active experimentation, preferring practical application, little affect, and specific interests.
2. *Divergers* are comfortable with concrete experiences and reflective observations and can view situations from varied perspectives.
3. *Assimilators* are comfortable with abstract conceptualization and reflective observation and work with theoretical models and inductive reasoning.
4. *Accommodators* are comfortable with concrete experience and active experimentation, rely on others' information, adapt easily, and solve problems intuitively (Stage, Muller, Kinzie, & Simmons, 1998, pp. 70–71).

When you read these descriptions, you may begin to feel overwhelmed in terms of how to assess with sensitivity to those differences, but they offer some beginning guideposts to address with our learners. Helping our students identify their learning styles or preferences will contribute significantly to their lifelong learning as well as to their success in our courses. In the process of identifying their style or preference, they are able to suggest or collaborate with us in the design of evidence to demonstrate their learning.

More Differences to Consider in Assessment Designs

Interestingly, researchers have found that the differences in learning styles are not related to age, gender, prior experiences, and educational attainment (Cavanaugh, Hogan, & Ramgopal, 1995), but may be connected to attitudes toward education (Bodi, 1990). Much of the research on learning styles concludes that particular modes of assessment are advantageous to students with particular learning styles.

There are also indications that your own learning style influences classroom assignments and evaluations of course work. When students match your learning style, pedagogy and assessment are comfortable and supportive for them. Otherwise, students who do not match are forced to use other learning styles (whether comfortable or effective) or risk failure. Sometimes it takes an entire course or sequence of courses for learners to figure out how to match an instructor's learning style, and it may be too late when they do. From my perspectives as a former faculty member and a facilitator of faculty dialogue, I consider that information about the influence of our own learning styles as a critical awareness focus. Once again, if we are going to be learner centered in our pedagogy and assessment, the research tells us to start with ourselves and develop an awareness of our learning styles and preferences. From there, we need to commit to learning about our students —especially their learning styles, preferences, and intelligences. This information will be a major informant to our pedagogy and assessment, but the match or mismatch with our own information can be used to achieve student-centered education.

Ideally, our classrooms must offer direct experience and active experimentation as well as abstract conceptualization and reflective observation in both pedagogy and assessment. Those who teach service learning courses blend direct experience with reflection for a powerful pedagogy, but few faculty members have been prepared to use either form of pedagogy prior to those courses. Even when such pedagogy is practiced well, our assessment often reverts to traditional assessments or forms of evidence.

Asking students to consider the best way to show that they have met the learning outcomes is often a very effective strategy. Not all students can prescribe for their learning accurately, but many can, and the resulting assessments are both interesting and engaging. Students will have a significant impact on the learning of their peers with their diverse evidence and related discussions. When students can produce relevant evidence that engages them and their peers, their learning is enhanced and expanded.

One more consideration about the differences of our students is less concrete but it is one that has important implications for student success. Students' conceptions of what it means to be intelligent can affect their performance (Dweck, 1989) on the assessment tasks (evidence) that we assign. If they think that intelligence is a fixed entity, they are likely to be performance oriented and concerned about the appearance of being successful (translated as intelligence) (Bridglall, 2001). They will not be thinking about the learning aspects of a task; instead, they will worry about making mistakes and will avoid risks. By contrast, if students think that intelligence is malleable, they are more willing to struggle with challenging tasks, to take risks, and even to fail if the learning is visible and valued (Bridglall, 2001).

The implication of these differences for us is that we must come up with evidence tasks that are challenging yet manageable. It is such a fine line between challenging students and discouraging students. In addition to knowing their knowledge and skill level, learning preferences and styles, and previous educational experiences, we must converse with them about intelligence, learning, and success. Such rich conversations inform both our pedagogy and assessment. We have been stunned and delighted when listening to students describe their perspectives on these topics. We have also gleaned good insights for designing assessment.

Fair Assessment Practices: Equitable Opportunities for Students

Linda Suskie (2000) reminds us that if we are to "draw good conclusions about what our students have learned, it is imperative that we make our assessments—and our uses of the results—as fair as possible for as many students as possible" (p. 116). She describes steps to fair assessment that begin with the attention to student diversity much as we explained in the previous section. She adds additional steps that really support our learners, such as the following: Help students learn how to do the assessment tasks.

Suskie (2000) describes such help in her own teaching. She says that she provides extensive directions for the tasks—"sometimes my assignment descriptions for student projects can run three single-spaced pages"—(p. 117) but affirms that the quality of student work is far higher than when she provides less detail. She also provides examples of projects or other assignments from previous classes. Many of us have been hesitant to do that, fearing that it would reduce creativity or effort, but many of us have discovered that examples promote confidence and clarity of student work. Some of our colleagues at CSUMB had students critique and evaluate previous student work as a preparation for doing similar work themselves. They unanimously reported that the quality of the resulting evidence was indicative that the approach should be continued. The bottom line for this advice about helping students learn is to be sure that learners have the skills and information they need to produce the evidence.

A second step recommended by Suskie is to review the results of your assessment to determine whether the assessment supports or jeopardizes students' capacity to demonstrate their learning. Sometimes, in spite of our best intentions, we design assignments or projects or other evidence in ways that do not align with our outcomes, are not clear, or are at odds with the way we taught the curriculum. For example, a colleague of ours, Burke Pease, taught an on-line business course and had students complete all of their assignments in collaborative learning groups. He was pleased with the quality of work on those assignments. However, when he followed each set of assignments with a multiple-choice exam, he was dismayed by the dismal results. Upon examining the results of his assessment and talking with his students, he discovered two problems: the exams did not emphasize the content of what was practiced in groups or even emphasized in the classes, and the conflict of styles between the practice and traditional assessment discouraged and confused many of his learners. Burke's first response was to redesign the exam; the results improved. Not yet satisfied, he designed a new assignment that he integrated with the collaborative learning assignment to assess the terminology that had been the focus of his exams; the results were exciting. Ultimately, Burke wanted his students to be able to use the technical vocabulary, and the new assignment really demonstrated students' ability to do so. He truly achieved student-centered practices by attending to the lack of consistency in student achievement between his two main forms of assessment.

In addition to her useful steps to fair assessment, Linda Suskie (2000) encourages us to question when we see unfair assessment practices, work to improve our own assessment methods, and find ways to share our learning and practices (p. 118). We will find a great deal of support for our fairness in the innovations of assessment currently being disseminated, by the sharing of colleagues at conferences and in publications, and in the work of our professional associations and accreditation agencies. We join Suskie in urging our colleagues to work to make fair assessment of student learning a reality.

Our discussion about fairness leads indirectly to our last major topic of this chapter: formative and summative assessment. One of our unfair practices is to move students quickly to summative assessment without ample opportunity to practice or engage in formative assessment. In the next section, we amplify that statement with descriptions of each form of assessment and examples of the kind of evidence that would be appropriate.

Formative and Summative Assessment

Before jumping into recommendations, it's necessary to define each form of assessment. *Formative assessment* is ongoing assessment that provides information about progress, misunderstandings, need for clarification, and so forth. It's the kind of assessment that we need to use consistently through the learning process to determine whether students are learning. It often tells us whether to slow down and provide more explanation or to move on because learners are getting bored. As we conduct formative assessment, we are able to provide feedback to students so that they will know whether they are "getting it," "need to work harder," "are off track," or "are ready to start new information." Most important, formative assessment provides opportunities for students to practice new learning and make mistakes without the risk of earning a low grade or reducing grade averages and so on. Let's look at a couple of examples before moving on to summative assessment.

Students are working on analysis of community issues as a learning outcome. After learning about and practicing the process of analysis with some simple class issues, they study several significant community issues and work in collaborative learning groups to analyze an assigned community issue. This is their first formative assessment. Following the group analysis, students critique another groups' analysis. This is their second formative assessment. In one of their class sessions, the students engage in a simulation of a community issue and write a news story analyzing the issue. This is their third formative assessment. Finally, students are ready for their last assignment: summative assessment. They each select a community issue of interest, conduct interviews and read news reports and stories, and develop a Web site analysis of the issue.

Throughout the three formative assessments, the faculty instructor examines the evidence and provides feedback to support the continuing learning. Although students are given points for completing each step or assessment in the learning process, their analysis evidence is not graded, only reviewed for purposes of giving feedback. When they complete the summative assessment, the Web site analysis, their evidence is graded.

Designing a sequential set of evidence assignments to support student practice with feedback is a sophisticated process and requires much effort. However, those faculty members who do so feel strongly that their efforts are worthwhile because they experience such satisfaction with the quality of student evidence for the summative assessment. One of our colleagues at CSUMB, Dan Shapiro, assigns a major final research paper in one of his courses. After his students complete each component of the paper (guiding questions, rationale for topic, literature review, and so forth), they hand in that component and receive extensive feedback on their work. Throughout the semester, there is a continuous cycle of learning, production of evidence, review and feedback, revision, and improvement well in advance of summative assessment. Dan says that when students complete their final paper (summative evidence), they have clear self-assessments of the quality of their work, and there are no surprises when grades are assigned. He also confesses that his final grading work is minimal, although he works quite intensely all semester long. In addition, his students comment enthusiastically and with real sincerity about how much they have learned both about writing and about the content of their research. We think that such comments affirm the importance and effectiveness of formative assessment in an ongoing and iterative way for student learning.

As a final comment on formative assessments, faculty learn that formative assessments that are conducted in an ongoing and systematic way "make students' thinking visible to both teachers and to students" (Bridglall, 2001, p. 5). That window into students' thinking allows faculty to revise their teaching plans, both pedagogy and curriculum, to be as learner centered as possible. An extra bonus of students being able to examine their own thinking is that it makes it possible for them to revise and improve their thinking and learning. They can see their own progress and identify their own problems. One quality of formative assessments that makes much of this possible is their "learner friendliness" (p. 5); they are less threatening and more supportive of learners.

By now, you might not need a definition of summative assessment, but we will provide one. *Summative assessment* is a final process that follows the sequence of teaching and learning. Evidence of summative assessment should provide students with an opportunity to summarize what they have learned; possibly to synthesize and pull it all together; and, it is hoped, to integrate it with new ideas or experiences.

Again, all of those qualities of authentic, aligned, diversified, and fair assessment need to be considered in summative assessment. In fact, it is essential that summative evidence be designed more carefully than other types of assessment, because they have the potential to be harmful in the form of low grades, failure of a course, a need for repeating a course, denial of graduation or certification, and so on.

When students are engaged in the consistent production of evidence, we and they often intend to organize that evidence to demonstrate progress completion of a set of outcomes for a major, or as a comprehensive summative assessment for meeting graduation requirements. In the last 20 years, portfolios have emerged as a comprehensive and reflective way of assessing student learning.

Portfolios: Engaging Learners in Assessment

Portfolios have appealed to faculty and students alike as an attractive alternative to comprehensive exams. Basically, portfolios are collections of student evidence accompanied by a rationale for the contents and by student reflections on the learning illustrated by the evidence. Portfolios are best when planned and purposeful and containing evidence of efforts, progress, and achievement. Portfolios are a good fit with the kind of authentic assessment that we have advocated in this chapter. The best quality of portfolios is that when they are used most effectively learners "actively participate in the evaluation process" (Banta, 2003, p. 2). Learners have an intense say in the development of portfolios: selecting evidence, connecting and explaining evidence items, and describing how the evidence illustrates learning. The process of developing a portfolio is full of possibilities for self-assessment and reflection, and that important potential for extended and enriched learning.

It would take a complete chapter to teach you how to use portfolios. I think portfolios work well with outcomes-based assessment, but my intent here is not to address all of the considerations and steps for their use. Instead, I will discuss their use just enough to suggest some possibilities.

To begin, portfolios can "demonstrate a learner's accomplishments, reveal the range of her work, and capture the work completed in a particular period of time" (Larson, 2003, p. 7). Portfolios are adaptable to the needs and intentions of individual learners and the expectations of individual faculty members, programs, and degree requirements. Examples of how portfolios can be structured illustrate their flexibility:

- Portfolios can be structured to include evidence produced early in a course or program, evidence produced midway, and evidence produced at the end.
- Portfolios can be structured to include drafts of evidence, feedback about the drafts, and final finished evidence.
- Portfolios can be structured with both required evidence (determined by faculty) and evidence submitted by the learner, with both sets of evidence demonstrating achievement of a set of learning outcomes.
- Portfolios can be structured around learning outcomes with evidence generated by varied learning experiences, in varied learning contexts, and in varied forms (e.g., written, video, graphic).

Portfolios go beyond the potential of a single piece of evidence of learning in that they provide a holistic picture of the learner's achievements. That versatility I described in the previous list enables us to see firsthand "not only what students are learning but how they are learning" (Banta, 2003, p. 4). The information derived from portfolios goes beyond the documentation of student learning. Portfolios reveal strengths and gaps in our curriculum and pedagogy as well as strengths and gaps in student learning.

After using portfolios for more than a decade, Lorie Cook-Benjamin (2003) realizes that there is no one right way to create a portfolio and that the benefits of using portfolios far outweigh those of other summative assessment. She advises us to be sure that our portfolios reflect the course or program for which students are demonstrating their learning (p. 13). We've recently seen a superb example of such a fit. A history professor teaches one of his courses using five major forms of communication and records: works of art; music; diaries and journals and narratives; maps; and artifacts. The class explores each form with multiple examples to study history. Their portfolios are organized around the five forms and students provide photocopies of a journal, painting, and so on for their reflections on a movement.

Cook-Benjamin's (2003) next suggestion is to accept and even embrace the nature of portfolios as evolving (p. 13). Throughout this chapter we have emphasized the importance of knowing our learners. We'll extend that knowledge to include awareness of the changing nature of students as they are learning with us. As students change with their new information, additional skills, and even enhanced confidence, portfolios may change. As students gain experience with portfolios, they expand their capacity to reflect, self-assess, and monitor and improve their learning. Many students gain an awareness of the value of portfolios, develop pride in their efforts to document learning, and use their portfolios for later classes and future employment. As Cook-Benjamin acknowledges, students seldom take such pride in or find practical use of traditional assessments (p. 13).

In sum, using portfolios of evidence assembled by students to demonstrate achievement of their learning outcomes is a learner-centered way to provide integrated and multidimensional assessment for our students. More than a decade ago, Simmons (1994) encouraged us to keep track of student work and referred to such tracking or collection as a "record of understanding" (p. 22). We think that portfolios of evidence provide such a record with all of the potential for well-developed outcomes-based evidence:

- Concrete evidence of learning
- A basis for ongoing feedback to students about their learning
- A springboard for student self-assessment and reflection on learning products and processes
- Information for adjusting the curriculum and pedagogy to better meet student needs and progress
- An opportunity for students to understand the process of learning-assessment-feedback, learning-assessment-feedback, . . .
- An elaboration of the understandings and skills that have been developed, demonstrated, and consolidated

One final consideration when we provide students the opportunity to demonstrate their achievement of outcomes is the development of a set of directions to accompany our assignments or assessments. As you will read in the faculty interviews in chapter 9, our faculty were repeatedly surprised by the lack of agreement between what they asked students to do and what they looked for when they assessed the students' work. Directions have the potential either to support students as they demonstrate their learning or to jeopardize students' capacity to succeed. When directions are not clear, students' confidence and competence are damaged. I think that faculty's confidence and competence can also be damaged. Remember Juan's disappointment in our first story. One of the best ways to avoid that situation (and it's a common one) is to have a colleague or student read the directions and describe what they say.

We do not have any magic formulas for writing clear directions that actually support students, but we do strongly recommend that you have someone else review your directions. Get that person's feedback and interpretation before you provide the directions to your students. We also know of faculty who ask students to critique their assignments and assessments. Talk about being learner centered. These faculty members' requests are sincere probes for information to help them improve their assignments and assessments. Such requests communicate important messages to learners about their importance, about the value of their feedback, and about faculty intentions to study and improve their practices.

A Conversation With Swarup

Writing this chapter was transformative for my thinking—that is, it helped me pull together a whole series of experiences related to student evidence. I was therefore anxious to ask Swarup about his thoughts on student evidence. Here is our conversation:

In the past and early in our assessment work, we thought that developing evidence was the easy part. In fact, I used to say, "This is the fast part of the process, because faculty have been doing this, creating assignments and assessments, for a long time" and even added, "And they're good at it." Recently, two experiences have made me pause about that perception: our review of student evidence, which you describe in chapter 6, and our reflection for preparing this book. We've come to realize that it takes skill and lots of careful consideration to create evidence that provides a truly aligned and learner-centered experience for students to demonstrate their achievement of outcomes. I'm curious about how that is affecting your practice. Now, when you stop to design evidence, what are all the considerations that go through your head? How does that compare to your processes of five years ago? Talk with me about that.

Great question! I take a great many things into account in designing my assignments. In the not so distant past, I've had students say, "Gosh, that exam didn't look anything like what I studied for or what we did in class." It burned to hear that because it was true. My evidence now looks like the same kinds of things that we've been doing; by the way, that has also really helped align the kinds of learning activities of my class.

My evidence gets at both knowledge and skills. Almost all of it requires students to do things: solve problems, make connections, analyze data and error.

My evidence is connected to the learning outcomes. I am careful to look back at the outcomes for each section of the course and make sure that there are several assessment items for each outcome from different angles. I really try to serve different learning styles with my efforts here.

My evidence includes problems with different levels of difficulty and I frequently give students a choice regarding which level they want to work. I really want to stretch them without overwhelming them.

My evidence frequently includes problems and questions that I've collected from students, that is, questions that they think should be on the exam. It shares the ownership with them.

Wow! I never knew that I had so much to say about my evidence. Do I go through this list every time I develop a new assignment or assessment? No, but this is what my assignments look like. I can say with certainty that I used to do a miserable job—focused on what was easy to grade, whatever came to my head the night before, etcetera. My assignments didn't align with learning outcomes because I didn't have any.

The most powerful insight I've gained from all of this work on student evidence is the realization that my students' success is largely a function of the learning processes of my class and how well I craft my assessment. Yes, their study and efforts make a difference, but it is so easy for students to blow a poorly worded assignment, and it has nothing to do with their ability or studies or real understanding. It's very painful to think that my assignments have the potential to communicate otherwise to students. It is a huge responsibility to create good evidence *with* directions that support them. Thanks for asking that question—I needed to think about this.

A final note here—Swarup's answers sound like a summary of this chapter, but the truth is that we don't read each other's chapters until after the conversation. It's good to hear the changes that have happened in his practices and his own clarity about them. I hope that you are as inspired as I am by them.

References

Association of American Colleges and Universities. (2002). *Greater expectations: A new vision for learning as a nation goes to college.* Washington, DC: Author.

Banta, T. W. (2003). *Portfolio assessment: Using cases, scoring, and impact.* San Francisco: Jossey-Bass.

Bodi, S. (1990). Teaching effectiveness and bibliographic instruction: The relevance of learning styles. *College and Research Libraries, 51,* 113–119.

Bridglall, B. L. (2001). Research and practice on how people learn. *Pedagogical Inquiry and Praxis, 1,* 3–6.

Cavanaugh, S., Hogan, K., & Ramgopal, T. (1995). The assessment of student nurse learning styles using the Kolb Learning Inventory. *Nurse Education Today, 15*(3), 177–183.

Cook-Benjamin, L. (2003). Portfolio assessment: Benefits, issues of implementation, and reflections on its use. In T. W. Banta (Ed.), *Portfolio assessment: Uses, cases, scoring, and impact* (pp. 11–15). San Francisco: Jossey-Bass.

Dweck, C. S. (1989). Motivation. In A. Lesgold & R. Glaser (Eds.), *Foundation for a psychology of education* (pp. 87–113). Hillsdale, NJ: Erlbaum.

Education Commission of the States. (1996, April). What research says about improving undergraduate education. *AAHE Bulletin, 28,* 5–8.

Gardner, H. (1983). *Frames of mind.* New York: Basic Books.

Gardner, H., & Hatch, T. (1989). Multiple intelligences go to school. *Educational Researcher, 18*(8), 4–9.

Kolb, D. (1976). *Learning style inventory technical manual.* Boston: McBer & Co.

Kolb, D. (1985). *Learning style inventory: Self-scoring inventory and interpretation booklet.* Boston: McBer & Co.

Krechevsky, M., & Gardner, H. (1990). The emergence and nurturance of multiple intelligences. In J. A. Howe (Ed.), *Encouraging the development of exceptional abilities and talents.* Leicester, UK: British Psychological Society.

Larson, R. L. (2003). Using portfolios to assess the impact of a curriculum. In T. Banta (Ed.), *Portfolio assessment: Uses, cases, scoring, and impact* (pp. 7–10). San Francisco: John Wiley & Sons.

Riordan, T. (2005). Education for the 21st century: Teaching, learning, and assessment. *Change, 37*(1), 52–56.

Schilling, K. M., & Schilling, K. L. (1998). *Proclaiming and sustaining excellence: Assessment as a faculty role.* Washington, DC: ASHE-ERIC Clearinghouse on Higher Education, The George Washington University.

Simmons, R. (1994). The horse before the cart: Assessing for understanding. *Educational Leadership, 51*(5), 22–23.

Stage, F. K., Muller, P. M., Kinzie, J., & Simmons, A. (1998). *Creating learning centered classrooms: What does learning theory have to say?* Washington, DC: ASHE-ERIC Clearinghouse on Higher Education, The George Washington University.

Staples, L. (2006). *Syllabus example for VPA 320, Museum Studies.* Seaside, CA: Department of Visual and Public Arts, CSUMB.

St. Mary's College. (2006). *Learning outcomes.* Moraga, CA: Author.

Suskie, L. (2000, May). Fair assessment practices: Giving students equitable opportunities to demonstrate learning. *AAHE Bulletin, 32,* 116–118.

Wiggins, G. (1989, May). A true test: Toward more authentic and equitable assessment. *Phi Delta Kappan, 70,* 703–713.

Wiggins, G., & McTighe, J. (1998). *Understanding by design.* Alexandria, VA: Association for Supervision and Curriculum Development.

5

CRITERIA AND STANDARDS FOR ASSESSMENT

No Longer a Faculty Secret

Story: Students' Surprise

One of the original faculty members at California State University Monterey Bay (CSUMB) is a colleague in the Department of Earth Systems and Science Policy by the name of Bill Head. Bill has spent the last five years writing major national grants to attract minority students to the sciences. He has been quite successful and has been able to attract, encourage, and support significant numbers of students to graduate with science majors. One of the unique components of his funded internships is the student portfolio developed in coordination with the students' work in community placements. The framework for the portfolios includes a set of common core outcomes, specified evidence, and criteria by which the interns' work will be evaluated. The framework also requires a second set of those items to be developed by the intern in collaboration with his or her community partner. This second set of outcomes, evidence, and criteria is intended to reflect the unique focus and kind of work to be achieved in each internship.

"Will students be able to design criteria?" we asked. We knew that they had learned about and experienced and even practiced developing outcomes. We felt certain that our students could plan work and projects that could demonstrate achievement of their outcomes. However, criteria had been the property of faculty members, a kind of manifestation of their expertise. Much hesitance and some resistance surrounded the decision to require our student interns to design criteria for us to judge their work. We heard comments such as, "I'm not ready to trust their capacity for such specific self-assessment" and "That's putting a lot of responsibility on students and their community partners." Many of the community partners responded with vague assent, a "wait and see" stance. Some admitted a lack of experience with criteria themselves.

For the first group of interns, we facilitated a mini-workshop on criteria with review of outcomes and evidence. We defined criteria, provided examples, and described their usefulness. Students were quiet, but they practiced writing criteria and responded to each other's criteria, and they appeared to be at ease with this new responsibility. Within a week, each intern submitted a framework for the second set of outcomes, evidence, and criteria. We held our breath as we began to review their submissions. Those same faculty members who had hesitated quickly became strong supporters of the role of students in designing their own assessment. They were especially impressed by the kind of criteria students developed for themselves: "Those are the same criteria that I would have posed," admitted one faculty member. "They have set high standards for themselves," commented another faculty member.

It was an exciting experience and several faculty colleagues reflected on their new awareness of learner capacity and described their intentions to integrate some of the student development processes into their courses:

> "I'm going to start involving students more in my course outcomes and criteria."
>
> "Usually it feels like my students just brush over the assessment information in my syllabi, but this makes me think that they could have a more active role in developing some of those components."
>
> "It's a little startling to think that I am not the only one who can do this."

Throughout the internships, the topic of student autonomy and students' development role in assessment emerged. Community members interacted quietly and with agreement in those conversations. Months later, in an exit interview, several community members described their own use of criteria in project planning and evaluations and affirmed that they had experienced useful learning with the interns' assessment. Here is what one community member had to say: "Those criteria and how my intern developed them just stuck in my head. I kept thinking that we should be using them in our agency. We recently planned a new project for our institute and I decided to try integrating criteria into our planning model. I asked my staff, 'What qualities would tell us that this project would be successful?' At first, everyone was quiet, but then we started with a few ideas. Those ideas escalated into a lively discussion, and we now have an agreed-upon set of criteria to use in evaluating our project. My staff members appear quite satisfied and have commented on having a greater voice in what matters."

This story isn't as entertaining and lively as some of our stories, but it has deep implications for our learner-centeredness and for the way we develop outcomes-based assessment.

This chapter is about criteria for assessing student evidence. It is also about the related standards that explain those criteria and define them for varied levels of achievement. From our perspectives, this chapter is about a very exciting part of our work. Swarup sees criteria and standards as a guarantee of the respect and autonomy that students deserve in the assessment process. He says that it puts students on equal ground, or as co-learners with teachers. For me, developing criteria and standards represented the "high point" in our faculty development processes. Those work sessions were scenes of the highest energy and understandings that we had experienced, the zenith of faculty taking ownership of outcomes-based assessment. So, be prepared for a lot of enthusiasm in these pages. Be prepared also for arriving at some of your deepest insights and "ahas" about your own teaching and about student learning when you begin articulating criteria and standards.

Criteria and Standards: What? Why? and How?

Each of the preceding chapters has begun with definitions and descriptions of what we are talking about, along with quotes from our colleagues in assessment to give you an expanded conceptual understanding. We looked for such definitions and descriptions to discuss criteria and standards here, but all of the glossaries and indices in our favorite assessment books listed criterion-referenced tests or exams and standardized tests. We mention this because we do not want you to get confused when you browse the assessment literature. Our use of criteria and standards is not different. It's simply broader and more generic, relevant to all forms of assessment, rather than limited to tests and exams.

What Are Criteria?

When I define criteria for faculty, I usually call criteria the qualities we look for in student evidence. *Criteria* describe the skills, understandings, structures, and kind of thinking we want our learners to reveal in the work that they produce to demonstrate achievement of outcomes. Maki (2004) refers to criteria as "dimensions" and "performance levels" (p. 121), while some of the terms used in the literature are *primary traits* or *performance indicators.* Let's look at some examples:

> When students write a research paper to demonstrate that they can explain the concepts of power and equality, we want to see *reflection* and *multiple perspectives* in those papers.
>
> When students design a math project to demonstrate that they can use mathematical processes, we want to see *accuracy, appropriateness*, and *analytic thinking* in their designs.

Maki (2004) differentiates between two kinds of criteria: criteria for the kind of thinking, knowing, and behaving we look for in student evidence; and criteria that reflect characteristics of the evidence itself. I developed a list of descriptions from varied sources to get you started in developing criteria; I used Maki's two kinds of criteria (table 5.1) along with a few of her examples. Some of the criteria originated from the Visual and Public Arts Department (2006), CSU Monterey Bay. Table 5.1 illustrates the two kinds of criteria. Some of the criteria could probably be listed on both sides of the table, so the distinction between the two kinds of qualities is blurred. It may not even be important to focus on that distinction, but I found it helpful in trying to illustrate what criteria look like.

In developing criteria for our outcomes-based assessment approaches, we realized that criteria really describe lifelong goals or skills, that is, the habits that we hope our students will take into their personal and professional lives when they leave the university. I definitely want students to leave with habits of being reflective and organized and clear. As we worked together on the campus designing criteria, faculty members realized that they seldom made those qualities public to students. Most of us carried those criteria around in

TABLE 5.1
Kinds of Criteria (Descriptions)

Descriptions of thinking, understanding, behaviors	Descriptions of evidence
Creativity	Clarity
Integration	Organization
Reflection	Technical competence
Synergy	Accuracy
Multiple perspectives	Citations
Analytic thinking	Accuracy

Source: Adapted from *Assessing for learning: Building a sustainable commitment across the institution* by P. L. Maki, 2004, Sterling, VA: Stylus and *VPA program learning outcomes, evidence, criteria and standards* by Visual and Public Arts Department, 2006, Seaside, CA.

our heads and used them when it came time to review student work and assign a grade, hence the use of "faculty secret" in this chapter's subtitle. You may be conscious of your criteria but it's also likely that you may not be aware of them when you review student evidence. When we began reviewing and analyzing student work in our faculty groups (see chapter 6), we also learned that, as faculty members, we were often swayed by unintended criteria or subjective response to individual students, even though we were committed to not being influenced. Students' writing quality or presentation is often a major distracter from our intended outcomes and criteria.

The explanations and examples that we have provided here respond to the "What?" of criteria and begin to develop some strong "Whys"—reasons for why it is important to articulate them to our learners.

Why Not Leave Criteria "Secret"?

After years of this work of developing outcomes and criteria, Swarup and I developed a list of the kinds of learning that come from articulating criteria for both students and faculty. We have since expanded the list with ideas from our colleagues, shared our lists in workshops, and gotten very positive feedback about them. We often hear comments such as, "I had not thought of what those criteria were doing to the learning process for students or for ourselves."

Most important, those criteria have an impact on student learning in the following ways:

- Promoting confidence in their learning efforts
- Promoting habits of self-assessment (Shepard, 2000, p. 8)
- Promoting a sense of fairness of evaluation for students
- Motivating students with increased security in the assessment processes
- Promoting qualities of work for personal and professional roles
- Promoting timely and meaningful feedback on evidence (Stevens & Levi, 2005, p. 17)

That last advantage needs expansion because it is more complex than it looks. The "timely and meaningful feedback" can actually begin when students complete an assignment or assessment because criteria allow for self-assessment before submitting the evidence. In collaborative learning environments, when learners have experience with peer assessment or group assessment, they may ask a peer to review their work using the criteria before final submission. We have met a number of faculty members who actually structure such peer review into their schedule so that evidence is improved before submission. Huba and Freed (2000) connect those opportunities for self-assessment and self-improvement with intrinsic motivation (p. 59).

Once the evidence is submitted, criteria and related standards actually make it easier and more efficient for faculty to provide feedback to students in timely and more meaningful formats than usual. Educational research supports the influence of timely feedback on student learning (Rucker & Thompson, 2003; Taras, 2003). In addition, the more detail or information provided in the feedback, the more effective the feedback can be (Brinko, 1993). Such feedback enables us to be learner centered in our assessment practices.

For faculty, the process of articulating and reaching agreement on criteria has the following impact:

- Faculty move closer to student perspectives in their assessment approaches.
- Faculty reflect on and draw upon their disciplinary expertise.
- Faculty dialogue with colleagues about relationships among pedagogy, curriculum, instructional design, and educational practices (Maki, 2004, p. 121).

- Faculty consider learning patterns and their own interpretations of learning.
- Faculty make public their rationales for evaluative judgments.

There are surely other reasons why articulating criteria is important, but the reasons we have given are enough to convince you of the importance and power of criteria for student learning. Once you begin the development process for articulating criteria, a good reflection activity is to develop such a list with some faculty peers and see what learning is occurring for them and their students.

Now that we have addressed the question of "why," it's time to address the question of "how."—How do we arrive at criteria for our student work? In other words, now that we know what criteria look like and do, and are convinced of their great benefits, how do we produce them?

How Do We Design Criteria?

To begin, criteria are not new information. Most of us who have taught or currently teach have carried criteria around in our minds. However, we have not typically discussed them or made them public. For most of the faculty members at CSUMB, discussing criteria was a brand new experience, one that was slightly uncomfortable at first. It probably helped that those discussions followed intense discussions of outcomes and evidence, and that there was a sense of community. As faculty continued to articulate criteria, their comfort level rose and they found much satisfaction in the process. Swarup talks about their insights and learning from the process in chapter 6.

You are probably thinking, "So, how did you begin? How did you get faculty to grasp those criteria that had been with them but not articulated?" This was one process in which telling faculty would have been disastrous, so I stayed constructivist in my approach. I facilitated a discussion using a scenario that would probably be familiar to most faculty:

You are reading student final papers and you encounter three very different pieces of student work (evidence). All three papers have followed your directions well. They all have introductions, summaries, citations and references, and the required number of pages. The first paper is so excellent that it is a pleasure to review and evaluate. It meets the outcome at a very high level, and you easily point out its strengths in your feedback. The second paper definitely satisfies the outcome, but it leaves you wanting. You experience minor disappointment in its quality and suggest to the student how to improve the paper. The third paper clearly does not demonstrate that the outcome has been met, and you are greatly disappointed. It's hard to know where to start with your feedback. Although each of the papers followed your directions, provided the components you outlined, and appear to be earnest submissions, the quality of the work is different. What makes the papers different? Or, with the outcome in mind, what differentiates these three papers? What are the qualities of the excellent work and what qualities are missing from the satisfactory work? What do you usually look for when you begin making judgments, assigning grades, and providing feedback?

I continue with these kinds of questions and prompts and faculty begin carefully with ideas such as "clarity" and "organization." At first, the discussion yields fairly generic criteria upon which most faculty members agree. Later it moves to criteria that are specific to the goals and outcomes and then begins to reveal faculty values. The discussion becomes complex and intense. Sometimes, it is difficult to name the criteria. Faculty make comments such as, "I know it when I see it but I don't know what to call it." Faculty collaboration and that trust we discussed in chapter 2 are essential here.

We began these discussions to get faculty to articulate criteria in the faculty learning communities and then moved to departments. The discussions have been and continue to be rich with faculty disciplinary expertise, teaching experiences, insights and successes, as well as problems and challenges that faculty have wrestled with over time. The time spent articulating and narrowing the criteria ultimately helps students, making it worthwhile. In a few departments, students have joined the discussions or have been asked to review criteria, and not surprisingly, those have been powerful learning experiences for everyone.

Another possibility for getting started is to begin with actual student evidence: three projects that have all followed the appropriate steps in development, have the requisite components, and appear to be the result of hard work. Begin by reviewing the assignment and learning outcomes, and then have faculty evaluate the projects with a simple rating scale: "Decide which of these projects should be rated excellent, which should be rated satisfactory, and which should be rated unsatisfactory." Once everyone has reached agreement on the ratings, have faculty members ask themselves why they rated the project as excellent, satisfactory, or unsatisfactory. Even if there is no agreement about the ratings, your discussion will quickly turn to criteria and yield qualities that can be agreed upon. For example, you might hear comments such as the following:

"I don't think that this project is excellent because it has no complexity of design, or sense of its audience."

"I rated this project excellent because there is a clear sense of community research in its development, and you can almost see the design principles in action when you analyze the designer's rationale."

Such comments immediately submit qualities for the group discussion: complexity, audience sensitivity, community research foundations, and design principles. The members of your group may end up using different language or terms, but the basic idea is within their rationales and descriptions. This is an interesting process in terms of learning from each other. One faculty member may say, "I looked for some depth and openness to change in the project development," while you may say, "I chose this project because there was so much detail and ongoing revision." Often you realize that you are talking about the same thing. From there, it's a matter of giving the criterion a name that you can agree upon, and then defining it with the language that you both have used in your discussion. You may agree to call your criterion *reflection and adaptability* and define it with words such as *detail, ongoing revision, rethinking, raising questions,* and *open to change.* Those definitions begin the process of developing standards.

Standards: Continuing the Learning Process

We began with criteria being the qualities that we seek in students' evidence as they demonstrate achievement of outcomes. Articulating criteria builds a good support for student learning, but not providing definitions for the criteria leads to ambiguity for both faculty and students. As we described earlier, one faculty member's notion of complexity may be different from your notion of complexity. Your students' notion of complexity is probably even different from those notions. In this case, students are left with defining complexity and determining what you mean and what your colleague means by complexity. That kind of situation is not learner centered, so the next step, then, is to define and describe what the criteria mean. Standards provide that very necessary explanation and description of criteria, how to demonstrate the criteria, and what expectations faculty have for student evidence. Standards really help students both to understand and demonstrate the criteria.

Standards further support student efforts by explaining and describing the criteria for different levels of achievement. The following example illustrates standards for three different criteria at the levels of excellent, satisfactory, and unsatisfactory. We begin with an outcome and related evidence so that you have a context within which to understand the criteria and standards. The outcome derives from an institutional value that states, "Emporia State University has a commitment to academic and personal integrity" (Emporia State University, 2006, p. 1). The value statement is attached to the university mission.

OUTCOME: Students articulate an individual code of ethics and apply it to personal decisions of integrity.

EVIDENCE: Written personal code with discussion of two different decisions of integrity

Multimedia presentation of personal code and decisions of integrity

Dramatization of ethical dilemmas and decisions of integrity

Letter of application for employment responding to questions of ethics

CRITERIA: Reflection
Multiple perspectives
In-depth analysis

STANDARDS FOR *Reflection*

Excellent: The student consistently raises questions, analyzes assumptions, connects with previous experiences, acknowledges biases and values, engages in self-assessment, and elaborates on implications for future actions.

Satisfactory: The student raises questions, identifies assumptions and assesses them, connects with previous experiences, begins to acknowledge biases and values, and occasionally assesses thinking as decisions are being made.

Unsatisfactory: The student moves through the decision-making process with few questions and an unawareness of the influence of assumptions, biases, and values and seldom assesses thinking and process before making decisions.

STANDARDS FOR *Multiple Perspectives*

Excellent: The student examines his or her own thinking and experiences and those of others with consistent integration of both for perspectives on issues, empathically considers those affected by decisions and responsibilities, and weighs diverse possibilities before moving to action.

Satisfactory: The student focuses on his or her own thinking and experiences, occasionally listens to or considers another perspective and may revise his or her own perspective according to those considerations, considers those affected by decisions and responsibilities with some empathy, and considers more than one possibility before moving to action.

Unsatisfactory: The student remains focused on his or her own thinking and experiences for a singular perspective, considers those affected by decisions and responsibilities from his or her own perspective, and commits to one possibility early in the process and moves to action.

STANDARDS FOR *In-Depth Analysis*

Excellent: The student consistently reviews and evaluates all aspects of decisions, responsibilities, and related processes; reviews comprehensive pros and cons of possible decisions; consistently considers ethical principles of issues and decisions and questions his or her own code of ethics; studies related examples; and identifies a broad group of individuals influenced or affected by decisions and responsibilities.

Satisfactory: The student reviews and evaluates most aspects of decisions, responsibilities, and related processes; considers pros and cons of possible decisions; checks with his or her personal code of ethics and some ethical principles; may ask for others' opinions; and identifies those affected by decisions and responsibilities.

Unsatisfactory: The student occasionally checks on some aspects of decisions, mentions ethics in decision making, and refers to others who may be affected by decisions and responsibilities. There is no suggestion of using ethical principles, evaluating decisions, or weighing pros and cons.

We decided to elaborate three full examples so that you could begin to see how helpful criteria and standards can be to students as they learn and demonstrate their learning. You can also see how valuable those criteria are in developing lifelong habits in thought processes and work. Most of you are no doubt committed to supporting students to be reflective and to use in-depth analysis and multiple perspectives in their lives, so your standards put those commitments into your communication about what's important in student work.

Standards Support Faculty Too

Just as standards help students learn more and demonstrate their learning effectively, standards help you in your faculty role. Faculty reported that the reflections and discussions that yielded standards had an enormous impact on their thinking about pedagogy, curriculum, and assessment—an unanticipated benefit. Faculty individuals admitted to a consistent gnawing concern that their grading standards were too strict or rigid or too easy or insignificant, whether they had years of teaching experience or were neophytes. One faculty member had this to say about standards: "It's just not something we have ever talked about unless you planned a course together or team taught, and even then, it wasn't articulated very openly." Another commented, "I've always wondered and worried a bit that I was too easy on students or too hard. I've never asked any of my colleagues about their standards even when we were teaching the same course."

Often our faculty work sessions for articulating criteria and developing standards ended with faculty feeling much more secure in their evaluation decisions, or contemplating a revision of their standards. Like our colleagues, you can achieve both competence and confidence in your evaluation practices as a result of developing standards.

In chapter 1 we described a concern in higher education for the lack of academic currency, that is, agreed-upon standards so that grades have a common meaning or so that course completion has an established meaning. When you and your faculty colleagues come together to articulate criteria and develop standards, you can achieve academic currency. Your decisions provide a powerful response to the calls for accountability from all around the academy.

Another benefit of developing standards with their helpful definitions and objective expectations is that students perceive an ethic of fairness about the whole assessment and evaluation process. They make comments such as these:

> "I know where I stand even when I hand in my assignments because I understand the criteria."
> "I hate it when you have no idea how you are going to be graded, but these standards make it clear and I feel like it's fair."

One of our colleagues describes a significant change in her teaching that has resulted from using criteria and standards:

> "I used to be so hassled by students when I returned assignments and exams. They always wanted to express their disagreements and convince me that they should have received a higher grade. I didn't mind the discussions about alternative answers—they were interesting—but the hassling always extended beyond a learning experience. Now they use the criteria and standards themselves and they agree and seem satisfied with my judgments. I really think that the quality of their work is better too, and that's worth everything. I feel so much better about my teaching."

Often when colleagues are talking about standards, they use the term *rubrics*. You may have heard or used the term, and I think that it is important to differentiate between standards and rubrics. They both accomplish the positive effects on student learning that we have described, and they can help you with assessment processes and evaluation decisions.

Rubrics: Another Way of Supporting Students

Rubrics are tools for grading student evidence with detailed descriptions of the expectations for the work as well as of the levels of performance for each component. Stevens and Levi (2005) recommend rubrics to help with a variety of teaching issues:

- Complex assignments with extensive directions that need to be explained over and over and that remain a mystery for some students up until the time that they are due
- Assignments that are going to be time intensive both for students to complete and for you to grade

- Assignments that cause you to struggle with explanations in terms of directions, expectations, and grading (and if you're struggling, then students will have great difficulty)

Basically, rubrics bring the same benefits that I described for criteria and standards. They do so with a slightly different format. Rubrics start with a description of the evidence required of students; a list of work tasks to produce the evidence; and for complex tasks, a set of components that comprise the tasks. The following examples will help clarify that description of the starting point for rubrics.

If the evidence is a debate, then the requisite components of the debate are the research preparation, introductory statement, outline of arguments, defense and support of arguments, summary statement, and responses to opponent's arguments. That analysis of a debate into required components is the first step for developing a rubric.

From there, each component is described with levels of performance, much like standards, into ratings. So, the introductory statement is described as either excellent, satisfactory, or unsatisfactory. Stevens and Levi (2005) suggest alternative terms such as *competent* or *needs work, proficient* or *marginal, intermediate* or *novice*, or *average* (p. 8). The very process of discussing and agreeing upon terms for ratings is an excellent context for assuring that your practices are learner centered. We have heard faculty members' concerns about the messages being sent to students when terms such as *not competent, marginal*, or even *average* are used. Naming your ratings is a good opportunity to be as student centered as possible. There probably aren't any ideal descriptions, so it is wise to choose those terms carefully to closely align with the message you wish to send. The terms you choose are an important part of your feedback and may influence how your intended help is received.

With those ratings, it will be important to then describe the expected behaviors, understandings, thinking, and so forth that comprise each level of rating. Back to our debate example, when the introductory statement is excellent, it poses challenging questions, raises compelling issues, and previews the arguments that will follow. When excellent, the introductory statement engages listeners and prompts interest. Once again, students are supported and guided as they produce evidence of their learning. They are clear and feel certain about the expectations for their evidence and can self-assess their work before submission, and it is hoped that they can do this with confidence.

Our colleague Dan Shapiro analyzed the capstone requirement for his department into a comprehensive rubric so that students could have complete and useful information about how to proceed through each step of achieving completion of the capstone. His development efforts in collaboration with his colleagues forced a rethinking of what individual faculty members expected and consensus about departmentwide expectations for the sake of students. Students now have a kind of "road map" for their capstone work. That final summative assignment is a bit overwhelming, and students occasionally put it off because its enormity leaves them unsure of how to begin or how to organize their efforts. When you look at the rubrics provided by Dan in figure 5.1 and by Susan Agre-Kippenhan, a former colleague at Portland State University, in figure 5.2, you can see how students receive guidance and assurance from the information within.

After reviewing Dan and Susan's work (both collaborative but with them taking the lead), you might feel overwhelmed (again!), so I wish to keep my promise to support your efforts and be realistic. As you have no doubt noticed, almost everything I have described in this chapter calls for the collaboration of colleagues. Yes, you can design criteria and standards by yourself for your courses without any input from others and create good supports for students. I'm one of those people who works well independently and gets more done. I do good work too, but I am continually made aware that the ideas and perspectives of others always make me pause. I consistently reflect, "I've never thought of it that way." It does take longer to think and design with others, but the payoff for learners is well worth it. And I always learn from the discussion.

That collaborative design process is one of the challenges of creating criteria and standards for assessment of student learning. Unfortunately, once that information has been developed, other challenges appear. We think that they're the right kind of challenges if we are working toward being student centered in our approaches.

Criteria and Standards: Another Responsibility and Challenge

This chapter could have stopped when we finished describing how to articulate criteria and develop standards, and we were tempted by that ease of completion. We would be remiss, however, if we didn't point out the responsibilities and possible challenges that you could face once you provide

FIGURE 5.1
Capstone Assessment Outcomes Criteria and Standards

Assessment Outcomes, Criteria, and Standards for:

1. Cover Letter
2. Abstract/Summary
3. Systems Approach to Environmental Decision Making (MLO #6)
4. Areas of Depth:
   - Knowledge in the Physical and/or Life Sciences (MLO #3)
   - Economic/Political Knowledge (MLO #4)
   - Scientific Inquiry (MLO #8)
   - Service Learning (MLO #11)
   - Science Education
   - Independently Designed Area of Depth
5. Ability to Complete an Original, Complex Independent Project
6. Real-World Application
7. Written Communication (MLO #9)

Assessment Criteria and Standards for Project Originality, Complexity, and Student Initiative

CRITERIA: Capstone project was *original* and *complex*; student demonstrated *initiative* and *self-direction* in designing, carrying out, and presenting the capstone project.

STANDARDS:

Exemplary: Capstone project was highly original, involved significant logistical challenges, and required frequent problem solving and reassessment of project methods and goals throughout the duration of the project; student demonstrated exceptional and frequent initiative and self-direction in identifying and overcoming problems as they arose.

Commendable: Capstone project was original, challenging and required consistent problem solving and reassessment of project methods and goals throughout the duration of the project; student demonstrated consistent initiative and self-direction in identifying and overcoming problems as they arose.

Satisfactory: Capstone project was challenging and required minor problem solving and reassessment of project methods and goals throughout the duration of the project; student demonstrated some initiative and self-direction in identifying and overcoming problems as they arose.

Needs Work to Meet Satisfactory Standards: Capstone project was simplistic and required little or no problem solving; student failed to demonstrate initiative and self-direction in identifying and overcoming problems as they arose.

Assessment Criteria and Standards for Real-World Application

CRITERIA: Capstone project made, or has the potential to make, a contribution to the community outside of CSUMB.

STANDARDS:

> **Exemplary:** Project made, or has the potential to make, a substantial contribution to the community outside of CSUMB.
>
> **Commendable:** Project made, or has the potential to make, a moderate contribution to the community outside of CSUMB.
>
> **Satisfactory:** Project made, or has the potential to make, a minor contribution to the community outside of CSUMB.
>
> **Needs Work to Meet Satisfactory Standards:** Project does not make, or does not have the potential to make, a contribution to the community outside of CSUMB.

Source: From *Capstone Assessment Materials*, by D. Shapiro, 2006, Seaside, CA: Earth Systems and Science Policy Department, CSUMB. Reprinted with permission.

criteria and standards for student work. As Tim Riordan (2005) reminds us, "Learning outcomes that emphasize ways of thinking and acting have implications for the way we envision our pedagogy" (p. 55). That same statement can be made for criteria and standards and their implications. Those implications for your teaching and curriculum cannot be ignored when you expect students to demonstrate the criteria of *multiple perspectives* in their work, or look for *in-depth analysis* in their assignments. We have to ask ourselves questions such as the following

- Where will they learn about multiple perspectives?
- Have they seen examples of multiple perspectives?
- Have I modeled in-depth analysis?
- Have they had an opportunity (or opportunities) to try out multiple perspectives?
- Have they practiced in-depth analysis?
- Have they had practice identifying multiple perspectives?

Earlier in this book, we told of faculty members admitting that they did not know how to teach students varied skills such as analysis or the understandings of ethics theory. One of the problematic skill areas that was

FIGURE 5.2
Graphics Design Sophomore Portfolio Quality Levels

Level 5

Excellent. Level 5 work clearly differentiates itself from other work and requires extra effort. It has memorable impact and pursues concepts and techniques above and beyond what is discussed in class. It exhibits what is done by a highly self-motivated student who puts forth above and beyond effort. The work meets/surpasses all of the criteria set in the project/assignment description. The content is exceptional with outstanding critical thinking, superb formal mediation of the concept, and impeccable craft. Ideas are original, thoughtful or imaginative. Spelling, punctuation, or grammar errors are nonexistent. A level 5 documents the ability to think critically and work independently. It demonstrates strong methods and process, the ability to research, explore, investigate, and experiment.

Level 4

Good. Level 4 work is good/very good and requires extra effort. Impact is good. The work demonstrates an ability to pursue idea and suggestions presented in class and work with extra effort to resolve required projects. Content is good. The work demonstrates better than average design sensitivity. Methods are good, demonstrating an understanding and utilization of process. Above average craft and attention to detail are shown.

Level 3

Satisfactory. Level 3 work is average and competent. The work has fulfilled the requirements of the project, has acceptable levels of impact, conceptual development, and visual interest. Content is sufficiently developed. Work doesn't demonstrate the additional effort needed to excel. It lacks thoughtful, original, and imaginative resolution or attention to detail and craft. It employs process but does not demonstrate notable solutions.

Level 2

Poor—Below Average. Level 2 work is lacking in many or most areas that show any understanding of design. The impact is weak with unsound, unoriginal, or unimaginative thinking. There is a lack of understanding of general design principles including form, typography, or image making. Problems may include lack of interest, procrastination, poor planning, and poor craft.

Level 1

Unacceptable. Level 1 works shows no overall understanding of the assignment on many levels. Work shows a severe lack of interest. Work that is so substandard that the project holds few if any redeeming characteristics.

N/A

Not an applicable consideration.

Graphic Design: Sophomore Portfolio Review Evaluation Sheet

(1–5 HIGH)

Methods

Quality of the procedures and processes used to develop work	1	2	3	4	5
Research/process	1	2	3	4	5

    Quality of research

    Quality of exploration discovery

Work Habits (familiar faculty to evaluate)	1	2	3	4	5
Oral and written communication (written sample, faculty input)	1	2	3	4	5

Impact—Success based on purposes, goals and desired results, risk taking, personal voice. Visual choices support ideas, appropriate and inventive uses of historical references, and development of original concept that address audience/purpose/context

Creativity	1	2	3	4	5

    Originality, quality, and appropriateness

Concepts	1	2	3	4	5

    Strength of underlying ideas

    Understanding of audience/purpose

Content—Mediated through form: design principles, typography, form, materials

Composition and layout	1	2	3	4	5

    Spatial relationships, placement, formal principles (scale, direction, etc.), organization

Color/contrast/value	1	2	3	4	5
Typography: type as Image	1	2	3	4	5
Typography: line, paragraph, page	1	2	3	4	5

    Sensitivity and sensibility, visual hierarchy, grid, layout

    Typeface choices/combinations

    Expert typography and attention to typographic detail

Use of Imagery	1	2	3	4	5

    Choices/skills

Creation of original imagery (if applicable)	1	2	3	4	5
Use of materials	1	2	3	4	5
Content and form relationship	1	2	3	4	5

Craftsmanship—Overall polish, organization, and rigor; use of technology and skilled production

(continues)

FIGURE 5.2 (Continued)

Polished craft	1	2	3	4	5
Hand skills	1	2	3	4	5
Quality of execution	1	2	3	4	5
Presentation of work	1	2	3	4	5
Use of technology	1	2	3	4	5
Sophistication of performance—Overall impression of portfolio: complexity, maturity, selection of pieces					
Overall impression of portfolio	1	2	3	4	5

Source: *Art Department Sophomore Portfolio Review*, by S. Agre-Kippenhan, 2006, Portland, OR: Author. Reprinted with permission.

repeatedly brought up in our discussion was the capacity to synthesize. In one work session, several faculty members admitted not knowing how to teach students to synthesize. After a pause, one faculty member spoke very quietly, "I'm not sure that I know how to synthesize myself." Others shook their heads in agreement. It is this admittance by faculty that they do not know how to teach students varied skills that leads us to recommend that you become very comfortable with your own criteria as a starting point. Once you achieve clarity about criteria—and standards will help with that— your pedagogy and curriculum will need examination, revision, and expansion to include content and learning activities focused on the criteria.

Here's where I get uncomfortable—because it feels like I'm piling more work onto your already huge set of responsibilities, and I don't have any easy answers to reduce that additional responsibility. This discomfort prompts my questions to Swarup as we end this chapter.

A Conversation with Swarup

I begin without hesitation, and end up asking a set of questions:

When we finished our extensive discussions and development work on criteria and standards, you and your peers probably talked about the impact of such work on your teaching and on your courses. Since most faculty whom we know are usually overwhelmed by the amount of content "to cover," by the number of outcomes that they are supporting, and by the fleeting amount of time in each course offering, what does it feel like when we add the responsibilities that come with

*criteria and standards? How have you accommodated those implications in your
teaching, your courses? How have you handled that new responsibility?*

[Swarup pauses to consider my questions before responding.] I feel philosophical as I respond to that. Shall we teach to deliver content or use content to help students answer meaningful questions? Judging from the size
of the introductory chemistry texts that I receive from publishers, I would
say that they are mainly in the "live to deliver content camp." For me,
outcomes-based assessment has forced me to prioritize what I deem important. Looking at those texts, what are the three or four ideas in that 30-page
chapter that are essential? How can I organize my teaching and learning activities to help students develop deep and meaningful connections with, between, and among those three or four ideas? For me, criteria and standards
enrich, clarify, and support the outcomes.

Coming back to your question, one could experience the "adding on"
of criteria and standards as a stressful extra responsibility, burden, but for the
most part, they have simplified things for me. My memory of our work tells
me that the outcomes became considerably less vacuous upon completion of
our criteria and standards. The outcomes didn't stand alone well. Criteria
and standards provide a well-defined rationale for our evaluation decisions.
And they direct our teaching, make it more intentional—directed toward
those life skills and habits of mind that each of us care about and want for
our students.

Let me use an example from my chemistry courses in which accuracy is
an important quality in professional work and, thus, criteria for students'
research papers. When students understand that inaccurate calculations un-
dermine the integrity and validity of their claims, they have insight into why
scientists pay great attention to detail and into the values of the scientific
community. In that case, working toward accuracy is an integral part of my
teaching and learning approaches. I can't imagine teaching my chemistry
content without emphasizing accuracy.

References

Agre-Kippenhan, S. (2006). *Art department sophomore portfolio review*. Portland,
    OR: Author.
Brinko, K. T. (1993). The practice of giving feedback. *Journal of Higher Education,
    64*(5), 575–593.

Emporia State University. (2006). Affirmation of values [On-line]. Available: www.emporia.edu/about/values.htm.

Huba, M. E., & Freed, J. E. (2000). *Learner-centered assessment on college campuses.* Boston: Allyn & Bacon.

Maki, P. L. (2004). *Assessing for learning: Building a sustainable commitment across the institution.* Sterling, VA: Stylus.

Riordan, T. (2005). Education for the 21st century: Teaching, learning and assessment. *Change, 37*(1), 52–56.

Rucker, M. L., & Thompson, S. (2003). Assessing student learning outcomes: An investigation of the relationship among feedback measures. *College Student Journal, 37*(3), 400–405.

Shapiro, D. (2006). *Capstone Assessment Materials.* Seaside, CA: Earth Systems and Science Policy Department, CSUMB.

Shepard, L. (2000). The role of assessment in a learning culture. *Educational Researcher, 29*(7), 4–14.

Stevens, D. D., & Levi, A. J. (2005). *Introduction to rubrics.* Sterling, VA: Stylus.

Taras, M. (2003). To feedback or not to feedback in student self-assessment. *Assessment and Evaluation in Higher Education, 28*(5), 549–566.

Visual and Public Arts Department, CSU Monterey Bay. (2006). *VPA program learning outcomes, evidence, criteria and standards.* Seaside, CA: Author.

6

FACULTY RESPONSES TO DEVELOPMENT OF OUTCOMES-BASED ASSESSMENT PROTOCOLS

Story: Learning From My Colleagues

I t was the fall of 2000, I (Swarup) had been chair of the science general education faculty learning community (FLC) for a couple of years, and all of our FLCs had recently finished developing examples of evidence, criteria, and standards for their learning outcomes. There was a sense of pride among the faculty, and when the opportunity to showcase our work came along, there was genuine enthusiasm for "showing off" the work. We arranged a poster session in which every FLC's outcomes, criteria, and standards were displayed in huge attractive posters on the walls of the university center for external visitors as well as our colleagues. Chairs of each committee walked both campus guests and our own administrators through the poster display of what we had accomplished.

During a lull in the festivities, I perused some of the posters and visited with Seth, a colleague who chaired the community participation FLC, and asked him about his group's process. He began with, "Oh my gosh, you wouldn't believe" and then spoke nonstop for five minutes about all that the group members had learned, how they had to rework their outcomes, how positive the work had been, and so on. I immediately began to regale him with my experience in the science FLC: "You can't believe how fascinating it was to sit with scientists from different disciplines and energetically debate the meaning of the word *fact*. We never came to a consensus and had to remove it from one of our outcomes." I described how the work continually brought us up against our assumptions, particularly around our use of language, and how challenging developing the criteria and standards had been for us, even though it is what we require of our students. As I considered our discussion, I thought to myself, "I wonder what everyone else has learned? Do they share our experiences, our enthusiasm?" I broke off my conversation with Seth and walked over to Amy (the coauthor of this book), who had been listening to our animated discussion with one ear while she talked with the provost. I pulled her aside and wondered aloud what she thought of me doing an interview study of other FLC members. The excited but somewhat hushed discussion that ensued started me on much of the scholarship and collaborative projects that would later earn me tenure, and form the basis for my contributions to this book. That first interview study (there was another) is the content of this chapter.

Interviews: Inquiry, Motivation, Approach

I hope that the previous story provides insight into why our faculty development work sessions compelled and insisted that I, a science professor, needed to conduct an interview study. Given that the focus of my three-year-old dissertation was soil microbiology and secondary plant chemistry, ethnography (I can honestly say that at the time I didn't know the meaning of the word) was not exactly a match for my educational experience. Conducting an interview study of my peers was a nontraditional form of scholarship for me, a science professor seeking tenure, but I was so hungry to hear my peers describe their experiences. It was the kind of passion and commitment that I needed for my research, so I crossed a boundary and began studying what our faculty had learned from their experiences developing examples of evidence, criteria, and standards for our learning outcomes.

Even though you are probably reading our chapters in order and already know about how to develop learning outcomes, examples of student evidence, criteria, and standards for learning outcomes, it is important that I give a good overview of the process that we used as I introduce my research. I experienced the development of examples of evidence, criteria, and standards for our general education learning outcomes through assessment-focused faculty dialogues and work sessions, as chair of our science general education FLC and as the interviewer of faculty participants. What I share here derives from both experiences. You've already been introduced to California State University Monterey Bay's (CSUMB's) general education FLCs, and those communities are an important context for my study. In this chapter I discuss the results of my first interview study, what we learned from developing examples of evidence, criteria, and standards for our general education learning outcomes. This work had a profound impact on my teaching and assessment. In truth, it had a profound impact on many who experienced it and on the culture of the campus, as I learned in my interviews.

Study Context: Faculty Learning Communities

Our general education FLCs, one for each of the 13 general education areas, are responsible for developing and maintaining the general education learning outcomes and reviewing courses that deliver and assess the learning outcomes and function as discourse communities on how to teach to the learning outcomes effectively. The general education learning outcomes had been in place for several years before our director of the Center for Teaching, Learning, and Assessment (Amy) was hired. As you've read, it took about a year before we worked with her, but when we did, we began by developing examples of evidence, criteria, and standards for our previously developed general education learning outcomes. The work was essentially a faculty-centered collaboration between Amy and the FLCs. Amy provided the leadership; expertise in teaching, learning, and assessment; tough questions; and encouragement. Faculty provided expertise in their subject areas, knowledge of students, and the learning outcomes previously developed by them. All of the partners were passionate about student learning.

Looking back on that work, I am amazed at how much we (the faculty) assumed about outcomes-based assessment and how little we actually knew. As individuals, we understood the outcomes and what students had to do to meet those outcomes in our own courses, and we assumed that we had a shared understanding of what the outcomes meant. That is, we did not actively question each other's understanding of the outcomes but assumed we were all on the same page with respect to their meanings. We had not compared terminology, analyzed the overall meaning of each outcome, or described how assessment of the different outcomes transpired in each of our courses. This assumption would later become an intense source of learning that impressed me deeply.

Once faculty began to approach this task, the chairs of the FLCs began to take responsibility for completing the assessment details. To begin the work sessions, the director of Teaching, Learning, and Assessment prompted us with questions such as, "How would students show us that they had achieved the outcomes?" or "What evidence could students provide to demonstrate their mastery of the outcomes?" I remember the ringing silence that followed these questions, a silence caused, I believe, by the whirr of many mental cogs thrown into neutral all at once. Most of us earned our disciplinary Ph.D.s at R1 institutions and had received very little training as educators. We were used to thinking about teaching (primarily in the context of subject-based courses), but we had never approached course design from the perspective of learning. We had not considered what would be the evidence of that learning, nor what qualities we would require of the evidence. I know that many of you design your learning activities so that students can see into the design and understand the intention of both your instruction and assessment. That is certainly a strong part of my instruction now, but at the time, the idea of unpacking and delineating our expectations for each of the learning outcomes was a new way of thinking. For some faculty members, it was intuitively obvious. They thought, for example, "Of course, this is how we can help students understand the outcomes better; this will help increase students' performance on the outcomes." Others thought, "Hey, aren't we giving too much away?" It was a quantum leap from their own educational experience in which expectations of students (implicit outcomes, criteria, standards) were an assumed part of these professors' power and held very close to their chest if not consciously or unconsciously kept secret.

Along with her questions, Amy facilitated by explaining that learning outcomes were just the first part of our assessment designs, and that we had to engage in this work further to really support student learning. The FLCs responded by working collaboratively with her to develop a process of inquiry. They discussed, developed, and articulated the ideas that faculty used in their personal assessment of student work and made them "public and visible."

Developing Criteria and Standards Through Inquiry

The work sessions in which we developed examples of evidence, criteria, and standards were fascinating in that they were simultaneously intense work experiences (we accomplished much) and learning experiences. Most of us had never engaged in anything like them. For two days, learning community faculty sat at a round table and worked on one learning outcome at a time. Developing the examples of evidence was easiest, but because we were encouraged to be inclusive in what kinds of student work we would require, and to develop evidence that was learning centered, it was also difficult. Developing the criteria and standards was much more challenging. As our facilitator, Amy, worked with us in developing the criteria for a learning outcome, she listened as we struggled to understand different aspects of the outcome. For example, as we began to discuss the first outcome, she guided us as follows: "Okay, your first learning outcome asks students to explain five physical science concepts. What could students do to show you that they can explain it?" Our response was, "A poster or an oral presentation." She then asked, "What qualities will you look for in the poster or oral presentation?" You can imagine that many times her questions would be followed by considerable head scratching. We were much more used to thinking about what we wanted from students in terms of assignments than we were about the criteria that we would use to evaluate those tasks.

Another example of how Amy prompted us to think about the criteria is as follows: "Visualize three pieces of student work that demonstrate achievement of a given learning outcome. One is excellent, one is passing but not remarkable, and one is not satisfactory. Now describe the differences between the papers." This was a wonderful way of getting us to actually describe the qualities that we wanted in the student evidence; you can see how the criteria would emerge naturally from these descriptions. In developing the standards, Amy continually asked us questions such as, "What does that mean?" or "If you had a piece of student work in front of you, what would the work need to receive an excellent grade?" When we said that the student evidence had to be accurate, Amy asked, "What does accuracy look like in a piece of student evidence? How will students know when they've achieved it?" One of our big discoveries during this time together was that most of us were much more comfortable using terms such as *accurate, depth, critical, analysis, synthesis,* and *reflection* in our assignments than actually explaining what the terms meant and how to achieve them. This significant discovery led to the richness and enthusiasm of our ensuing conversations. Together with Amy, we were asking questions, encouraging and prodding each other, trying out ideas, and sharing our thoughts. We used this kind of back-and-forth discussion in developing the standards, which we used to unpack the criteria and to illustrate levels of student achievement of the outcomes. From my descriptions, you are probably not surprised that many of my interview subjects said that this process was a very significant learning experience and required them to wrestle with learning outcomes in different ways and in considerably more depth than they had ever done previously.

Methods

Before describing what we learned from the interviews, it is important to share my interview and analysis methods so that the insights will have credibility in our academic world. Data were gathered from interviews of faculty members (9 of 40) who participated in developing examples of evidence, criteria, and standards for their general education learning outcomes. The data were collected through semistructured (in-depth) interviews. Interviews were tape-recorded and the recordings were transcribed. The selected interview subjects broadly represented the experience of general education (GE) FLCs. Interviews were conducted in person in subjects' offices, and the questions reflected my experience:

- What did you learn from the process?
- What did you like best about the process?
- What was your biggest epiphany?
- Was any part of the process painful?
- Is there anything else you would like to add?

The entire set of transcripts was read twice and coded to determine themes that emerged in more than four interviews. Transcripts were then read a third time and scored for the presence of the different themes and for the identification of examples as recommended in the ethnographic literature (Esterberg, 2002; Johnson & Christensen, 2000).

Implications for Individual Faculty Members, Faculty Development, and Institutions

Five different themes emerged from my interview study following the general education FLCs' work on developing examples of evidence, criteria, and standards for their general education learning outcomes. Here I discuss the themes and their implications for our faculty, but also for your work and your institutions. Each of these themes is probably not unique to the CSUMB campus. When you read them, see if they apply or have implications for your institution.

1. Value of the assessment work
2. Shared understanding of learning outcomes
3. Concerns about the outcomes-based education (OBE) agenda
4. Influence of faculty status on participation
5. Consideration of learning outcomes from a student's perspective

Value of the Assessment Work

To anticipate the experience that our faculty had with the work sessions and to think of how faculty on your campus might respond, you might consider how many of your colleagues have ever sat down and talked about the kinds of assessment they are using or about how much students are learning. How many of them have been observed in their teaching role? How many would be comfortable with such observations? Even a conversation about the possibility of being observed would yield an in-depth discussion of what is missing, and what might be learned by working collaboratively to develop examples of evidence, criteria, and standards.

When I present this interview study at conferences I introduce the talk by asking my audiences to reflect for a few minutes on what faculty on their campuses would learn if they spent several days together developing examples of evidence, criteria, and standards for their learning outcomes, and what issues would arise. In general, my audiences are very good at anticipating what our faculty experienced, and I think, at least to some degree, this means that many of the results are rather predictable.

In stark contrast to the well-documented faculty resistance to assessment, every one of my subjects said that the work was valuable. As you can imagine, some of them were surprised by this revelation. Faculty valued the development of criteria and standards for many different reasons, including "being able to collaborate with colleagues" and "having to approach their learning outcomes from a student's perspective." Several faculty members praised getting to see the kinds of teaching and assessment that were going on in their colleagues' courses. They enjoyed seeing "the creative thinking their colleagues used in teaching activities, assignments, and assessment practices as they addressed the different GE [general education] outcomes in their courses." One lamented, "I routinely get to collaborate with students, but rarely with faculty on campus." Other faculty members appreciated the process because it forced them to determine just what they intended for students to learn.

Deepening Our Own Learning

I believe one of the biggest reasons that faculty valued the assessment work was the intellectual challenge of having to articulate the qualities that they require of student work and the obvious immediate value of doing this in their efforts to increase student learning. Most of us have great expertise in our subject areas, and because of our own depth of understanding, we see and can analyze the deep patterns and connections that exist in our disciplines. This depth of expertise does not necessarily translate into effective, learning-centered pedagogy, into understanding how to engage our students in meaningful ways such that *they too* understand the connections. These kinds of faculty development processes are challenging because they require us to prioritize important content and process areas within our disciplines and articulate the relationships between and among them. The adage "You don't really understand something until you've taught it" applies here. Thinking about how to connect students deeply with a subject can intensify our own thinking. I believe this occurred with faculty at CSUMB, and I suspect that many of you will gain insight into your own understandings as you grapple with the process of developing criteria and standards for your learning outcomes.

Refining the Outcomes

In addition to the intellectual challenge of the process, many faculty members experienced the development of criteria and standards as the first significant "road test" of their learning outcomes. Almost all of the learning outcomes in all 13 general education areas were changed as a result of the work. Some outcomes were written more clearly, and some were simplified. Developing criteria and standards really helped faculty understand the level of the learning outcomes, and many groups saw that their supposedly sophomore-level outcomes were overly ambitious (i.e., challenging for a graduate student), so they changed them accordingly. Many felt that this work took the campus's assessment to another level in our understanding and implementation of OBE. After the work was accomplished, the level of faculty buy-in to the process and to the learning outcomes was incredible; faculty were proud of what they had produced. From our work with faculty here and in our workshops across the country, we know that developing learning outcomes is challenging, insightful, and relevant to faculty work. However, overall, faculty find developing criteria and standards a much more challenging, deeper, and rewarding task.

The Importance of an Inquiry-Based Process

The fact that all of my faculty colleagues found the development work valuable warrants attention to the faculty dialogues that facilitated our successful work. Our faculty discussions directed to the development of criteria and standards were inquiry based and focused on the question: How would a student know if he or she had achieved (and could demonstrate achievement of) a given learning outcome? This open-ended approach allowed substantive exploration of the issues. Faculty did not feel as if they were being corralled toward specific ends. The process was constructivist and faculty centered and drew on faculty expertise. The work sessions were intense, and faculty were deeply engaged in issues that they both cared a great deal about and knew. I believe this aspect of the work was of paramount importance to the success of the process as well as the depth of the faculty learning experience. Most of the aspects of the faculty development share much with the qualities of excellent teaching, illustrating that faculty as well as students work harder and have deeper and more productive learning experiences when they are engaged in challenging, inquiry-driven processes that are relevant to their interests.

Shared Understanding of Learning Outcomes

The process of developing examples of evidence, criteria, and standards actually required faculty to develop a shared understanding of their learning outcomes by forcing many assumptions regarding the use of language, philosophy, and academic discipline out into the open. Each interview subject indicated that although he or she assumed a common understanding of the outcomes, different faculty members had very different interpretations. For example: "With respect to the general education outcomes, there was a sense that we were all doing the same thing in the courses. When it came to getting it down on paper, we discovered significant differences. Reconciling these differences was not an easy task." As I worked with the science FLC, I was continually surprised by how differently we used language, and how completely ignorant we were of those differences. An interview subject expressed my thoughts exactly when he said, "I liked the fact that this process has forced a lot of assumptions out into the open. In our area, we've had to deal with the fact that we use key terms in different ways depending on our background."

When you work in groups to develop outcomes, it is easy to assume a shared understanding of learning outcomes, and for differences in the ways you use key terms to remain hidden. However, when you must describe exactly what students have to do to demonstrate mastery of the outcomes, detail the qualities of the evidence, and describe levels of achievement (developing criteria and standards for outcomes), differences in your meaning and language quickly become apparent. This discovery was very powerful for the campus and has resulted in a culture that understands the need for active and ongoing dialogue about our learning outcomes and their meanings. I have since seen the assumption at play many times on different campuses. It is easy and perhaps natural to assume a mutual understanding of shared learning outcomes, but only when you make it a priority to discuss those meanings will the differences emerge.

On an institutional level, this result speaks volumes about the need to get faculty members together to come to terms (pun intended) with what their outcomes mean. But for individual teaching faculty members, this result gives insight into an even more insidious problem. The fact that faculty, with similar levels of education, interpret learning outcomes differently makes prominent the need to support our students as they struggle to understand and interpret the language we use in our teaching. How often do we assume that our language and instructions on assignments are perfectly clear and that our students share a common vocabulary?

In their work to become more learning centered, several of my colleagues have adopted the practice of having their students deconstruct and present different aspects of their assignments. This practice has led to marked improvement in their students' performance.

Building a shared language is one of Angelo's (1999) four pillars of transformative assessment. I believe his work assumes that until faculty have done the work of communally discussing the meaning of the terms they use they will not have a shared understanding of their learning outcomes and will consequently be teaching in different directions. Although Angelo discusses the need to build a shared language in the context of assessment models, my interview study suggests that developing learning outcomes requires a shared language as well.

Just as faculty members assumed common understandings of the language of our outcomes and criteria, they also assumed an agenda for the OBE model, which takes us to our next discussion.

Concerns about the OBE Agenda

It is hard to imagine a reader or a campus for whom concerns about OBE do not resonate. Our experience here supports a strong connection between faculty concerns about OBE and the need for faculty to take ownership of assessment on campuses. If assessment is to become a driving force in continuous renewal and to be used to support improvement of student learning, those concerns must be addressed and that ownership supported. Slevin (2001) expresses concern that current assessment models are likely to marginalize faculty members' perspectives and their work. He argues that faculty who teach must commit to assessment to improve the classroom teaching and programs, and that they must take leadership roles in assessment lest their values, expertise, and perspective be lost amid competing and less important interests. I witnessed similar tension regarding OBE at CSUMB in the years preceding our work on developing criteria and standards for the general education learning outcomes, as described in chapter 1. There were genuine concerns that OBE and associated assessment processes would take us away from the kinds of teaching and pedagogies to which we were committed. These concerns explain the commensurate disinterest and resistance to assessment. The following statements illustrate the kinds of concerns faculty had when describing OBE and assessment in the interviews:

"I was afraid I was being asked to run humanities courses (an understanding of the human experience) through a business model."
"We had been worried that outcomes would be used to endorse a particular style of measurement that we were very much against."

As it turned out, developing criteria and standards (and the beneficial effect it had on our learning outcomes) actually deepened and improved our teaching, resulting in faculty ownership of both the general education outcomes and assessment processes (Wiley, 2003). The following statements illustrate how some faculty members felt after developing examples of evidence, criteria, and standards for their general education learning outcomes. They very much reflect how the FLCs took ownership of the process and used it to promote excellence.

> "The process of developing standards and criteria alleviated our concerns. We saw that our outcomes still upheld the values of the CSUMB vision. We were able to develop the outcomes to meet our agenda rather than having the outcomes-based model develop us."
> "Our big epiphany, or at least mine, was recognizing that outcomes could be structured and measured as process rather than as a single-point measurement tool."

If you are adopting OBE, it is important to seek out faculty members who already use outcomes to facilitate learning and improve their teaching and to use their expertise to engage other faculty members. Campuses that focus on student learning must facilitate and engage in processes in which faculty experience the potential benefits of OBE or assessment in general regarding the improvement of student learning as well as the development of more satisfying, intentional teaching. I have no doubt that faculty ownership of our learning outcomes, criteria, and standards and faculty members' important contributions to the design of the process were fundamental to building excitement around OBE and assessment at CSUMB.

Influence of Faculty Status on Participation

Tenured, tenure-track, and part-time faculty (one third of my interview subjects) noted that the status of faculty influenced how they participated in the development of examples of evidence, criteria, and standards. Listen to one tenured faculty member as she discovers that some part-time faculty members were nervous about participating fully: "My biggest epiphany was that the degree to which faculty participated and their perspective was shaped by their status." She went on to say that this had not been apparent during the work meetings but had come up in conversations around the water cooler and at other times. Part-time faculty illustrate what some of these men and women felt during the process. For example, one part-timer commented, "As a lecturer, I became very concerned about my own retention." Another stated, "I often felt the tension of not being able to disagree. I was reserved." In light of this, it is important to address these issues in faculty dialogues and to acknowledge openly the differences in power of the respective faculty groups.

The literature on the extensive use of part-time faculty in higher education discusses problems with maintaining program coherence, as well as addressing how marginalization of part-time faculty affects both faculty and student learning (Caprio, Dubowsky, Warasila, Cheatwood, & Costa, 1999; Gappa & Leslie, 1997). At CSUMB and many other campuses, part-time faculty teach the majority of general education courses. Some of the part-time faculty members who have been at CSUMB long term have substantial experience with the general education learning outcomes. Thus, there is potential for faculty members who have the most experience with the learning outcomes to have a disproportionately small voice in the evolution and maintenance of the outcomes over time. In this case, the issue is that the university is not benefiting fully from the experience and expertise of part-time faculty and is ignoring the importance of their support for program outcomes.

In terms of promoting improvement, understanding this disconnect between part-timers and their experience in our general education FLCs is paramount. This finding allows us to showcase what we currently do to include part-timers (pay them for attending FLC meetings) and develop and implement strategies for developing more inclusive environments within these learning communities. An important consideration in any long-term change or improvement process must be the inclusion of part-time faculty.

When you work in administrative and faculty development roles with part-time faculty, you can serve your learning outcomes and these individuals more effectively by anticipating their reluctance to address thorny issues publicly and by understanding that they run risks when they do. You can do this by acknowledging publicly the power differences in groups that include tenure-track, tenured, and part-time faculty; investing in trust-building exercises; and creating venues where faculty can share anonymously.

Consideration of Learning Outcomes From a Student's Perspective

Several faculty members said that the process of developing criteria, standards, and examples of evidence forced them to address learning outcomes from a student's perspective and that it was a very valuable aspect of the work. Some of these individuals prided themselves on being very student centered, yet this process nudged them to rethink the learning outcomes from a student's point of view in new and different ways, as illustrated by this comment: "I think it is extraordinarily valuable to do this work—it forces people to talk about what they are doing in their classes and it makes us look at things much more from a student's perspective."

By approaching their learning outcomes from the perspective of what the outcomes really mean and how students can demonstrate them, faculty were forced to shift from the perspective of one who does the teaching to that of one who does the learning (and has to demonstrate that learning). I believe this student/learning-centered approach, that is, having to experience learning outcomes from a student's perspective, is very valuable with respect to improvement because it facilitates a deeper connection among faculty members, their teaching activities, and their learning outcomes. It also gives insight into how well students may or may not be able to use teaching and learning activities to master learning outcomes.

I would like to elaborate on what it was about the work sessions that led faculty to feel that they had been forced to approach their learning outcomes from a student's perspective, and why they thought that was valuable. Let's begin with an often heard question posed by a student: "What do I have to do to get an A?" If your answer to that question includes an "analysis" of something, the student's next question should be, "How will you evaluate my analysis, or, more accurately, what are the important attributes of an analysis?" From working with many large groups I know that many of you can easily extemporize on the qualities of an excellent analysis as well as the important aspects of a good synthesis, and that you do this with your students. However, there are a great many of us who can't (even though we use these and similar requirements in our assignments). One of the things our faculty liked about having to approach their work from a student's perspective was that we had to interrogate our teaching more deeply than we had before. The process in these work sessions required that we understand and articulate to our students exactly what we mean when we use terms such as *analysis, synthesis, depth,* and *critical.* It was powerful for our own learning, and many of us saw immediately its potential to increase student learning.

Summary

The themes from my interviews revealed that developing examples of evidence, criteria, and standards for our learning outcomes gave faculty insight into many important issues. The themes showed us the need for ongoing dialogue regarding learning outcomes, because without coming to grips with exactly what the terms we use mean, faculty will interpret the outcomes differently. The themes gave faculty confidence that they could use OBE and assessment to develop and improve the kinds of pedagogies valued on our campus. In some cases, the themes illustrated skills and abilities that our faculty needed to learn more about in order to teach the skills and abilities effectively, and assess them in our students' work. Finally, the themes illustrated that our faculty really enjoyed collaborating with each other in this very challenging work, and having to approach their teaching from the perspective of their students. For these reasons and many others, our faculty found this work very valuable.

A Conversation With Amy

Having experienced all of this work as a faculty member and having seen the effects it had on the campus's culture and its attitudes toward OBE and assessment, I was interested in understanding how Amy planned the process of developing examples of evidence, criteria, and standards. I began my conversation with Amy with this question:

These were such rich learning experiences for all of us, and from my perspective, it seemed like you pulled them off with the greatest of ease. What were your biggest concerns about working with faculty as we headed into the process of developing examples of evidence, criteria, and standards for our learning outcomes?

I had so many concerns that I hardly know where to start. Remember, Swarup, faculty were still coming to OBE unwillingly and didn't care much about assessment, but they were giving it a chance. I really sweated because it felt like a "make or break" situation. To tell the truth, I was mainly worried about the outcomes. They had been developed in a series of workshops before my arrival, and when I reviewed them beforehand, many of them were not outcomes and were so unclear that I knew they would be confusing to students and faculty too. If they weren't right, the work we planned would be difficult because outcomes are the foundation. Revising them should have been our starting point but I was reluctant to begin there—after finally getting faculty to engage with me in assessment. It seemed like a negative beginning with huge potential to discourage everyone—I just couldn't risk it.

I had to dig a little deeper.

Do you still think we should have revised the outcomes first? For me, this process took the outcomes out of the abstract and made them very tangible. Developing criteria and standards for well-developed outcomes is challenging enough, but doing this for poorly written outcomes would not work. In retrospect, what we did seemed like it was the perfect process for revising the outcomes because it illustrated and highlighted areas of weakness.

No, I agree. The process required us to revise the outcomes in an organic way which was both more natural and intrinsically deeper than if we'd started out to do it—but who knew that when we began! Also, and for me perhaps this is more poignant, I realize now that this was an example of *me* needing to trust just as I was asking faculty to trust. So I let go and planned to build off of the already developed outcomes with my initial question, "What do students have to provide to show that they have achieved this outcome?" to lead us to evidence. We could begin with momentum, and I had to trust that faculty would assess and improve their outcomes as we reflected on criteria and standards. They did!

My second concern was that I felt sure that few faculty had ever designed outcomes, evidence, criteria, etcetera, and I was certain that the work would be intensely time-consuming. The biggest issue was the time factor, especially with so much else to do on a new campus. I lost a lot of sleep over this one; I dreaded getting started and not finishing, because if faculty got worn out halfway through, I knew the process would falter. I guess there again I had to trust.

Amy, isn't it interesting that trust has been such a major theme in all of this work? Faculty trusting the facilitator/administrator, faculty trusting each other, you trusting the faculty, to let them guide and knowing it would work; it is interesting the extent to which community building and forming relationships may be required for this work. I can't imagine accomplishing what we did without a great deal of trust.

Now that we understand your concerns and how they played out during the process, tell us about facilitating the work sessions and your biggest challenge working with the faculty.

The challenge was one of balancing the incredible discussions about teaching and learning with the need to finish. It's just like teaching—knowing when to let the discussion go and when to guide it forward. I think that my teaching background helped a lot here, and that's why it's a good idea to have expertise and experience in teaching for this role. It was marvelous listening to faculty talk about both teaching and learning with such intensity and enthusiasm and to experience a culture of inquiry and faculty collegiality. For me, maybe for my whole career, this was collaboration at its best. It certainly was worth the time spent.

I really like the way you talk about the challenges and dilemmas you faced when you facilitated this work. I'm wondering if you could talk a little more of the value of this work for our campus and faculty. Of all that we learned, what do you think was the most important result of this work?

That is easy. Without question, the empowerment and ownership of faculty for OBE and assessment that emerged from the discussions and work were critical. Without that, the whole assessment program would have stayed in my lap—instead it became the faculty's pride and responsibility. I moved to the sidelines with resources, consultations, and food, but I no longer directed the development.

I would like to close this chapter by reflecting briefly on how this work influenced our campus. Peggy Maki (2004) writes that just as intellectual curiosity powers their disciplinary research, faculty are similarly curious about what and how their students learn. She says that this curiosity is the "wellspring of institutional commitment to assessment" (p. 2). When I read this I thought, "Of course, and all that is required to connect faculty members with this curiosity is a positive experience illustrating how assessment can benefit their teaching." It is clear from my interviews that the collaborative, inquiry-based processes that we used to develop examples of evidence, criteria, and standards for our learning outcomes achieved this, and further helped focus our intellectual energies on student learning. You'll see more of this curiosity and energy when we look at what faculty learned from CSUMB's collaborative analysis of student work in chapter 11, and in the vignettes at the end of the book.

References

Angelo, T. (1999). *Doing assessment as if learning matters most* [On-line]. Available: http://frontpage.uwsuper.edu/frc/Scholars/assess.pdf.

Caprio, M. W., Dubowsky, N., Warasila, R. L., Cheatwood, D. D., & Costa, F. T. (1999). Adjunct faculty: A multidimensional perspective on the important work of part-time faculty. *Journal of College Science Teaching, 28*(3), 166–173.

Easterberg, K. (2002). *Qualitative methods in social research*. Boston: McGraw-Hill Higher Education.

Gappa, J. M., & Leslie, D. W. (1997). *Two faculties or one? The conundrum of part-timers in a bifurcated work force*. Originally published by AAHE. Sterling, VA: Stylus.

Johnson, B., & Christensen, L. (2000). *Educational research: Quantitative and qualitative approaches*. Needham Heights, MA: Allyn & Bacon.

Maki, P. (2004). *Assessing for learning: Building a sustainable commitment across the institution*. Sterling, VA: Stylus.

Slevin, J. (2001). Engaging intellectual work: the faculty's role in assessment. *College English, 63*(3), 288–305.

Wiley, M. (2003). In an age of assessment, some useful reminders. *Exchanges* [On-line journal]. Available: www.exchangesjournal.org/viewpoints/1124_Wiley.html.

7

GOING BEYOND MAKING ASSESSMENT "PUBLIC AND VISIBLE"

Story: Syllabi as Communication

I t was an intense time for the campus. Accreditation deadlines were approaching and data gathering was moving at a frenzied pace. As we describe in *Taking Ownership of Accreditation* (Driscoll & Cordero de Noriega, 2006), most of those processes were directed at improvement of the institution, specifically to improving student learning. One of the most obvious and readily available data sources was our course syllabi, not because they provided direct evidence of student learning, but because they demonstrated the existence of behaviors, messages, and course provisions that support student learning. Pascarella (2001) talks about "effective educational practices or processes as one of the most common ways to identify excellence in undergraduate education" (p. 19). Examining those practices offers a reasonable way to check on student experiences that significantly impact students' academic learning.

Our syllabus review, as one of those ways to examine such practices, started out as a simple process with straightforward checklists. We reviewed every current syllabus, checking for the following:

- Learning outcomes
- Use of materials to support learning (beyond textbooks)
- Indications of "active learning"
- Criteria and standards for assessment

These inclusions were fairly easy to find—they were either there or not there. The data, translated as percentages for the campus and for departments, were efficiently recorded. Many of the findings were impressive. For example, 97% of the syllabi had learning outcomes, and 73% of the courses provided learning materials "beyond textbooks." With a growing uneasiness, we patted ourselves on the back. Then, with a sigh, our review group agreed that there was so much more in the syllabi. Within each syllabus, there were powerful messages to students, and those messages were hugely varied. The group was concerned. One member commented, "I keep thinking about the students who read these and feeling worried." The worst dilemma obvious to us all was that "laundry lists" of outcomes appeared at the beginning or end of syllabi, typically unconnected to pedagogy, and separate from the syllabus items that students care most about: schedule and assessment.

We reread the syllabi, no longer prompted by accreditation but by our commitment to student-centered learning and some deep, gut-level feelings about this very important communication with students. The months and months of developing outcomes and evidence with criteria and standards suddenly left us feeling heavy and disappointed. Group members made these admissions about the learning outcomes:

> "If I were a student, I would not pay any attention to those learning outcomes."
> "I would be annoyed by them."
> "I would be asking, What have these got to do with anything?"

Students might also use some choice expletives or names for the learning outcomes but more likely would ignore them. Our projections were the antithesis of the student- or learner-centeredness that we had hoped and worked for with our outcomes-based developments.

It was a painful reread and we attempted to do so with "student hats" on, that is, in the role of students, with empathy for how each syllabus would make them feel. Our reading was a digging process aimed at uncovering the underlying messages to our student readers. Our conversations best describe the categories of syllabi that we reviewed:

> "This syllabus strikes fear in me. I'm not sure that I have a chance to succeed. There are so many ways to screw up. I'm not sure of what's

expected of me, only what will happen if I don't meet deadlines or use specific formats. I feel dread—thinking of ways to get out of this." (8% of syllabi)

"I like short syllabi but this is ridiculous. I have no idea what we will be doing in this class—even what the course is about, except those learning outcomes. The schedule gives me no clue about topics, activities, etcetera. And I definitely don't know what I have to do to pass this class. I guess that we'll talk about the assignments and assessment when we get there." (11% of syllabi)

"This is going to be a tough one . . . so many expectations and so much information about how to do everything. At least it's pretty clear. I know what to do and I can plan my workload around my schedule and assignments. I wonder if any of this is negotiable." (38% of syllabi)

"A little overwhelming on the verbiage but I think this is going to be a good experience. I like the sound of how we are going to learn and the idea that I'll have a voice in some of the class decisions. Kind of different! I get a feel for this teacher and what we can expect of her." (19% of syllabi)

"Now I get it! I see what those learning outcomes are all about. That's why we are doing projects in this course—we'll be able to show that we can do those outcomes. I think that I like knowing why we are assigned certain work because I can see the connection with what I'm supposed to learn. Even our readings are related to specific outcomes!" (24% of syllabi)

Time was running out on us—so much else to do. We gathered samples of syllabi—the ones with messages that felt learner centered—and reflected on our own learning from the process:

"I think that I will ask students to describe how they feel when they read my syllabus—maybe in the first class. On second thought, they might not feel comfortable doing so publicly until they get to know me. Maybe I will have them write it anonymously."

"I like the tone of some of those long syllabi, so welcoming, so community oriented. I just wonder how to motivate students to read and process all of that."

"I just can't stand those lists of outcomes at the front of the syllabi with no connections! I'm going to analyze my syllabus to see how or where I can connect the outcomes to its [their] components. I saw some good examples in those syllabi we set aside."

"I'm going to talk about this in our department meeting—describe what we found and nudge everyone's thinking. I expect some resistance—people will think that we're trying to make all the syllabi look the same. I've got to try. Students deserve better than what they are getting in some of our syllabi."

"Academic freedom" and sensitivity to individual faculty style and intentions would have to be considered in order to act on the last sentiment.

We did collect exciting samples with encouraging messages for students. Later, we asked for permission from their authors and began thinking of how to expand the potential of those syllabi to promote learner-centered practices. We never intended for syllabi to look the same, just to provide information to our students in ways that help and support their learning.

Making Assessment Public and Visible: Why Go Beyond?

The previous story continues throughout the chapter as we describe how syllabi and other forms of communication make assessment "public and visible" along with other important information that students need. We conducted our review of syllabi because the practice of providing clear information about outcomes, criteria, and standards is one of those "best practices" of effective assessment. One of the American Association for Higher Education's (1992) "nine principles of good practice for assessing student learning" (p. 11) refers to clear, explicitly stated purposes and the importance of information about learning outcomes for students. Naively we thought that providing that information to students and others was enough. Our syllabus story demonstrated that we must unpack those qualities of "visibility" and "publicness" and extend them to "understood and useful" and "connected and meaningful." Those extensions are the topic of this chapter.

In this chapter, we promote a new "best practice" of making assessment publicly connected and visible, meaningful, and understood for students to use in directing their learning efforts and demonstrating their learning successes. We provide strategies and approaches at the institutional level, for programs and department-level support, and for individual courses. These three levels of approaches are all essential for learning outcomes to be integral to successful student learning. Furthermore, we look at strategies and samples from faculty. The vignettes at the end of the book are derived from faculty teaching experiences and extend the possibilities for "connected and meaningful" information. We also weave hints and suggestions about syllabi in general as a context for this chapter.

Beyond Public and Visible to "Understood and Useful": From Syllabi to Pedagogy

We chose to begin the process of making assessment public and visible with syllabi and at the course level because it's the core of students' programs and it's the most well known and intimate to faculty. Many of us as faculty do not have much voice in the creation of the programs within which we teach, but we are consistently the authors of our own courses. Tim Riordan (2005) agrees that course assessment is central to program and institutional assessment, so for me it's where we can make the most difference. As our story illustrated, once you analyze your syllabi and ultimately your courses from students' perspectives, you may not be content to have those learning outcomes "just sitting there." Remember in our story that faculty members were the authors of those outcomes, and that their sense of ownership prompted the concern that we heard from them.

We think that once you make connections among your learning outcomes and your pedagogy, curriculum, and learning activities in your syllabus, those connections in the actual course will follow. This result is not guaranteed but its possibility does nudge consideration of learning outcomes as you engage in the day-to-day or week-to-week planning. For that reason, most of our efforts were directed to syllabus design with individual faculty members at CSU Monterey Bay (CSUMB). We began with new faculty and oriented them to our outcomes-based approaches first. Then we showed them some of the excellent examples we found in our syllabus review. It was not hard for them to see those connections in the samples They saw schedules with the outcomes designated for each class, reading assignments with associated outcomes, assignments with the outcomes designated for the student work, and specific indications of how each outcome would be assessed. Groups of new faculty, some having taught at other institutions, described the connections as "making sense," "helpful to students," and a "guide for my planning." With the help of some mini-grants, each new faculty member agreed to design at least one syllabus with information about learning outcomes and assessment that was "understood and useful" to both faculty and students. Since we already had many faculty members who were making those connections in their syllabi (24%), several years of hiring new faculty brought the total number of these individuals going beyond "public and visible" in their syllabi with assessment information to a significant level. Student feedback on the following examples was increasingly positive.

Dr. Lila Staples (2006) designed and teaches in a new museum studies program at CSUMB. In her introductory course, VPA 320, Museum Studies, she poses an "overarching question" for students to examine in the course: "How do museums give voice to underrepresented populations and perspectives, and facilitate the transformation of social structures to create a more inclusive, interactive discussion of history, society, and culture?" (p. 1).

Following her question, Dr. Staples lists the outcomes that students will achieve as they develop their own response to the question:

1. Identify and analyze how museums serve and reflect multiple communities in terms of representation and relevance.
2. Analyze and articulate the internal and external economic and social pressures that influence the choices made by museum personnel, boards, and volunteers with regard to the development of collections and exhibits. (Staples, 2006, p. 1)

These are just two of her six learning outcomes, but it is apparent that the learning outcomes are directly related to the question. Thus, Dr. Staples paves the way for the outcomes to be connected and better understood in relation to the purpose of the course.

Later in her syllabus, Dr. Staples makes visible the connection between the course learning outcomes and the readings, lectures/discussions/slide presentations, assignments, and field component of the course (see figure 7.1). Those connections are useful because students are motivated and learn more easily when engaged in learning activities that make sense to them. Another way of saying "make sense" is that they can see a rationale for the activities or an end for their own learning. Diane Halpern (2003) urges us to "share our vision of teaching and learning with students." She states it simply, "Here's what I am doing and why."

FIGURE 7.1

Excerpt from Dr. Staples's Syllabus Showing the Connection between Learning Outcomes and the Elements of the Course

	Outcome					
	#1	#2	#3	#4	#5	#6
Readings						
Judith Boss *Ethics for Life*	X	X	X	X	X	
John Berger *Ways of Seeing*			X		X	
Ronald Wells *The Importance of Josiah Royce's California for Our Time*		X	X			
Martha Norkunas *The Politics of Public Memory*		X	X	X		
Will Joyner *A Few Thousand Years of Museums in a Nutshell*	X	X			X	
Boas and Black *Frozen in Their Tracks*						X
David Carrier *Restoration as Interpretation*		X		X	X	X
Ivan Illich *To Hell with Good Intentions*			X			
Rachel Naomi Remen *Helping, Fixing, or Serving*	X		X	X		
James Banks *Educating Citizens in a Multicultural Society*	X				X	
Lectures/Discussions/Slide Presentations						
Staples: "Museum boards, where responsibilities begin and end"		X		X		
Staples: "Looking at historical 'truths,' the power of presentation and interpretation."	X	X	X		X	
Staples: "High art and low art, dissolving boundaries"			X	X	X	
Staples: "The role of art/craft in a cultural context"			X	X	X	
Staples: "Ethical issues surrounding collections management"	X		X	X	X	

(continues)

FIGURE 7.1 (Continued)

	Outcome					
	#1	#2	#3	#4	#5	#6
Lectures/Discussions/Slide Presentations						
Mesa-Bains: "Looking at museums and their diverse stakeholders"	X	X		X	X	
Staples: "Learnt assumptions: beauty, truth, genius, civilization, taste, status. . . ."				X	X	
Staples: "The museum and community: role and responsibility" (guest speaker: Mary Murray, MMA)	X	X		X	X	
Guest Curator: "What to exhibit?"	X	X		X	X	X
Pollack or Staples: "What it means to be of service: exclusion and belonging."			X			
Staples: "What it means for a museum to serve."	X	X		X	X	
Assignments						
Write a description and analysis of your own biases and personal lenses and how they might affect your assessment of artifact value.		X	X		X	
From an ethical perspective, as described in *Ethics for Life,* write a paper addressing a personal ethical dilemma you have faced.					X	
Write an analysis of an ethical dilemma surrounding a specific object/artifact in a museum collection, approaching it from dual perspectives.				X	X	X
Select a personal artifact and describe to the class how you define its meaning, history, and importance.			X		X	

FIGURE 7.1 (Continued)

	Outcome					
	#1	#2	#3	#4	#5	#6
Select a museum artifact and write a description and analysis of it from multiple perspectives, in multiple contexts.	X		X		X	
Visit a local museum and write an analysis of a specific exhibit with regard to perspective and representation and display.	X				X	X
Consider and analyze and write about the relationship between viewer and maker in a museum context.				X	X	X
Final project: As a group select artifacts around a central theme and design an exhibit showing an understanding of multiple perspectives, educational components, accessibility, cultural sensitivity, proper handling, design and exhibit requirements. Assign different responsibilities within the group. Project will involve written, oral, and graphic presentations, both individual and collaborative.	X	X	X	X	X	X
On-Site Field Work (Monterey History and Art Association, Maritime Museum, Monterey Museum of Art, Steinbeck Center, Airport Gallery, Carmel Mission)						
Students will learn, use, demonstrate competency with, and be assessed on the following skills: archival research, exhibit fabrication, art handling, oral history skills, computer research, exhibit installation, registration of artifacts, photo documentation, desktop production, preventive care, resume development.					X	X

Source: From *Syllabus example for VPA 320, Museum Studies*, by L. Staples, 2006, Seaside, CA: Department of Visual and Public Arts, CSUMB. Reprinted with permission.

Dr. Staples's syllabus offers compelling evidence of a practice that is encouraged in higher education: making careful choices about content. The very task of aligning curricular content with course outcomes, as she did in her syllabus, forces faculty to prioritize their teaching and learning efforts and class time. In addition, students immediately become aware of those priorities and can do their own prioritizing as they begin the course.

In the syllabus section in figure 7.2, students are immediately informed of why they will be studying the specific curriculum. Dr. Frauke Loewensen begins with the outcomes and follows with the content that will enable students to achieve the outcomes.

At the end of her syllabus, Dr. Loewensen provides the definitions of language proficiency levels as set by her professional association. As we described in chapter 3, a number of professional groups have articulated sets of common or core outcomes or competencies for their members to use in curriculum planning and course requirements. The American Council of Teachers of Foreign Language (2005) has blended outcomes, criteria, and standards into their levels. They are written in helpful language and guide students as well as teachers as they plan for learning. Figure 7.3 provides a section on one of those levels of proficiency from Dr. Loewensen's syllabus.

The syllabus descriptions continue with Novice-High Listening, Novice-High Reading, and Novice-High Writing. Those descriptions also put the course outcomes and content in the big picture of a national set of outcomes and professional expectations. Note how much information is provided for students to understand the expectations. Later in Dr. Loewensen's syllabus, students find descriptions of each of their assignments (e.g., projects, presentations) and a connection to the proficiency level and course outcomes.

In both of the presented examples of syllabi, the descriptions of learning outcomes and related assessment information really promote understanding and use. They are the kind of examples that help new faculty members, many of whom have no experience in syllabus or course design. Even for those faculty members with teaching experience, the actual design process for creating a syllabus and planning pedagogy is fairly undeveloped. Most of us in higher education have had to rely on the examples of syllabi and course design to which we have been exposed, and they are often poor examples. It is, however, a time of positive change.

Along with many of the changes in our profession, the shift from teaching to learning that we described in chapter 1 calls for "changes in how we think about our courses, how we design students' learning experiences, and

FIGURE 7.2
Excerpt from Dr. Loewensens's Syllabus Explaining Why Students Will Be Studying the Specific Curriculum

Learning Outcomes

This course incorporates the National Foreign Language Standards, especially Standard 1 "Communication", Standard 2 "Cultures", and Standard 4 "Comparisons." In connection with Standards 1 and 4, you will gain a better understanding of the nature of language through comparisons of Spanish and English, and you will learn to communicate in Spanish in three different modes: the interpersonal, the interpretive, and the presentational. With respect to Standards 2 and 4, you will be introduced to the relationship between some practices and perspectives as well as some products and perspectives of the Spanish-speaking cultures, and you will gain a better understanding of the concept of culture through cultural comparisons. You will demonstrate achievement of these standards through your work in regular class meetings as well as through special projects.

All three standards will be taught via the following content:

Chapter 8: "Los días festivos"
- You will talk about holidays and other important dates of the year,
- talk about events in the past,
- describe some important Hispanic celebrations,
- and learn some basic information about Cuba.

Chapter 9: "El tiempo libre"
- You will talk about how you spend your free time, including fun activities and household chores,
- describe and talk about what you used to when you were younger,
- express extremes,
- ask a variety of questions,
- and learn some basic information about Colombia.

Chapter 10: "La salud"
- You will talk about the human body,
- talk about health issues,
- create structurally more complex sentences,
- and learn some basic information about Venezuela.

Chapter 11: "Presiones de la vida moderna"
- You will talk about accidents, injuries, and the pressures of modern life,
- tell for how long something has been happening,
- tell how long ago something happened,
- express unplanned or unexpected events,
  and learn some basic information about Puerto Rico.

Source: From *Syllabus sample for WLC 102, Beginning Spanish,* by F. Loewensen, 2006, Seaside, CA: Department of World Languages and Cultures, CSUMB. Reprinted with permission.

FIGURE 7.3
Excerpt from Dr. Loewensen's Syllabus Providing a Description of the Language Proficiency Level Novice-High Speaking

Student Proficiency Outcomes

By the end of this class, you should be able to demonstrate a Novice-High level of proficiency in all four language skills as defined below:

American Council of Teachers of Foreign Languages (ACTFL) Novice-High Language Proficiency Levels

The following are detailed descriptions of the **Novice-High** ACTFL LANGUAGE PROFICIENCY LEVEL that has been adopted by CSUMB, and is the level of achievement that students should attain upon completion of a language course at the **102** level. Note that these descriptions refer to general language acquisition, and do not address the particular course learning outcomes addressed in your class syllabus.

Novice-High Speaking

Speakers at the Novice-High level are able to handle a variety of tasks pertaining to the Intermediate level, but are unable to sustain performance at that level. They are able to manage successfully a number of uncomplicated communicative tasks in straightforward social situations. Conversation is restricted to a few of the predictable topics necessary for survival in the target language culture, such as basic personal information, basic objects and a limited number of activities, preferences and immediate needs. Novice-High speakers respond to simple, direct questions or requests for information; they are able to ask only a very few formulaic questions when asked to do so. Novice-High speakers are able to express personal meaning by relying heavily on learned phrases or recombinations of these and what they hear from their interlocutor. Their utterances, which consist mostly of short and sometimes incomplete sentences in the present, may be hesitant or inaccurate. On the other hand, since these utterances are frequently only expansions of learned material and stock phrases, they may sometimes appear surprisingly fluent and accurate. These speakers' first language may strongly influence their pronunciation, as well as their vocabulary and syntax when they attempt to personalize their utterances. Frequent misunderstandings may arise but, with repetition or rephrasing, Novice-High speakers can generally be understood by sympathetic interlocutors used to non-native speakers. When called on to handle simply a variety of topics and perform functions pertaining to the Intermediate level, a Novice-High speaker can sometimes respond in intelligible sentences, but will not be able to sustain sentence level discourse.

Source: From *ACTFL guidelines: Speaking*, by American Council of Teachers of Foreign Language, 2006. www.sil.org/lingualinks/LANGUAGELEARNING/OtherResources/ACTFL ProficiencyGuidelines.htm

how we articulate our expectations of our students and ourselves" (Diamond, 1997, p. viii). Diamond (1997) says that the traditional syllabus of the past was never designed to communicate the student role in learning or to provide the kind of information that would help students understand how to make the most of their course experience (p. viii). For some faculty members at CSUMB, the syllabus represented their first opportunity to communicate the learner-centered philosophy of their pedagogy. They worked intensely designing that communication and made sure that all of their teaching plans including assessment were "understood and useful." For new faculty members as well as for current ones with little experience in learner-centered approaches or environments, a well-designed syllabus with "understood and useful" expectations and supportive pedagogy to meet those expectations (outcomes) offered a concrete way to get started. Syllabi such as the examples from Drs. Staples and Loewensen offered a beginning. Later, the course alignment process that we describe in chapter 8 will affirm the syllabus models and encourage your understanding and commitment to learner-centered pedagogy as part of course design.

Beyond Public and Visible to "Connected and Meaningful": Program Coherence and Value

Before a learner chooses a major and enters a program of study, the learning outcomes of that program can offer a meaningful preview of what is ahead. They represent the promise to learners, "here's what you will have when you complete this program." As we described in chapter 3, many high-quality programs have developed learning outcomes in collaboration with community partners, potential employers, and professional associations so that learners can preview the professional role and employment expectations of their choice of major.

Making Meaning of Our Program Outcomes

There are varied ways to introduce learners to the learning outcomes of a particular major. Brochures, program descriptions, and Web sites offer public and visible information for a wide audience. Beyond that, the learning outcomes and other assessment information can be made meaningful and connected in an orientation session, an advising/planning meeting, or an introductory class. With the exception of the class, there is always the possibility of the learning outcomes not becoming meaningful to learners. In chapter

3, we talked about how Professor Eric Tao used a coding scheme to get his learners to reflect on the learning outcomes at the beginning of his class. That same idea could be used with learners for several purposes, such as pre-post self-assessment of learners.

Let's examine a set of directions for rating learning outcomes:

> "Look at the learning outcomes of our major. Think of what you already know about the profession you are entering and the kind of work you hope to do. Rate those learning outcomes for their importance to your future employment: place a 1 next to those outcomes that you think are absolutely essential for success in the work, a 2 next to those outcomes that you think are important but not as essential as the 1s, a 3 next to those outcomes that you think are only minimally essential, and a 4 next to the outcomes that do not seem necessary at all."

This set of directions asks students to do three things:

1. Reflect on their future professional role and employment responsibilities.
2. Reflect on the learning outcomes.
3. Make connections between the future employment and the learning outcomes.

The act of rating the importance of the learning outcomes will increase both meaning and value and build connections for learners at the start of their program of studies. It will be advantageous to the program and its learners to repeat the process midway through the program along with a self-assessment by students of their own progress in meeting the outcomes, and at the completion of the program. The same connections can be requested of alumni after they have entered the professional world of work to ensure program coherence and value. This same reflective strategy is a useful one for you to respond to as well. Your responses will be useful in the program development process, in program review, and for new faculty.

Webbing Our Program Outcomes for Connectedness

A final strategy for connectedness specifically is a webbing activity, again useful for both faculty and students. Creating a web of program learning outcomes is appropriate for your departmental faculty meeting. Using the template in figure 7.4, reflect individually and then collaborate with colleagues to create a group web of those outcomes. For an institution that values interdisciplinarity, the web can extend to other disciplines to represent

FIGURE 7.4
Template for Creating a Group Web of Learning Outcomes (LO) for a Course Titled CST 321 Multimedia

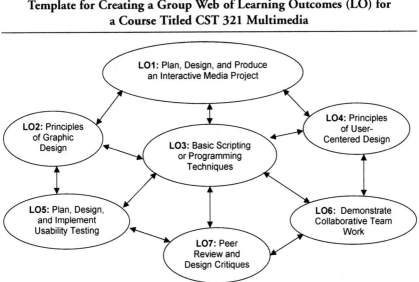

actual connections that exist in courses or program requirements outside the department.

This same webbing exercise would be an excellent summarizing activity for students or a pre-post assessment for the beginning and end of a program. Students usually make connections that most faculty members have not thought of, so if this happens you may wish to ask the students to explain and support their connections. Laura Lee Lienk's vignette at the end of the book uses a contextual web that reinforces the content of her course. Be sure to read how she webs the outcomes with her students. Any webbing exercise will provide information to help you review your program and to address its capacity to be meaningful and connected.

Program Review Processes: Toward Meaningful and Connected

The use of learning outcomes and assessment information can go beyond providing meaningful and connected information to your students and contribute to strengthening or improving your programs, making them meaningful and connected. CSUMB's program review model probes such components as clear description of learning outcomes, capacity to collect and analyze student evidence, improved advising for students, connection with institutional mission and values, and capacity for program improvement. All of these components rely on public and visible as well as meaningful and connected assessment in program structure and components.

I urge you to ask questions such as the following as a focus of program review:

- Are the learning outcomes, evidence, criteria, and standards clear and well understood by students?
- Are the learning outcomes, evidence, criteria, and standards clear and well understood by faculty?
- Does the advising system track a path for students to achieve the learning outcomes?
- Is there a tracking system to keep a record of students' achievement of the learning outcomes?

These types of questions and the evidence to support their answers will prompt the kind of assessment and reflection that lead to program improvement and, ultimately, student-centered programs.

Ensuring Public and Visible: From First-Year Experiences to Graduation

When you open a CSUMB catalog, it is immediately "public and visible" that learning outcomes are a dominant theme in the pedagogy and learning approaches of the campus. Much discussion and decision making preceded that inclusion in the catalog, along with worries about the legal issues associated with making the promises of learning outcomes. In some ways, articulating the learning outcomes in such a public format represents a contract with students who decide to attend the institution. The inclusion of learning outcomes in brochures, program descriptions, and the catalog sends a message that the university will provide resources (faculty, library, technology, and so forth), teaching and learning approaches, curriculum, and other forms of learning support to ensure that all students have every opportunity to develop the skills and knowledge that are described in the learning outcomes. The message represents an institutional commitment not only to provide those resources but to assess and evaluate that the promise is being kept. Later in chapter 9, we will watch faculty review and analyze student work to check on that commitment and to ensure that students are achieving the promised learning outcomes.

With such institutional commitment came the realization that learning outcomes in courses and programs were not enough. After about eight years of requiring students to meet learning outcomes in their courses and to satisfy program learning outcomes for both general education and their majors, a group of faculty worked to redesign the first-year–experience course. One of the group's intentions was to reflect the importance of outcomes in the overall CSUMB baccalaureate experience. "We realized that if learning outcomes were central to our educational approach, then our learners needed to become familiar with them early in their educational program here" (R. Perry, personal communication, 2003). The faculty committee developed an important learning outcome for the first course:

> "Students will define outcomes, describe the benefits of outcomes for their learning, and design individual learning outcomes for their CSUMB experience."

With that outcome as one focus for first-year curriculum, faculty members then faced the challenge of designing teaching and learning approaches for their courses. Natasha Oehlman provides a vignette of her pedagogy directed to that outcome at the end of the book. She and her colleagues frequently came back to the outcome as they collaborated on varied pedagogical decisions, such as selection of a common text, readings, course resources, and assignments.

Throughout varied sections of that first course, students had multiple opportunities to write their own outcomes, connect outcomes to their activities, and assess how the outcomes were influencing their learning and study approaches. I still remember sitting in a meeting with several students—a meeting focused on planning an unrelated social event—and asking about their first-year seminar. The students knew nothing about me or my role on campus, and it was a friendly environment for candid conversation. One of the students didn't value the first-year course he was completing, but another student enthusiastically reported, "I'm learning all about outcomes and they make sense. . . . I think that they will help me in my education." He went on to describe how his family was trying to understand the outcomes approach and set some outcomes of their own.

After revising the first-year curriculum to include attention to an understanding of outcomes, related abilities for using them, and appreciation for their value and usefulness, we looked to the end of students' baccalaureate programs. All of the institutional programs required a capstone project that was intended to be a synthesis of major programs of study as well as the general education requirements. Most departments used their major learning outcomes (MLOs) to frame the capstone requirements while adding other outcomes or new criteria. Only recently have most departments revised capstone descriptions to specifically call for a synthesis of the MLOs of the major with criteria that were already threaded through the program assessment. It does not make sense to familiarize students with particular outcomes and criteria all through their major and then switch to new ones. It does make sense to further integrate some of the most significant general education outcomes that align with the institutional vision and values with those capstone requirements.

At another institution, Portland State University, students work toward four main learning outcomes areas throughout their four years of study. For their capstone, they must show evidence of achieving those outcomes as well as participate in a campuswide assessment process of those outcomes. The capstone itself is designed and structured to extend the learning associated with those outcomes. One of the outcome areas is collaboration. Without the team approach to capstones—that all capstones must be achieved in teams of students—the goal of collaboration would be a bit elusive.

After the vignettes at the end of this book, with permission, we reprint the graduation speech of Megan Jager, the outstanding student in 2000 at CSUMB. We will let her words describe the potential for learning at an institution in which learning outcomes frame the educational program. When you read her words, it will be clear that our assessment information was consistently "public and visible" throughout the baccalaureate experience for our learners.

After reading Megan's speech and hearing a first-year student describe the impact of learning outcomes, I reflected back on our syllabus review process and the discomfort of seeing disconnected learning outcomes in syllabi. I still worry about the possibility of faculty moving beyond "public and visible" to "meaningful, useful, connected, and understood." I check in with Swarup and ask questions to probe that possibility.

A Conversation With Swarup

I continue to worry that faculty are not yet making meaningful connections between learning outcomes and course components. I have to ask a tough and revealing question. After your years of developing outcomes, evidence, criteria, and standards, how do you approach your syllabus (or your course design)?

Don't worry, I definitely do things very differently than I used to. Whereas I used to teach subject-based courses largely driven by the order of the chapters in the textbooks that I used, I now teach very thematic courses in which the themes are groups of related learning outcomes. My syllabus and course design are the wheel that surrounds the hub, my learning outcomes. That hub is central—everything that I do is connected to the learning outcomes. All of the teaching and learning activities—lectures, inquiry-based exercises, labs, manipulatives, group work, readings, assignments, assessments (both formative and summative)—revolve around the outcomes and are connected intentionally and directly to them.

I continued with my probe with a concern about syllabus length and engaging learners in the content of informative syllabi, reflecting the worry voiced in our story at the beginning of this chapter: the moment you insert all of the learning outcomes, evidence, criteria and standards, syllabi get long. So I posed this question:

Do you introduce and review your syllabus with students, or engage them with the assessment information in any way?

Getting students to engage with the syllabus is a perennial lament. I've tried arranging the students in small groups on the first day of class and having them present different sections of the syllabus to the class. Throughout the course, I refer students to the syllabus as a way of getting them used to using it as a reference for the course.

Swarup's lament is not an isolated one. It's reported by many faculty members. I wonder if you experience that challenge. Grunert (1997) urges us to introduce and review syllabi thoroughly from the very beginning, much like Swarup does: "Be sure to allow sufficient time for students to discuss their respective roles in the course" and "turn to the syllabus often to encourage students to develop the habit of using it as a common reference throughout the course" (p. 20). In *The Course Syllabus: A Learner-centered Approach*

(1997), Grunert suggests the following for getting to understood and meaningful:

1. Ask students to review the syllabus and/or the learning outcomes outside of class and write a brief response to both following the class discussion.
2. Include key terms in the syllabus and define them, as well as ask students to extend the list of terms and supply their own definitions.
3. Refer to the syllabus when discussing new assignments and reinforce the connection with learning outcomes.
4. Encourage students to make notes on the syllabus elaborating the discussion about particular items.
5. Provide concrete examples ("exemplary but realistic") of assignment and assessment requirements to clarify the connection with the learning outcomes (pp. 20–21).

Grunert's second suggestion is especially important with technical learning outcomes or outcomes with language specific to a discipline. Students often come into a course without enough knowledge to understand the outcomes, so it will be important to begin your course by making your language "understood and meaningful."

Knowing this chapter has come to a close is a bit frustrating because there is so much more to consider in going beyond "public and visible" with our assessment information for students. Knowing that syllabi and program descriptions are such influential communications with students adds more tension considering the brevity of this chapter. Fortunately, there are new resources like Grunert's (1997) book (we bought copies for all new faculty) and Huba and Freed's (2000) assessment guide, *Learner-Centered Assessment on College Campuses*, so we close our chapter by urging you to go "beyond" this text.

References

American Association for Higher Education. (1992). Principles of good practice for assessing student learning. In L. F. Gardiner, C. Anderson, & B. L. Cambridge (Eds.), *Learning through assessment: A resource guide for higher education* [A Publication of the AAHE Assessment Forum] (pp. 11–12). Washington, DC: Author.

American Council of Teachers of Foreign Language. (2005). *Standards and criteria for foreign language instruction.* Washington, DC: Author.

Diamond, R. (1997). Introduction. In *The course syllabus: A learning-centered approach* (Grunert, J., author) (pp. viii–x). Bolton, MA: Anker.

Driscoll, A., & Cordero de Noriega, D. (2006). *Taking ownership of accreditation.* Sterling, VA: Stylus.

Grunert, J. (1997). *The course syllabus: A learning-centered approach.* Bolton, MA: Anker.

Halpern, D. (2003). *Applying the science of learning to the university and beyond.* Presentation at the annual meeting of the Association of American Colleges and Universities, Long Beach, CA.

Huba, M. E., & Freed, J. E. (2000). *Learner-centered assessment on college campuses.* Needham Heights, MA: Allyn & Bacon.

Loewensen, F. (2006). *Syllabus sample for WLC102, Beginning Spanish.* Seaside, CA: Department of World Languages and Cultures, CSUMB.

Pascarella, E. T. (2001). Identifying excellence in undergraduate education: Are we even close? *Change, 33*(3), 19–23.

Riordan, T. (2005). Education for the 21st century: Teaching, learning, and assessment. *Change, 37*(1), 52–56.

Smith, D. (2004). *Syllabus sample for ESSP 260, Introduction to Geology.* Seaside, CA: Department of Earth, Systems, Science, and Policy, CSUMB.

Staples, L. (2006). *Syllabus sample for VPA Museum Studies.* Seaside, CA: Department of Visual and Public Art, CSUMB.

ALIGNMENT

Making Explicit Connections Between Teaching Decisions and Learning Outcomes

Story: Comparing Perceptions

Professor Guidry starts every class the same way—with her outcomes for the day's session. Sometimes she states them directly. For example, she might say, "Today we will work together so that by the end of class you can explain and apply the theory of supply and demand." Other times she writes the outcomes on the white board or in PowerPoint and asks, "How many of you think that you can already explain this?" Students offer explanations when they think they already know the material, and she offers feedback. Sometimes she has to rethink the class session. Or she might provide a scenario of economics and ask students what theory will explain what is happening. In this case, if her students reply that the theory of supply and demand will explain the scenario, she might respond: "Yes, the theory of supply and demand will help us understand that scenario. Today we will focus on that theory so that you can explain what is happening and use it to make recommendations." Professor Guidry has been using this strategy since she read some of the research on effective teaching that advised teachers to communicate to students the outcomes or expectations for their learning at the beginning of the class. The research promised that students would learn better.

Dr. Guidry finds a connection between that research insight and a faculty development session at her university. During the semester break, she attends an orientation session on the Course Alignment Project being offered to all faculty members. Faculty could receive $250 in professional development funds for participating in the project. "I need some travel money for my annual conference," she thinks. She agrees to create a course alignment grid for her introductory course in economics before the semester starts.

Using the grid, Professor Guidry is to plot the learning outcomes for each class session across the top of the grid. Along the vertical axis, she is to list her course components: class sessions, readings and other materials, assignments, and assessments. She also agrees to ask her students to identify the learning outcome focus of each session at the end of each class. As she sits in the orientation session, Professor Guidry reflects on her opening strategy of informing students of the class outcome. She describes her strategy to her colleagues and the orientation leader and asks, "Won't this make it easy for my students to identify the outcome focus of each class?" She thinks to herself, "I will have high agreement on this one. . . . My students will always know what outcome we are working on." The orientation leader agrees with her prediction but suggests that it would be interesting to test it out.

Three weeks pass and Professor Guidry's hypothesis is supported each week at the end of her class sessions when her students identify the same outcome(s) that she did for each class session. She is feeling smug in week 4 as she begins her session with, "Today's class is focused on supply and demand (Outcome 3 on her syllabus). By the end of class, I want you to be able to explain several economic crises using the theory of supply and demand, and I expect that you will be able to apply the theory with some recommendations." That learning outcome comes straight from her syllabus.

The class session is lively, with discussions focused on news clippings of economic crises, role plays of upper-level management explaining crises to stockholders, and integration of global trade issues that influence supply and demand. It is a fast-paced, content-rich session, and there is little reflection or review time at the end of class. Professor Guidry hurriedly passes out the weekly forms (see figure 8.1) with the course learning outcomes listed for students to select the day's focus. She repeats her directions: "Think about our class today and check off the outcome that we worked toward today."

Later that day, Professor Guidry reviews the student forms and is puzzled. In her class of 32 students, 18 selected an outcome different from the outcome she stated at the beginning of class. The 14 remaining students chose the outcome about "using the theory of supply and demand to explain

FIGURE 8.1
**Example of a Weekly Form Providing Outcomes for Students
to Select as the Day's Focus**

Course Outcomes:	1	2	3	4	5	6
Class Session: 4					X	
Comments:						

Source: "Course Alignment Grid," by A. Driscoll, December 1998, California State University, Monterey Bay, Center for Teaching, Learning and Assessment.

economic crises." After she mentally reviews the class activities, she begins to understand why some of the students focused on global economics (Outcome 5) in their choice of outcome. She decides that at the start of their next class she will ask the two groups to describe for each other why they made their choices. She believes that their explanations will provide valuable information that will enhance her teaching. "I will probably learn some good information for my teaching from their explanations of their outcome choice. Maybe I can ask each group to describe why they think their choice is a good fit for the class focus."

Most of us would like to follow Professor Guidry to her next class session and listen to her students. We would all learn with her. This chapter, however, is focused on the alignment of teaching and curriculum with intended learning outcomes.

Alignment of Teaching and Curriculum With Learning Outcomes

Aligning teaching and curriculum with learning outcomes is a simple "best practice" in education and fairly easy to monitor and adjust in your courses and your programs. Another way of stating the practice is that when you plan your course you design teaching and learning activities that will help students meet the desired outcomes. That sounds very simple, but without the clear direction provided by learning outcomes, our planning, implementation, and assessment of curriculum become difficult. According to Gardiner (1994), "Much of the disjunction between curricular requirements and results can be explained by the lack of outcomes for direction" (pp. 32 and 37).

Frequently, when I (Amy) remind colleagues of this practice of alignment, I get a look of disbelief—amazement that I would mention anything quite so simple, that I am insulting their professional expertise. It feels like such common sense to most of us that we cannot believe that anyone would need to articulate the idea. "But of course I align or plan my course to meet the outcomes," you may think and say, and I know that I thought and said the same thing when I was teaching. However, my experiences with faculty have reinforced the need to check alignment of courses on a regular basis. Those experiences have also taken a deceptively simple process and demonstrated that there is complexity to course design and that alignment is an important component of that process. Faculty teachers who have studied the alignment of their own courses have described significant insights and have been able to revise their courses to improve student learning. They provide compelling reasons for studying alignment.

Reasons for Studying Alignment

You might be asking why alignment has become so important in the recent assessment movement. It's not something that we have talked about in the past. In chapter 1, we noted that many reforms are occurring at the same time as changes in assessment. Some of those reforms are curricular in focus, with a growing recognition of the need for coherent curriculum.

Curriculum in higher education is quite suspect today with evidence and critics arguing that college curriculum is not contributing to the needs of students or society (Gardiner, 1994). Criticism of efforts to revitalize curriculum has been intense, with descriptions of curriculum continuing to be disappointing, insufficient, inadequate, and incoherent. The research and critique both suggest that curriculum "is no longer achieving its intended purpose" and "do [does] not produce the results we intend" (Fife, 1992, p. xii). Having worked with a large number of institutions around the country, I defend many of those efforts as well aligned with societal needs of our time. Gardiner (1994) summarizes that what is needed is "a clear definition of intended outcomes and knowledge of how each course or curricular component interacts with what students bring to the course and contributes to each outcome produced" (p. 35)—and I agree. Thus, a starting point for effective curriculum is our clear expectations for students. From there, we need to understand how the curriculum produces those learning outcomes. That understanding can work toward coherence in our curriculum. According to Huba and Freed (2000), an important quality of learner-centered curriculum is coherence in the learning process in terms of both curriculum content and pedagogical processes.

Quality curriculum is at the heart of learner-centered education, and alignment studies promote both planning and reviewing of syllabi and program descriptions for the quality of coherence. Another focus of a learner-centered approach to curriculum is faculty attention to experiences and activities leading to student learning. Huba and Freed (2000) ask the question, "Do faculty focus on experiences leading to outcomes as well as on the outcomes themselves?" (p. 77). It is easy to become so involved in the outcomes that we focus little on how we will support our learners to achieve those outcomes. Huba and Freed's question again seems like a basic or simple question, yet we noted that many of our California State University (CSUMB) faculty colleagues focused intensely on the development of outcomes only to revert back to a previously developed course to achieve them. The course alignment grid described in this chapter can guide and focus faculty to think and plan using such experiences, that is, the pedagogy and curriculum, to support student achievement of learning outcomes.

Studying course alignment is an important inquiry process. When faculty members ask themselves, "Am I doing all I can to help students achieve these learning outcomes?" the Course Alignment Project provides one level of answers in terms of how the teaching and learning time is spent and to what ends it is directed. You will find it a satisfying and compelling approach to answer that question yourself.

Initial Experiences: Easing Faculty Into Assessment

At this point, a personal anecdote will reveal the potential of course alignment for different results. About eight years ago, when I first introduced the idea of course alignment to faculty, some of the early comments were as follows:

> "Well, first, I've got to be clear about what the outcomes of my course are."
>
> "I'm not sure that my students can understand my outcomes."

That was a breakthrough to focusing on assessment because a number of faculty members decided that they had to spend time clarifying their outcomes. That clarification is a significant result of the course alignment process. One faculty member had so many outcomes (30 +) that it became impossible to determine whether or how his teaching and learning was directed to them. A second result, then, is the review and prioritization of outcomes in order to have a reasonable number for your course. It's important to pause here and acknowledge that the Course Alignment Project was introduced at that time when few faculty members wished to collaborate with me on assessment. The resistance that I described in chapter 1 was frustrating. Out of desperation, I introduced the Course Alignment Project, a kind of backdoor approach, with the intention of bringing faculty to assessment through a self-study of their own courses. The resulting faculty engagement in assessment was an exciting extension of the project.

The course alignment process is an ideal starting point for involvement in assessment because it is nonthreatening and efficient. The fact that it does not consume an inordinate amount of your time or energy is especially important. The data from your individual projects do not have to be shared or made public in any way. The course alignment process was designed for you to use to study your own teaching, and how you use it is your choice. For our campus, eight years ago, it relieved the pressure in terms of what faculty feared from assessment. The process seemed so simple, and it was. Remember, too, that I had a large grant and could offer those mini-grants like Professor Guidry needed to faculty who agreed to conduct an alignment study of their own courses.

Our use of course alignment heeded the advice of Tom Angelo (1999, 2002) to build trust and support before expecting faculty to engage in assessment. At CSUMB, the "hearts and minds" of faculty were focused comfortably on teaching and learning. To begin the process of steering their efforts to assessment, work needed to begin in the comfort zone, teaching and learning. The Course Alignment Project was designed to achieve that placement of comfort—beginning to look at assessment through a study of teaching and learning. As faculty examined their own courses, they were actually studying their overall assessment approaches with ease, with confidence, and with interest. The understanding that must precede involvement was also emerging (Wehlburg, 1999).

Directions for Using Course Alignment Grids

For those faculty members (about 80 percent) who submitted proposals for those first mini-grants, the directions provided a simple way to check their course alignment, that is, the alignment between the teaching and learning activities of their courses and their student learning outcomes.

The samples in figures 8.2 and 8.3 are the kind of grids that faculty at our campus were asked to produce. They used an Excel spreadsheet and filled in their course outcomes on the vertical axis. On the horizontal axis, they listed their class sessions, readings and other resources (e.g., videos, Web sites, newspapers), assignments, and assessments. They were urged to include labs, service learning activities, guest speakers, and any other distinctive teaching and learning activities that they planned for their classes. Once both axes were complete, faculty were asked to plot the outcomes for each of the items in the horizontal axis.

The grids served as matrices, and Banta (1996) urges the use of simple matrices as tools to help faculty to conceptualize assessment with student outcomes. For course alignment, the matrix or grid allowed faculty to chart the relationship between their course activities and course learning outcomes. Such grids make this relationship visible and easy to analyze and understand. One faculty member described the advantage of the grid: "The form provided a way for me to cross-check my activities with my stated course objectives. It was clear, succinct, and easy to use. I will definitely use this form again for other courses and for my scholarship of teaching—a great tool."

The grids in figures 8.2 and 8.3 make the relationship between course activities and course learning outcomes visible and easily analyzed and understood.

What to Look for in an Alignment Grid: Analyzing the Data

The alignment grid is a visual that reveals gaps, patterns, and integration with very little analysis. In the rest of this chapter, I provide examples of the

FIGURE 8.2
Sample Course Alignment Grid A

Course Information:
Professor:

	Outcome 1	Outcome 2	Outcome 3	Outcome 4	Outcome 5	Outcome 6
Class 1	X					
Class 2	X					
Class 3	X	X	X			
Class 5		X	X			
Class 10		X				
Class 11		X				
Class 12	X	X				
Class 20				X		
Class 21				X		
Class 22	X			X	X	
Class 23	X			X	X	
Class 28				X	X	X
Class 29	X					X
Class 30	X	X	X	X	X	X
Reading A	X	X				
Reading B		X	X			
Reading C						X
Reading D						X
Assignment 1	X	X				
Assignment 2	X	X				
Assignment 3						X
Assignment 4						
Assignment 5						
Assessment 1	X	X				
Assessment 2	X	X			X	
Assessment 3						
Assessment 4				X	X	

FIGURE 8.3
Sample Course Alignment Grid B

Course Information:
Professor:

	Outcome 1	Outcome 2	Outcome 3	Outcome 4	Outcome 5	Outcome 6
Class 1	X	X				
Class 2	X	X				
Class 3	X	X				
Class 5	X		X			
Class 10		X	X		X	
Class 11		X	X	X	X	
Class 12		X	X	X	X	
Class 20				X		
Class 21		X				X
Class 22		X				X
Class 23		X				X
Class 28	X			X		X
Class 29		X	X	X		X
Class 30	X	X	X	X		X
Reading A		X				
Reading B		X				
Reading C		X	X			X
Reading D			X	X		X
Text Selections	X	X	X	X	X	X
Assignment 1	X	X				
Assignment 2	X	X				
Assignment 3		X		X	X	
Assignment 4		X	X	X		X
Assignment 5		X	X			X
Assessment 1	X					
Assessment 2	X	X				
Assessment 3		X	X	X	X	X
Assessment 4			X			X

kind of findings that emerged from our use of alignment grids in 1999, 2002, and 2004. I share the insights that have emerged as faculty have analyzed their own grids and describe how we have used alignment exercises in varied ways to consistently check our practices and improve student learning. A few of the typical findings from our first round of course alignment will illustrate the grid's usefulness.

Gaps in the Alignment

The first and most obvious finding is related to gaps, that is, outcomes that are forgotten, do not get attention, and do not have teaching and learning activities directed to them. Figure 8.2, Sample Course Alignment Grid A, depicts a course in which Outcome 3 gets very little attention in class sessions, no practice opportunities in assignments, and even a lack of assessment. Although this is not a frequent finding, it is important to verify whether it is intended or not. Outcome 6 is addressed minimally but with no assessment. Faculty were surprised by such findings and reflected consciously on the difficulty of assessing and even teaching some outcomes. In our experiences at CSUMB, outcomes with the skills of synthesis and analysis were often difficult to teach and to assess, and we saw those gaps when outcomes reflected those critical-thinking skills. Remember in chapter 3 when we described processes for designing outcomes and urged you to prioritize them? It just may be that Outcomes 3 and 6 were the kind of outcomes that could be described as "interesting but could be skipped."

Patterns in the Alignment

The most common pattern that faculty find in their alignment grids is the uneven allocation of time and activities, emphasizing some outcomes and not others. In figure 8.3, Sample Course Alignment Grid B, Outcome 2 is addressed in more than half of the class sessions and in all of the assignments and half of the assessments. It could be that the teacher intended to emphasize Outcome 2 and/or to integrate it with other outcomes and, thus, is satisfied with this pattern. When prioritizing outcomes, this instructor may have said, "This is so important that I cannot teach the course without it" or "This is the central focus of my course." Or it could be that this instructor was not aware that Outcome 2 was getting so much attention and could really use the time to work on other outcomes. The same could be true for an outcome that is not getting much attention, such as Outcome 5 in figure

8.3 and, again, it could be that the instructor deliberately prioritized how his or her time would be used.

In situations such as that portrayed by figure 8.3, many of our faculty members have expressed surprise and concurrently described a past concern about students' poor achievement of an outcome that was not getting attention. Faculty were both relieved by the revelation and enthused about changing the pattern, because they felt that they had found the answer to an important question.

Another type of pattern that emerges from an alignment grid is the sequence of outcomes being addressed. Sometimes it appears to be random, and sometimes it appears to be carefully designed based on complexity or a scaffolding of outcomes. There is no right or wrong in the sequencing of outcomes, but it is an aspect of planning to consider when looking at the outcomes individually and in relation to each other and to related teaching and learning activities.

Integration of Curriculum and Pedagogy

In our first use of our alignment grids, we did not set out to determine whether the outcomes were addressed with integrated pedagogy or curriculum. However, in the initial round, the pattern of integration was vivid in a number of faculty grids. Figure 8.4, Sample Course Alignment Grid C, illustrates a course with such integration. The outcomes are seldom addressed individually. Outcome 1 is almost always addressed with Outcome 4, and Outcomes 3, 5, and 6 are addressed together 50 percent of the time. In the latter half of the semester, all of the outcomes are addressed in many of the class sessions, which is probably an ideal approach. Note that the outcomes are seldom assessed individually either—in the kinds of assessment listed for the course, it makes sense that several or all of the outcomes are assessed simultaneously in projects and presentations.

Benefits of Course Alignment Processes

The most important aspect of analyzing the alignment of teaching and learning with student learning outcomes is the intentionality of your course design. If the grid reveals the intended alignment, you will be assured that your planning will be coherent and directed to the intended student learning outcomes. If, however, the grid reveals unintended patterns, you will become

FIGURE 8.4
Sample Course Alignment Grid C

Course Information:
Professor:

	Outcome 1	Outcome 2	Outcome 3	Outcome 4	Outcome 5	Outcome 6
Class 1	X					
Class 2	X			X		
Class 3	X			X		
Class 5		X				
Class 10	X			X		
Class 11	X			X		
Class 12			X		X	X
Class 20			X		X	X
Class 21	X		X	X	X	X
Class 22	X			X		
Class 23			X		X	X
Class 28			X		X	X
Class 29	X	X	X	X	X	X
Class 30	X	X	X	X	X	X
Reading A	X			X		
Reading B			X		X	X
Reading C		X				
Panel	X	X		X		
Comm. Visit	X	X	X	X	X	X
Assignment 1	X			X		
Assignment 2	X			X		
Assignment 3		X	X		X	X
Assignment 4			X		X	X
Assignment 5	X	X	X	X	X	X
Assessment 1	X			X		
Assessment 2			X		X	X
Assessment 3	X	X		X		
Assessment 4	X	X	X	X	X	X

aware that you need to make important changes to improve alignment in your course planning.

The second most important aspect of the entire project, both the plotting of alignment and the analysis, is faculty satisfaction with the processes. In a survey of 80 faculty participants in the 2002 Course Alignment Project, only 1 individual expressed a lack of satisfaction with the alignment process. Others described a wide variety of insights, uses, improvements, and understandings, and with them, affirmations of the usefulness of the process. Much of their satisfaction resulted from the constructivist nature of the course alignment process. With this process, you produce your own learning when you analyze the data. After analysis, you are empowered to make improvements or to be confident in the alignment. Changes and recommendations do not come from an outside source but from within your faculty expertise and decisions.

The following comments by participants in the project encouraged plans for continued use of the course alignment process and related extensions of alignment for improved student learning:

> "I shifted some films around and changed the focus of some lectures."
> "In the service learning course, the grid forced me to tailor learning activities and reflective exercises so that students could now connect questions, readings, and community activities with their outcomes."
> "I did notice that one of the outcomes lacked any assignments, so I designed new assignments for students to practice that outcome."

Continued Use of Course Alignment Projects

The latest round of Course Alignment Projects comes a year after our accreditation visits and reports (extremely positive results), and it is prompted by faculty interest rather than accreditation. Funding for faculty development is directed to the projects and, again, a majority of faculty members are participating. The projects are part of ongoing self-study and institutional improvement directed at promoting student learning. Many faculty members have begun to use their alignment grids as a focus for reflections in their scholarship of teaching and learning for both annual evaluations and promotion and tenure reviews. Depending on the reward system of your institution, the course alignment constitutes legitimate scholarship when analyzed, when implications are drawn, and when the insights are shared with peers.

Possible Extensions of Alignment for Expanded Improvement

For the last few years, the alignment grids have been used to support new faculty as they design their courses for the first time on our campus. After a workshop about outcomes-based education and assessment, course alignment is introduced and samples of well-aligned courses are provided. New faculty submit their syllabi to the Center for Teaching, Learning, and Assessment for review and feedback. They are encouraged to make alignment visible in their syllabi so that students are aware of what outcomes are being addressed in their readings, assignments, and class sessions. The excerpts of syllabi in chapter 7 demonstrate the various ways to make alignment visible.

As you read in our introductory story, we have also involved students in the study of course alignment. In the first round of using the alignment grids, many of the faculty members engaged their students in the study. At the end of each class, students were asked which outcome or outcomes were addressed in the class. Using the list of course outcomes that matched the top of the course grid, students indicated the outcome or outcomes that they thought were addressed in class. In general, their perceptions agreed with those of their faculty instructor. However, as in the situation that Professor Guidry encountered, there were many cases when the faculty instructor's designated outcome for a class session was different from what students perceived it to be. For example, when the instructor designated the class session as directed to Outcome 3, 80 percent of the students thought that it was Outcome 5. Such disconnects raised questions for faculty and led to re-teaching, reviewing, and informative discussions with students. Most faculty members addressed the disconnect in the following class and gained useful insights when students described why they thought that the previous class was directed to an outcome different from the one the instructor had designated for the class.

Program Alignment: A Larger Coherency

Alignment grids can also be used with entire programs. For those departments that have well-articulated outcomes for their major programs of study, the outcomes are again lined up on the horizontal axis. Courses (names or numbers) are lined up on the vertical axis. Faculty plot the attention given in their courses for each outcome with a *P* for primary emphasis and an *S* for secondary emphasis. The grid reveals gaps, integration, and patterns. Again, there is no right or wrong, just a check on intentions. As with the individual alignment grids, there are usually some surprises, and often faculty collaboration emerges from conversations about connections or similarities among the instructors' individual courses. When faculty stepped back and reviewed the grid in figure 8.5, they immediately began discussing a redistribution of courses for their outcomes.

Alignment grids may also be used for nonacademic programs such as residential life or first-year experience programs. Many student affairs units are developing learning outcomes for students to be achieved through such approaches as developmental advising, residence programs, work-study assignments, mentoring, and tutoring. The same kind of coherency as in formal curriculum is important in the informal curriculum of such programs and can lead to increased effectiveness in terms of student learning.

Going Beyond Alignment: A Simple Check on Learner-Centered Courses and Curriculum

The Course Alignment Project is an ideally generic strategy that requires little training as well as limited time and resources and engages faculty in a process that makes sense, yields useful data, and prompts intrinsic motivation to improve. Course alignment and improvements in course designs and syllabi are easily documented for campus self-study, accreditation, and strengthening the quality of learner-centered education. The rationale for starting the alignment process with courses is that courses are the "flesh of higher education's curricular frame" and the primary means for promoting student learning (Gardiner, 1994, p. 37). Courses are familiar and comfortable for faculty and ideal starting points for institutional alignment. Once faculty have achieved course alignment, they are ready for program alignment with potential for improvements in course distribution and program coherence for student learning.

Huba and Freed (2000) developed a framework of inquiry for use in assessing a campus assessment program or practices. The Course Alignment Project that we have described responds to some of the significant questions of their framework:

FIGURE 8.5
Program Alignment Grid

Courses	Program Outcome 1	Program Outcome 2	Program Outcome 3	Program Outcome 4	Program Outcome 5	Program Outcome 6	Program Outcome 7
100							
101							
102							
200							
201							
202							
235							
236							
237							
238							
239							
240							
241							
242							
243							
Capstone 240							

- Does assessment lead to improvement so that faculty can fulfill their responsibilities to students and to the public?
- Does assessment focus on using data to address questions that people in the program and at the institution really care about?
- Is assessment based on a conceptual relationship among teaching, curriculum, learning, and assessment at the institution?
- Do faculty feel a sense of ownership and responsibility for assessment?
- Do faculty focus on experiences leading to outcomes as well as the outcomes themselves?

When one considers the Course Alignment Project in response to those five questions, the answer is easily yes. Granted, there are other questions, but checking alignment is a simple, efficient approach that accomplishes a broad array of assessment functions while engaging faculty and responding to important assessment questions.

Alignment studies promote that culture of inquiry we described at the beginning of this book. That inquiry is focused on student learning and prompts improvement when groups of faculty or staff come together to review alignment. The grids prompt discussions and reflections that yield shared insights, new understandings, collaborative decision making, and collective improvements. According to Maki (2004), those kinds of discussions ensure that assessment is developing and being refined. We think that those discussions stay focused on student learning as well and continue to promote a learner-centered teaching environment. They are also curricular discussions that have the potential to integrate the campus community on an intellectual level (Boyer, 1990).

The development of outcomes and subsequent alignment takes extensive time, but the end results are valuable in terms of student learning. Allen (2003) elaborates on the possibilities:

- Students experience a more cohesive curriculum in which important concepts and skills are introduced in a logical sequence and they have opportunities to synthesize, practice, and develop increasingly more complex understandings.
- Faculty can better appreciate how their courses contribute to overall student development.

- Department chairs can share agreed-upon learning outcomes for the courses of new faculty and integrate them into departmental functioning.

As we described in the previous chapter on developing syllabi, sharing learning outcomes and making their connections with the learning activities visible is significantly advantageous to students and faculty. Students can use the information to guide their studying and faculty can use them to structure activities and assignments to promote learning (Allen, 2003, p. 2).

As the criticisms of curriculum have indicated, we have directed extensive efforts to improving curriculum with less than satisfying results. It is encouraging to know that such a simple process as course alignment has the potential to achieve the end results described by Allen (2003).

In sum, checking alignment is an important inquiry process probing *what* and *how* our students are learning. Finally, the process of studying alignment within individual courses highlights and promotes faculty instructors' intentions in their planning processes of curriculum design. The grids display patterns that are sometimes intentional and sometimes not, but they provide data so that faculty can make decisions about those patterns. Faculty instructors have expressed satisfaction with the use of course alignment and have elaborated on the value of alignment for their teaching and student learning. Course and program alignment engage faculty in assessment in ways that encourage and support ongoing attention to assessment in a learner-centered context.

Reflections from Faculty: Impact of and Insights on Alignment

We are breaking tradition here and reaching out to our colleagues for reflections on the impact of alignment. Swarup and I decided that hearing varied experiences rather than just his would be useful to you, our readers. We asked faculty at CSUMB about the Course Alignment Project and its meaning for their teaching. Here are some of their responses:

> "It was helpful to see how the outcomes were being met, which ones were well covered and which ones were a little thin."

"I learned a great deal in that I was able to spot the gaps as well as those areas that were covered, perhaps too much, and adjust my syllabus in order to bring balance to each of the outcomes."

"The course alignment process helped me think deeper about the connections between the course content, course assignments, and learning outcomes . . . a good exercise for course design."

"I have expanded my syllabus to integrate and display alignment with my course schedule. As a result, students can easily see the linkages between lectures, assignments, and learning outcomes on a weekly basis."

"You can bet the syllabus shifted quite a bit once I aligned it according to the outcomes I was trying to support students to meet."

"I actually learned how many projects were connected to certain outcomes. It was a confidence builder to see that most of my assignments and assessments were right on."

"The grid gave me the opportunity to 'inventory' all the materials and activities for each session and reexamine their efficacy to the stated outcomes. It prompted some prioritizing and helped focus sessions around just a few key concepts that I wanted students to learn and demonstrate through the lab activities and session assignments."

"I strongly resist 'overprogramming' my syllabus, so this was a real pedagogical stretch for me. It forced me to clearly think out the relationships between teaching activities and outcomes. I still think that we tend to overdo the degree to which we map out an entire course for our students, sometimes precluding the 'discovery factor' as knowledge unfolds, or the flexibility to respond to students' needs. But I have to admit that having to consider activities and outcomes deliberately and thoroughly was a good strategy to keep myself in line."

"The course alignment process made me more aware of pursuing course outcomes. I have a creative, flexible teaching style (which I and my students appreciate) but I need to be aware of direction for how I spend time in class, and the process helped with that awareness. Like a 'strategic plan' it offered a concrete representation of my course, even if we occasionally strayed from the plan."

These faculty comments reveal a range of teaching styles and rationales for using and appreciating the course alignment process. The process was designed to respond to varying priorities, needs, teaching experiences, and interests without adding time-intensive responsibilities. It can be used in the process of designing a syllabus or program or as a check on the alignment of an existing course or program. In chapter 7, we demonstrated how that alignment can be communicated to students to motivate and inform their learning efforts.

In addition to the benefits outlined in this chapter, the course alignment process represents a widely accepted "best practice" of aligning teaching and learning with learning outcomes (American Association for Higher Education, 1992) as well as an inquiry and improvement process for both individual faculty members and the institution.

References

Allen, M. (2003). Faculty engagement in assessment. *Perspectives on Assessment, 6*(1), 2.

American Association for Higher Education. (1992). Principles of good practice for assessing student learning. In *Learning through assessment: A resource guide for higher education* [A Publication of the AAHE Assessment Forum] (pp. 11–13). Washington, DC: Author.

Angelo, T. (1999, May). Doing assessment as if learning matters most. *AAHE Bulletin*.

Angelo, T. (2002). Engaging and supporting faculty in the scholarship of assessment: Guidelines from research and best practice. In T. W. Banta and Associates (Eds.), *Building a scholarship of assessment* (pp. 185–200). San Francisco: Jossey-Bass.

Banta, T. W. (1996). The power of a matrix. *Assessment Update, 8*(4), 3, 13.

Boyer, E. L. (1990). *Campus life in search of community*. Princeton, NJ: Carnegie Foundation for the Advancement of Teaching.

Fife, J. D. (1992). Foreword. In W. Toombs & W. Tierney (Eds.), *Meeting the mandate: Renewing the college and departmental curriculum* (pp. xi–xii) (ASHE-ERIC Higher Education Report No. 6). Washington, DC: The George Washington University, School of Education.

Gardiner, L. F. (1994). *Redesigning higher education: Producing dramatic gains in student learning* (ASHE-ERIC Higher Education Report Vol. 23, No. 7). Washington, DC: The George Washington University, School of Education.

Huba, M. E., & Freed, J. E. (2000). *Learner-centered assessment on college campuses*. Boston: Allyn & Bacon.

Maki, P. (2004). *Assessing for learning: Building a sustainable commitment across the institution*. Sterling, VA: Stylus.

Wehlburg, C. (1999, May). How to get the ball rolling: Beginning an assessment program on your campus. *AAHE Bulletin, 31*, 7–9.

REVIEWING AND ANALYZING STUDENT EVIDENCE

Constructivist Faculty Development

Story: Faculty Know Best

B efore we begin our story, it's important for you to know that our faculty were immediately enamored of our faculty-centered collaborative approach to analyzing student work because the process revealed so much about their teaching, much that they had never been aware of. Now, let's move on to our story.

By the time of our accreditation's educational effectiveness visit, many of our general education and departmental faculty had participated in this process twice, and we planned an inquiry audit as part of the team's visit. An inquiry audit is a process in which the data sources (faculty) are shown the findings and conclusions and asked if the data represent their experience. The purpose of our audit was to determine whether the results of my second interview study (see chapter 10) were valid for faculty who had not participated in the study as well as for several who had. You can imagine the setting: a couple of the accreditation team members; several faculty members; our Teaching, Learning, and Assessment director; and myself all sitting in a circle. It was fascinating how each of the themes that emerged in my second interview study resonated with all of the faculty members in the room. When I shared the theme of how our collaborative review of student work had helped faculty identify disconnects among learning outcomes, teaching activities, and assessment activities, one faculty member said, "I was very surprised to discover that several people in the group were not using the criteria (which we had agreed upon two years previously) in the evaluation of their students' work. I had taken it for granted that everyone understood that *that* is what we had agreed to." Another faculty member, a little reticent, confessed to being one of the guilty, but that making all the changes in his courses required by developing criteria and standards for the learning outcomes had been more work than he had expected. The instructors shared anecdote after anecdote, especially how they had modified their teaching and assessment activities in light of what the collaborative review of student work showed them about their teaching and their students' learning. It was very gratifying to have such support for the themes that arose from my interview study, and with all the sharing of stories there was a great feeling of warmth in the room.

As time left in the session began to draw to a close, one of the visiting team members began to ask capacity questions around how often the review of student work would occur. Concerned that faculty would begin to tire of it over time, Amy said, "So far this has been done every other year, but I would imagine that we'll soon move to doing it once every five years or so." I remember fidgeting uncomfortably in my seat and thinking, "This will be interesting. . . ." The faculty were incensed and did not hesitate detailing to the visiting team members *exactly* why "every five years" would not suffice. "The reason general education faculty learning communities adopted a policy requiring this process to occur biannually is because of its educational value for our faculty. . . . Without ongoing discussion and regular review of student evidence, our consensus on what the learning outcomes and criteria mean drifts. This kind of process is required to maintain the high level of ongoing discourse we need to maintain our learning outcomes," one faculty member said earnestly. Another added, "We cannot hope to introduce new faculty to our learning outcomes, criteria, and standards, with any depth, without involving them in the collaborative review of student work. This kind of process forces new faculty to grapple with our learning outcomes, criteria, and standards in ways that nothing else can." A third stated, "I need to be involved in this kind of collaborative work at least this often to push me further into my teaching." From the strength of the faculty response and the awkward silence that followed, I think both our visiting team and Amy came to understand that our ongoing collaborative assessment of student work was a faculty-owned process that had immense value for our teaching and assessment and that faculty had pride in what they had learned from their work and what they had achieved in terms of implementing policy to institutionalize the process. Finally, it was clear that the process continued to have broad and strong faculty support.

I use our story here to intrigue you. I hope that any process that has this much faculty support will capture your curiosity and interest you in reading this chapter.

I am continually reminded how much there is to learn about teaching and assessment on the path to becoming a learning-centered faculty. This is not surprising given the dearth of training in the art of teaching or in the pedagogical design of courses or curricula that most of us received as we navigated through our doctoral programs. My personal experience, and one that the literature is beginning to validate, suggests that the collaborative review of student work has much to teach us about our practice of teaching and assessment, as well as about student learning.

This book is written to and for faculty in the hopes of sharing what have been very gratifying experiences in teaching, learning, and assessment. My colleagues and I have grown much from our collaborative assessment of student work; this growth has been very fulfilling and increased our level of engagement in teaching and assessment. I have a strong desire to share these kinds of experiences and have contributed to the book largely in the hope that this chapter will inspire you to initiate the collaborative assessment of student work on your campus. I believe that any venue for this work, whether you do this at a programmatic level or invite colleagues to sit down and discuss student work over a glass of wine some Friday afternoon, has great potential to educate you about and deepen your understanding of teaching and assessment. I hope to impress upon you that the collaborative analysis of student work is a wonderful way of learning about student learning. I'll provide more reasons to convince you in the section that follows.

Rationale for the Collaborative Analysis of Student Work

Why work collaboratively to analyze student work? Before getting into the "how to's," I want you to understand what you and your campus stand to gain by engaging in this kind of work and why it is essential in higher education's movement to become learning centered. For an institution to become learning centered, it must develop and establish practices that allow the campus to address four issues:

1. Learn about what its students are learning and how teaching and assessment activities support student achievement of its outcomes.
2. Develop and maintain a common understanding of the campus's learning outcomes, criteria, and standards.
3. Develop ways of making strong connections among learning outcomes, criteria, standards, and teaching activities.
4. Engage faculty in the fascinating craft of student learning.

Let's examine next how collaborative analysis of student work can serve all four of these issues.

Evidence of Student Learning

As focused on evidence as most us are in our areas of scholarship, it is curious how little time we spend studying the *evidence* of student learning: student work. If academia is truly to transition from being teaching-centered to becoming learning- and learner-centered institutions, this will have to change (Barr & Tagg, 1995; Tagg, 2003). I believe that this transition will require us to train the focus of our intellects and our love of evidence on student learning. Toward these ends and that future, I ask, What could be more learning centered than to use student work as the source of learning about the efficacy of a university's teaching practices? What could be more productive than to use student work as the basis for our study of how to influence student learning in our classrooms?

For institutions that focus on delivering a learning-centered education, institutional research and self-study will focus on student learning. You can imagine that the analysis of student work will play a crucial role in institutional research cycles. As with any research, a framework is needed to develop questions and hypotheses. Developing learning outcomes and criteria will provide the foundation for that framework. Learning outcomes form the basis of hypotheses, and criteria will allow researchers to test their hypotheses (the efficacy of their teaching practices in facilitating student attainment of learning outcomes). As you can see, institutions will be able to use this research because the results will illustrate which practices helped students best achieve the learning outcomes and which did not. The results may also give insight on how teaching practices should be modified to help students better achieve the outcomes. Once institutions have implemented the changes, they will be ready to engage in another round of evidence collection and analysis to learn whether the changes in their practice have in fact improved student learning.

One of the questions that you will have to address is: What kinds of processes should be used to conduct the analysis and what are potential benefits of different approaches? In other words, should the analysis be conducted such that learning occurs solely from its results, the data produced by some external body (as is true of much large-scale assessment), or should it be structured to prioritize learning from the *process* of the analysis?

Although the collaborative analysis of student work is not yet common among college and university faculty, judging by the number of books, Internet resources, and conferences devoted to it, elementary and secondary educators have considerable experience with these kinds of practices (e.g., Bella, 2004; Blythe, Allen, & Powell, 1999; Langer, Colton, & Goff, 2003). A picture is emerging from this literature, as well as that devoted to postsecondary educators, that validates prioritizing learning from the process of the analysis, and it is beginning to illustrate the kinds of things that faculty can learn from engaging in the analysis of student work. Robert Garmston says in his foreword to *Collaborative Analysis of Student Work* (2003), "We are realizing that teachers do not learn from their (teaching) experience; they learn from *reflecting* on their (teaching) experience" (p. viii; parentheses and italics mine). In addition to giving us insight into our teaching practices, assessment processes can inform curriculum development as well as illustrate how students learn from and interact with teaching and assessment activities (Blythe et al., 1999; Langer et al., 2003; Wood, 2006).

A Common Understanding of Outcomes, Criteria, and Standards

One of the biggest benefits of faculty engagement in the collaborative assessment of student work is that it can lead to common understanding of exactly what an institution's learning outcomes, criteria, and standards mean among those who participate. Blythe et al. (1999) believe that the only way to achieve a common understanding of outcomes, criteria, and standards is through the collaborative examination of student work. Furthermore, Jeana Abromeit, chair of Alverno College's Council for Student Assessment, says that faculty dialogue and collaboration are essential in reaching a shared understanding of the meaning and applications of outcomes and criteria. Through that shared understanding, a community of judgment is possible with regard to assessing student performance (personal communication, June 26, 2006). At California State University Monterey Bay (CSUMB), we found that without our collaborative assessment of student work, our learning outcomes would mean different things to different faculty members. Similar to our experience, Little, Gearhart, Curry, and Kafka (2003) found that discussions about student work led faculty to grapple with gaps in their own understanding of criteria (i.e., "Exactly what is and how do I teach students to write an effective *persuasive* argument?"). You can see that such discussions and faculty work sessions provide excellent opportunities for faculty members to learn from each other, particularly if the work groups are interdisciplinary.

Connecting Teaching and Assessment Activities to the Learning Outcomes

Another important reason for engaging in collaborative assessment of student work is its potential for generating tight, explicit, and intentional connections among teaching activities, learning outcomes, and assessment practices. Langer et al. (2003) state that engaging in the collaborative review of student work can help align teaching standards (outcomes) with classroom practice as well as assessment practices, and this has certainly been our experience at CSUMB (Wood, 2006). Our collaborative review of student work illustrated many examples of how teaching activities, learning outcomes, and assessment tools were routinely not well connected to each other. Examples included courses that did not address or devote significant teaching resources to agreed-upon learning outcomes, courses in which learning outcomes were not assessed, assignments that were only loosely connected to the learning outcomes and/or did not effectively assess what the instructor intended, evaluation rubrics that did not use the agreed-upon criteria as standards, and assignments in which faculty asked for one thing and inadvertently graded as if they had asked for something else (Wood, 2006). Keep in mind that these are intelligent, dedicated, hardworking, well-meaning faculty living stereotypically harried faculty lives. From my experience, these kinds of disconnects are probably more the norm than the exception.

Benefiting From Collaboration

As you read, I hope you are asking, "What is in this for me and why should my campus engage in the collaborative analysis of student work when educators have been doing it on their own for millennia?" According to Blythe et al. (1999), because consultation and collaboration is common and expected in other professions, it would be surprising if teaching professionals did not benefit greatly from the practice. Working collaboratively allows faculty members to examine student work, and their own teaching practice, differently than when working alone. It can provide a lens through which faculty can look into student thinking and how it interacts with teaching and learning activities/materials. You may be thinking, "This is so powerful—why doesn't it happen when we work alone?" I think the answer to that question is that seeing our teaching through the eyes of our colleagues allows us to view it from a very different perspective. After all, our colleagues bring to our discussions different life and professional experience as well as many more years of experience. Because they did not create it, our colleagues look upon our work anew and are frequently able to spot assumptions that are very difficult for us to see. Their experience and fresh insight help us to step back, adding distance and an objectivity in viewing our work that are sometimes impossible to achieve when working alone. Jeana Abromeit and Sharon Hamilton at Alverno College and IUPUI, respectively, two campuses that have many years of experience in the collaborative review of student work, described to me again and again the value of faculty members looking together at student work and how much their campuses had benefited from this practice (personal communication, June 19, 2006). In her work with mathematics teachers, Angela Krebs (2005) found that working in groups to assess student work can give teachers deeper insight into students' learning processes. It can help them to recognize areas in which students did not meet the expectations, areas in which students need further help, and misconceptions in students' thinking. It also allows teachers to challenge their own assumptions on what students are learning and to learn from each other as well.

Returning to my rationale for the collaborative analysis of student work, I ask, If academia *is* to become more learning centered, what could be more appropriate than to use student work to study a university's efficacy? I hope this section has convinced you to engage in collaborative review of student work, and that you're ready to consider a process for doing so.

Qualities of the Process of Collaborative Review of Student Work

I devote this section to discussing the qualities that support successful processes for the analysis of student work and then share with you the practical issues that you will need to address in developing a process in the next section. It is important to think strategically about how the purpose of your analysis of student work and the qualities of the process will facilitate your campus's progress toward becoming learning centered. You may find it useful to explore potential relationships between faculty learning and student learning and the degree to which faculty engage in the study of their teaching practice.

If we can assume that student engagement and student learning are positively correlated with faculty engagement (in teaching and learning) as well as faculty learning, then as we develop our method of analysis, we are justified in prioritizing the kinds of qualities that are most likely to engage faculty deeply in the process. These qualities are the ones that Amy referred to in chapter 2 and are exactly the same as those that you use in your most engaging learning-centered teaching. They are important here for the same reasons. I am sure that many of you could expand and enrich the following discussion; the qualities that call most strongly to me suggest that a process for the analysis of student work should be inquiry based, constructivist, collaborative, and faculty centered and should focus on questions and issues that are important to faculty.

Making It Inquiry Based

Processes for reviewing and analyzing student evidence should be open ended and inquiry based, with no prescriptive destination, because engaging learners with questions and using a framework of problem solving engages them more deeply than merely providing information. We are naturally curious about the relationships between teaching and learning, yet many of us approach the assessment of student work solely through an evaluative lens (grading). An inquiry-based process can help approach assessment with an eye on what we can learn about student learning and about our teaching (Blythe et al., 1999; Langer et al., 2003). Approaching student work through the lens of "how do we know?" can engage faculty on many different levels, prompting questions such as the following:

- Did the student make sense of the assignment, or is there evidence to the contrary?
- Is there evidence of confusion or misunderstanding of key concepts being taught?
- What is the evidence of student mastery of the outcomes?
- Is there evidence that students understood or misunderstood the evaluation criteria?

An inquiry-based process may also give insight as to how well the learning outcomes were connected to learning activities and the assignment under consideration (that the evidence of student learning responded to), how well the grading rubric was connected to the assignment, and how well the grading rubric was connected to the original evaluation of the student work (Blythe et al., 1999; Langer et al., 2003; Wood, 2006).

Engaging Faculty with Valuable Experiences

I know that most of you have experienced traditional faculty development. Much like traditional teaching, it focuses on content delivered via lecture with a question-and-answer session. Yet when we intend to promote deep learning along with long-term retention, we engage learners in activities that give them *experience* with the concepts and processes that we want them to learn, rather than just talk to them about the ideas. For teaching faculty like you and me, this means engaging our colleagues in activities that draw them into the cause-and-effect relationships between teaching and learning.

From a teaching and learning perspective, it is understood that activities and multiple opportunities to practice are essential for learners to embody the knowledge and skills being taught (Halpern & Hakel, 2003). From a neurobiological perspective, it is understood that engaging learners in activities and giving them multiple opportunities to practice uses different parts of the brain and stimulates the formation of more neural connections than passively listening to a content-filled lecture (Zull, 2002). In developing and facilitating long-term retention with our colleagues, ample time is needed so that we can practice the same activity multiple times.

Drawing on Faculty Expertise

The process of collaborative review of student work should be a constructivist one in which faculty draw on their own experience and expertise to make meaning of the work being studied. That does not mean that the process will not benefit from your expertise should you decide to facilitate this work with faculty colleagues, particularly your experience in teaching and assessment. You should, however, lead from the side and from behind, as you would in your best teaching, soliciting the experience and knowledge in the group before interjecting. In addition, just as teaching activities go further with student learners when learning outcomes are presented in a context that is relevant and important to students, you need to present your assessment processes in a context that is relevant and important to the professional lives of faculty.

Understanding the Value of Collaboration

Assessment of student work is typically a solitary endeavor, probably owing to both expedience and fear (Little et al., 2003; Shulman, 1993; Wood, 2006). However, collaboration is an important facet of this kind of work for several reasons. Tina Blythe and her colleagues at Harvard's Project Zero (1999), and Margaret Price (2005) in her work on communities of practice in higher education, suggest that collaborative discussion is required for institutions to develop a common understanding of their learning outcomes, criteria, and standards, which is a prerequisite for transparent and consistent application of criteria and standards.

Collaboration is the heart, the essential quality, of the collaborative assessment of student work and is lauded by every one of the references I have provided in this chapter. With respect to using it as a pedagogy and as a way to engage your colleagues, collaboration allows you to see your own teaching through different lenses and multiple lenses simultaneously. A powerful synergy can develop from the various perspectives and different life and academic experiences within the group. You learn from others' areas of expertise, see into others' teaching practice, and help others understand the experience of your students' learning (Blythe et al., 1999; Langer et al., 2003; J. Abromeit, personal communication, June 26, 2006). In addition, one of the best and least appreciated aspects of working in collaborative groups is that it can provide a wonderful venue for positive feedback and validation of your work (Wood, 2006). Finally, collaborative work groups, especially those comprising members of equal or nearly equal footing, help lessen the power dynamics that exist in many teaching and learning situations. My chemistry students frequently remind me of this when they extol the virtues of working collaboratively with their peers; they say that they learn much more from the other students than they do from me.

In the classroom, many of us strive to share power with our students, to make them part of the teaching and learning process, because this practice helps students "buy in" to our model of teaching, learning, assessment, and yes, even evaluation. When we facilitate the process of reviewing student work and keep it faculty centered, it has much the same potential for engagement and stimulation of our learning as for student learning. There is another reason that making the process of assessing student work collaborative and faculty centered is important: In my opinion, engaging and facilitating assessment processes in ways that engage us in our practice of teaching and assessment is the single most important factor in dampening our resistance, and protecting faculty ownership of campus assessment (Schilling & Schilling, 1998). If we have bought into the vision of becoming a learner-centered institution, and we are using the analysis of student work to help actualize that vision, then the qualities of the process we use *must* build fires in the intellects of faculty around teaching, learning, and assessment. In addition, they must give us intimate experience with the value of this kind of work and, ultimately, help faculty assume leadership roles in assessment across campus (Wiley, 2003).

We've talked about the importance of the qualities of your process for analyzing student work (faculty-, student-, and learning-centered qualities in particular). In the next section, we'll shift into the more practical issues around developing a process for the collaborative review of student work.

Process: Practical Issues to Consider

This section is devoted to the major "how to's" that you will have to consider in developing the collaborative review of student work on your campuses.

Determining the Purpose

The first issue to consider for the collaborative analysis of student work is the purpose of the analysis. This issue must be carefully considered because it will inform almost all of the other issues that you will have to address. Different purposes will require and predicate different processes. For example, developing more intentional learning-centered teaching is likely to have a much different focus and process than developing a statistically valid proto-col for studying student mastery of learning outcomes across 20 sections of a single course.

Like many of you, when we initially developed this work, our intentions and perhaps our agendas were mixed. Amy, our director of Teaching, Learn-ing, and Assessment, and many others were acutely aware that the final stages of our initial accreditation were approaching. Having made the claim of being an outcomes-based university, some of us understood that we were obligated to show that our students were, in fact, mastering our outcomes. However, after the rich learning that our faculty experienced as a result of developing criteria and standards, Amy was determined to make our analysis of student work collaborative, inquiry based, and faculty centered. Thus, rather than design a process that would yield statistically valid claims on stu-dent mastery, we focused our process more on faculty engagement and faculty learning. As you might imagine, Amy involved faculty every step of the way.

Now that I have so strongly emphasized the importance of this work being faculty centered, I want to remind you, *especially* if you are gearing up for accreditation, to be sure to spend time thinking about how to bring fac-ulty on board in establishing the purpose. Some aspects of this work may be externally mandated (accreditation/program review), but opening the pur-pose up to faculty, to understand what they want to get out of it and to include them in the design of the purpose, is essential for the overall success of the program.

Providing Institutional Support

The second major issue to consider for the collaborative analysis of student work is that of institutional support. Little et al. (2003), in their research of three nationally recognized educational organizations that have developed collaborative processes for the analysis of student work, stress the importance of institutional commitment and organization. If your institution is going to use the collaborative review of student work as a strategy for long-term improvement and to help the institution become learning centered, it will have to devote resources to it. You will have to reserve time for this work; if you are going to be compensated, the institution must budget for it. In addi-tion, leadership to initiate and sustain the work must be either developed from within or sought from an external source. If you bring in help to initiate the process, then much of that help must focus on training campus leaders, preferably faculty, to sustain the work on campus. Ultimately, if the practice is to be retained long term, faculty will have to deem it valuable in order for it to become part of the campus culture.

One of the best ways that you can support and sustain the collaborative review of student work is through the use of faculty learning communities (FLCs). These have been used successfully and are lauded throughout the literature cited in this chapter as a way of organizing faculty around the collaborative analysis of student work. Ultimately, this kind of work involves looking at your successes and failures with your peers, and being open to asking and being asked tough questions regarding your teaching and assessment. It is paramount that you develop rapport and trust with each other as you engage in this kind of work.

Selecting Examples of Student Work

In developing strategies for your process, you will have to consider the volume of student work to be reviewed, from whose courses will it come, how much is needed, and how to protect faculty and students. If your focus is on learning from the process, one of the main goals is to slow down the procedure for analyzing student work relative to the time you would usually spend doing this alone (Little et al., 2003). When you and a group of colleagues really focus on a single piece of student work and study it through the lenses of several criteria, a few examples go a long way.

From our experience at CSUMB, we feel that in addition to having examples of student work it is important to understand the assignment and the learning outcomes to which students' work responds. Not only does this help faculty to penetrate the work deeply, but it also helps them to understand how well the assignment was connected to the learning outcomes, and how well the criteria were used in the original evaluation. However, not everyone agrees with this notion. For example, Blythe et al. (1999) suggest that including study of the assignment in the process narrows the analysis and faculty experience of the student work too much. Whatever your decision, develop explicit instructions, especially if faculty are submitting work on a voluntary basis. If the process requires the assignment and learning outcomes along with examples of corresponding student work, be sure to include that requirement in your instructions to faculty.

What quality of work should be studied? At CSUMB, we asked that faculty bring to the evaluation examples of student work that met the outcome or outcomes at a very high level (work that they considered to be excellent), work that presented a good solid demonstration of the outcome or outcomes, and work that was not adequate. Our experience has been that faculty learn more from and engage more deeply in excellent and satisfactory work than in examples of very poor work. However, again, differences in your strategy will be driven largely by purpose. Using the Collaborative Analysis of Student Learning process (Langer et al., 2003), faculty analyze the work of a few students over the course of a semester or year. Some of the focus of this method is on reaching and teaching effectively to poorly performing students. Using this method, faculty focus on some of the lowest-quality student work.

We first implemented our collaborative analysis of student work in our 13 general education areas. Faculty who taught in these areas and participated in the FLCs devoted to them were asked to submit work to the process on a voluntary basis. For us, it was very important to make participation voluntary. Others urge that faculty be able to make their students' work available on a voluntary basis as well (Blythe et al., 1999). Because students assume that their assignments will be read only by their instructors, which is generally true, we also strongly encourage campuses to obtain students' permission before they use their work in this way. CSUMB required that faculty obtain a signed permission form from each student, guaranteeing that students' names would be removed from the work prior to sharing it with other faculty or staff. Of course, students were also given the option of not having their work shared.

Providing Good Facilitation

It is said that good learning environments should be safe but never comfortable. The assumption here is that a tension arises from the right kinds of discomfort and that that tension facilitates a challenging and deeper learning experience. Our experience has been that collaborative analysis of student work can facilitate the "right kind" of tension and discomfort and that our excellent facilitation was fundamental in creating the kind of experience that both challenged and engaged faculty. Most of the authors referenced in this chapter have discussed this need for good facilitation. The qualities of the process that we have already discussed speak to the kinds of facilitation that will be needed for effective collaborative review of student work. In addition, it is important to make sure that the facilitator emphasizes faculty leadership and learning between and among faculty members. Of all the issues that may arise, anticipating issues around faculty safety are key.

As you develop your processes and facilitate this work, it is important to anticipate that your faculty may be apprehensive and nervous and to provide appropriate support. One of the things that keeps assessment such a private endeavor is that faculty may be nervous about putting their students' work in front of colleagues. Whether the process is voluntary or a systematic and randomized sampling, you should keep in mind that faculty whose students' work is being reviewed are also being scrutinized (Little et al., 2003; Wood, 2006). From my second interview study (see chapter 10), it is clear that faculty who are analyzing the work of someone else's students have a very different experience than those whose own students' work is being studied. It is also important to anticipate that your faculty colleagues occasionally may be defensive and, thus, to focus critique on student work rather than on faculty (Little et al., 2003).

Building Rapport and Trust

Before you begin your collaborative review of student work, you and your colleagues need to know what you are looking for. Getting together to talk about what you really want students to know and be able to do as well as the qualities that you will require in student work (developing learning outcomes and criteria, respectively) provides a great opportunity to tackle those issues. It is also a wonderful time to invest in the groundwork for your collaborative review of student work. While your campus is forming collaborative faculty groups to develop outcomes and criteria, by developing rapport and trust between and among your colleagues, you are laying the foundation for your future collaborative review of student work.

Developing a Method

Before diving into looking at student work with your colleagues, spend some time developing a method, or protocol. You may wish to create your own method, or modify methods presented in the literature or the one we developed at CSUMB. Blythe et al. (1999), Langer et al. (2003), and Bella (2004) all present methods for the collaborative analysis of student work, and I encourage you to read and borrow from them as you develop a method that suits your purpose.

At CSUMB, we analyzed student work through a three-step procedure similar to that used in qualitative research. We worked in small groups of four to eight faculty members. We have found that the process works better (participants are more comfortable with each other and willing to risk more) when participants know and are used to working with each other. Copies of identical pieces of evidence were given to each member, and the whole group worked on only one piece of evidence at a time. Participants read the same piece of student evidence three times, focusing on a different purpose with each reading.

In the first reading, we wanted to develop a broad understanding of the student's work and determine holistically whether or not the student had met the outcome. We used this as a kind of reliability check as well as a basis for the second reading. After all participants finished reading, we went around the group checking each person's evaluation of whether the work demonstrated achievement of the outcome or outcomes. In many cases, there was excellent agreement (both within the group of faculty members and with the original evaluation), and in many cases there was considerable disagreement. Either way, we saved discussion until we completed the second reading.

When student work demonstrates achievement of a given outcome, you should be able to point to examples of the criteria and standards within the work. In this way our second reading served as a kind of validity check in which we studied and substantiated the evaluation given in the first reading. Faculty again read the student work, this time using highlighters to document examples of the criteria and standards present in the student work. They used a different colored highlighter for each of the criteria. We found the process much more effective when faculty focused on only one criterion at a time.

I think it is important here to expand our discussion and talk a little bit about our experience. Conversations following the second reading tended to be very rich as faculty documented the presence or absence of the criteria and standards. Sometimes faculty found that the evaluation they gave a piece of work in the holistic reading was not substantiated in the second reading and that the work did not actually meet the criteria. In many cases, they struggled with the meaning of various terms used in both the outcomes and criteria; this experience is common throughout the literature. For example, our faculty struggled with defining exactly what was meant by "complexity, depth, and accuracy" as well as other terms used in the outcomes, criteria, and standards. While learning outcomes and assessment criteria must be established before the collaborative assessment of student work can begin, in our experience the process frequently calls for faculty to define again exactly what the outcomes and criteria mean. This occurs because as faculty see these ideas manifest in students' work they are forced to reconcile their own understandings with those of their colleagues.

The third reading was meant to build perspective, to look again at the work with an eye on what might be learned about the instruction/instructor, the teaching environment, and the student experience. Some of you may be put off by the subjectivity of this, and it is true that much of what we could see was inferential. Yet, frequently we were able to see deeply into some aspect of the teaching activities or classroom environment. In many cases, this final reading highlighted exemplars of learning-centered teaching and created excellent opportunities for faculty members to learn from each other. One instructor whose students repeatedly wrote poetry about intensely powerful, personal, and private aspects of their lives and their family histories was asked how she was so successful at getting students to write in this way. She replied,

> I really want students to explore the scarier, more vulnerable parts of themselves—places they are afraid to go. Socially we are taught to keep these pieces of ourselves secret, hidden, and yet great writers have to be able to explore tough issues. To get my students to do this, I spend several weeks being vulnerable, modeling vulnerability, sharing both poetry and other kinds of writing in which authors have taken great personal risk in exploring parts of themselves that most of us run from. Of course we do develop ground rules—about how what is shared in the class stays in the class—but once a few students are willing to risk being "seen," classes typically develop a very supportive community. After that, most of the students are willing to write and share deeply of themselves.

In another example, faculty members in the group were deeply impressed with the consistent level of questioning, discourse, and analysis present in some of John's students' work. John is a historian whose pedagogical approach requires students to study themselves both as products of history and as makers of history. One faculty member wondered aloud, "How do you get your students to produce this kind of depth? I cover much of the same material, and even my best students just seem to scratch the surface of what I see in your students' writing." This query inspired an impromptu but lengthy session on the ways that John methodically worked with his students, modeling the kinds of skills he wanted, and how he used praxis and self-examination to get his students to dig deeply into their own thinking on issues that they explored during the course.

There are many other wonderful examples of the kinds of things this third reading can bring to the surface. For instance, we have seen samples of student work in which students clearly felt safe to disagree strongly with the instructor. We have also seen examples in which students synthesized such a large variety of evidence in their summative essays that it was very clear that the instructor had used a masterfully broad body of evidence in exploring issues presented in the course. For me, the most significant aspect of this third reading was that it was a wonderful venue for seeing the beauty and expertise that many faculty members weave into their courses and for seeing how they learn from each other. From the examples provided here, you can see that most of what faculty members were drawn to in each other's courses were the ways in which some of these instructors excelled in making their courses student and learning centered.

Results of Collaborative Assessment of Student Work: Learner-Centered Decisions

In this section, I provide anecdotes from my own personal experiences and those of my colleagues, as well as examples from the literature. My intention here is to illustrate how analysis of student work has informed and influenced learner-centered decisions. I have gathered all sorts of examples, from faculty making classroom/teaching/assessment decisions to departments making changes to their curricula to departments making faculty line/hiring decisions to residence life directors making decisions around cocurricular activities. On a metalevel, I hope these examples illustrate how institutions can use this important form of self-study to become more learning centered. On a level more central to college teaching and to my colleagues who are passionate about teaching and learning, I hope these examples provide ideas about what might be in the collaborative review of student work for them.

After several successful rounds of the collaborative assessment of student work with faculty, Amy developed a workshop for our residence life staff and administrators that gave them a deep experience with our general education learning outcomes as well as the collaborative assessment of student work. The personnel from residence life really valued this entry into the academic side of the campus and in response developed a whole series of cocurricular activities (a film and lecture series) that focused on supporting several of our social justice outcomes.

One personal example of how this work influenced my teaching was that it brought up for me an ongoing frustration that my students were not achieving the level of mastery I sought in their ability to use the scientific method. I could see the lack of achievement very plainly in my students' work, as could my colleagues. In a very valuable work session, one of my colleagues asked what kind of teaching and learning activities I used in help-ing my students to master the outcome. The conversation that followed illus-trated several things for me—that it really was a challenging outcome for nonmajors, and also that I was not giving my students much opportunity to master the different components of the outcome before having them com-plete the assessment. As a result, I redesigned a whole section of the course. I began with some formative assessment in the form of a student reflection on what the "scientific method" meant to my students. I then used what they knew to introduce the module. I broke the outcome into its compo-nents and presented them one at a time, rather than all together. We then designed some simple experiments together as a class. I had them work on similar exercises in small groups, and then on their own. Finally, I had stu-dents practice designing experiments, diagramming the components, and de-tailing how they were using appropriate vocabulary on three separate occasions before giving them the assessment. As you can imagine, the changes in scaffolding and the increase in time devoted to that outcome yielded much more gratifying results on the assessment (for the students as well as for myself) and, I believe, a much deeper learning experience for my students.

In another example, a colleague of ours, Elaine, used the same protocol that we used in our collaborative review of student work with her students. She had been working for several years to connect her students with her course outcomes in a substantial way. She tried something different every semester, always with very limited success, and felt that the outcomes re-mained fairly abstract for most of her students. After participating in the collaborative review of student work for the first time, she decided to have her current students evaluate the work of previous students (after removing their names from the work) using the same criteria that she would later use to evaluate their work. They did not have to agree with her evaluation, but they did have to justify their evaluation via the criteria. She later shared with me that the change in the quality of her students' work and their connection to the course outcomes was monumental. She felt that this activity had been several orders of magnitude more successful than anything she had tried in the past.

Angela Krebs (2005) gives several examples of how the math teachers she studied modified their teaching in response to their collaborative review of student work. Their collaborative work focused on students' acquisition of math skills. As a result of their work together, they paid special attention to creating assignments that gave deeper insight into their students' thinking.

The collaborative review of student work can help faculty reach consensus on key terms and lead to improvements in curricular design. For example, the social sciences department at Alverno College discovered a disconnect between several of its outcomes and its curriculum when the instructor of the capstone course observed a pattern of student performance that suggested that some of the students were unable to meaningfully use theory in their analysis. This prompted a multifaculty examination of students' performances in the capstone course using criteria related to three outcomes for the social science major that confirmed the instructor's observation. Members of the department carefully examined the social science curriculum and specific assessments to identify when and how students were taught to use theory and for what purposes. They also established which theories were taught. Their analysis revealed substantial developmental gaps in the curriculum regarding social theory. The problem was exacerbated by the interdisciplinary nature of the social science department, in that members of the varied disciplines (i.e., sociology, urban planning, political science, and anthropology) drew on a wide range of theories.

As a result, department members incorporated specific theories in specific courses throughout the social science curriculum. In addition, they made major revisions in the advanced research course in order to strengthen opportunities for students to use social theory in their conceptualization of research projects and design (J. Abromeit, personal communication, June 26, 2006).

Sharon Hamilton, associate dean of faculties at IUPUI, shared with me how collaborative analysis of student work in its writing program surfaced concerns that some faculty members were rewriting too much of their students' work (personal communication, June 19, 2006). This led to faculty development that focused on how to comment on student work in the form of asking questions that engaged students in the issues that faculty wanted them to address. Dr. Hamilton said the influence of the faculty development was evident in faculty comments on student work in subsequent reviews of student work.

Collaborative analysis of student work has the potential to surface teaching issues about which faculty feel insecure and to provide help to those who wish to teach more effectively (Little et al., 2003; Wood, 2006). On our campus, the review of student work consistently led to musings such as, "I guess I'd have a hard time teaching my students how to synthesize, even though I ask them to do it all the time"; "I wish I had some good strategies for engaging my students in a thoughtful dialogue on reflection"; and "What are the qualities of a good analysis?" These thoughts pointed to an obvious need— that faculty needed a venue for exploring many of the criteria that we require of student work but with which we frequently have limited experience. The following year, our Center for Teaching, Learning, and Assessment responded with "Blooming Pedagogies," a workshop series in which faculty with expertise in teaching critical thinking, analysis, synthesis, reflection, and so forth engaged faculty participants in strategies for engaging students in these areas.

When my department conducted a collaborative review of our students' capstone projects in 2003, we validated as a group what many of us had been grinding our teeth over for years—that the quality of our students' writing was poor, and that as faculty instructors with disciplinary Ph.D.s, most of us were ill equipped to help our students meet our writing expectations. Six months prior to this review, we had conducted a significant scan of the local agencies and businesses that routinely hire our graduates. The single most important skill that they desired was the ability to write well. As a result of these two activities, help developing excellence in writing became our number one priority and, thus, our next faculty line was devoted to a person who could develop strong writing courses for our students, and a writing-across-the-curriculum program in which this individual would help the rest of us develop effective writing instruction in many of our courses.

Figure 9.1 depicts a research cycle of an outcomes-based learner-centered institution and summarizes much of what Amy and I have shared with you throughout the book. At a learning-centered campus, goals, outcomes, criteria, and standards begin with careful study of what is important to the campus; they are developed through faculty/learner-centered collaborative, inquiry-based processes. This work is then used to shape the curriculum and pedagogy and to facilitate student learning by making students aware of what we want from them as we partner with them in the process of teaching and learning. Numbers 4 and 5, the foci of this chapter, speak to collecting and analyzing evidence of student learning. What is learned from the analysis is then used to refine and improve learning outcomes, criteria, standards, curricula, and pedagogy—with the assumption that these changes will improve student learning. These changes form the basis of new hypotheses and the research cycle begins again.

FIGURE 9.1
Assessing Student Learning: Course, Program, and Institutional Levels

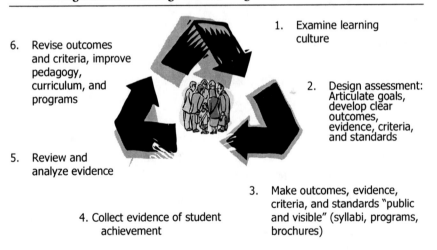

6. Revise outcomes and criteria, improve pedagogy, curriculum, and programs

5. Review and analyze evidence

4. Collect evidence of student achievement

1. Examine learning culture

2. Design assessment: Articulate goals, develop clear outcomes, evidence, criteria, and standards

3. Make outcomes, evidence, criteria, and standards "public and visible" (syllabi, programs, brochures)

A Conversation with Amy

In the discourse on assessment in higher education there is a conflict, never far from the surface, around the extent to which higher education should use a "one size fits all" approach (just as No Child Left Behind has done for elementary and secondary education) and the degree to which teaching, learning, and assessment activities should be idiosyncratic to individual campuses. This conflict raises many concerns on our campus, as I am sure it does on yours. Certainly there are excellent arguments for using common frameworks, such as basing teaching and learning activities and curricula on what we understand about how humans learn from cognitive psychology (Halpern & Hakel, 2003). In a recent conversation with Ralph Wolff, executive director of the Western Association of Schools and Colleges, he reflected on higher education's tendency to reinvent the wheel with respect to creating its own assessment processes rather than adopt and adapt what has been created elsewhere. As I read the literature in preparation for writing this chapter, I realized that reviewing and analyzing student work is not a unique process. This kind of process has been well used at all levels of education. It therefore seems that we could have adopted or adapted in our review processes, but we created from scratch. I discussed Ralph's comments with Amy and asked her:

As the person who developed our process, I'm very interested in your perspective. Why didn't we adapt a previously developed process?

I do agree with Ralph, but I also think that our "reinventing the wheel" is absolutely essential to making sure that our processes, be they assessment processes or curriculum development processes or community engagement processes, need to have a "grassroots" beginning in order to "fit" the culture of higher education in general and the individual institution in particular. The processes as well as the results must reflect the mission, values, intentions, priorities, student and faculty populations, and programmatic focus. Without a very active voice and role in designing and initiating processes, it's difficult to promote ownership of the processes. I recently worked with a group of public health faculty and they have a well-designed set of competencies from their professional organization [see chapter 3]. I saw those competencies as an asset, saving them from the time-consuming task of writing outcomes, but they corrected my assumption. They resented being handed a set of outcomes for their teaching, resisted "buying into" the competencies, and grumbled about the fact that "there is no room for the kinds of outcomes that we care about." Their dissatisfactions reminded me of the importance of constructivist faculty development, that is, having faculty create their own learning . . . and processes. At CSUMB, our processes for reviewing and analyzing student work emerged from our earlier processes of articulating outcomes, criteria, and standards. The processes also "fit" the faculty culture; that is, they emphasized the insights for improving our teaching rather than just assuring that outcomes were being met. Often processes for reviewing student work are intended for accountability purposes and do not connect to teaching. That approach would have been a disaster, with faculty resenting the time spent and not returning for another round of review. So I do think that it's helpful to review what others have done or accomplished or learned, and to keep it as wisdom for collaborating with faculty.

Taking Amy's response one step further, and returning to an earlier theme, I believe that faculty learning and faculty engagement in student learning are key in higher education's evolution toward becoming learning centered. If this is true, if harnessing our intellectual fascination and energy in the pursuit of more and more effective student learning is essential, then we have to invest in strategies that are likely to engage our colleagues. I hope that both this chapter and the one to follow call you to engage the collaborative review of student work and illustrate why this practice should become widespread in higher education's progress toward becoming learning centered.

References

Barr, R. B., & Tagg, J. (1995). From teaching to learning—A new paradigm for undergraduate education. *Change, 12*(6), 13–25.

Bella, N. J. (2004). *Reflective analysis of student work: Improving teaching through collaboration.* Thousand Oaks, CA: Corwin Press.

Blythe, T., Allen, D., & Powell, B. S. (1999). *Looking together at student work.* New York: College Teachers Press.

Halpern, D. F., & Hakel, M. D. (2003). Applying the science of learning to the university and beyond: teaching for long-term retention and transfer. *Change, 35*(4), 37–41.

Krebs, A. S. (2005). Analyzing student work as a professional development activity. *School Science and Mathematics, 105*(8), 402–411.

Langer, G. M., Colton, A. B., & Goff, L. S. (2003). *Collaborative analysis of student work.* Alexandria, VA: Association for Supervision and Curriculum Development.

Little, J. W., Gearhart, M., Curry, M., & Kafka, J. (2003). Looking at student work together for teacher learning, teacher community and school reform. *Phi Delta Kappan, 85*(3), 184–192.

Price, M. (2005). Assessment standards: The role of communities of practice and the scholarship of assessment. *Assessment & Evaluation in Higher Education, 30*(3), 215–230.

Schilling, K. M., & Schilling, K. L. (1998). *Proclaiming and sustaining excellence: Assessment as a faculty role* (ASHE-ERIC Higher Education Report Vol. 26, No. 3). Washington, DC: The George Washington University Graduate School of Education and Human Development.

Shulman, L. (1993). Teaching as community property—Putting an end to pedagogical solitude. *Change, 25*(6), 6–7.

Tagg, J. (2003). *The learning paradigm collage.* Bolton, MA: Anker.

Wiley, M. (2003). In an age of assessment, some useful reminders. *Exchanges* [Online journal]. Available: www.exchangesjournal.org/viewpoints/1124_Wiley.html

Wood, S. (2006). Faculty interviews: A strategy for deepening engagement in inquiry. In A. Driscoll & D. Cordero de Noriega (Eds.), *Taking ownership of accreditation* (pp. 205–228). Sterling, VA: Stylus.

Zull, J. E. (2002). *The art of changing the brain: Enriching teaching by exploring the biology of learning.* Sterling, VA: Stylus.

FACULTY RESPONSES TO ASSESSMENT OF STUDENT EVIDENCE

Story: Scientists Discover Grading Rubric Out of Alignment

We had spent the morning diligently analyzing students' science posters and checking to see if they had met the outcomes and criteria with their work. It had been an excellent session, and it was clear that Erica, whose students' work we had studied, had done a wonderful job of connecting her assignment to the science general education learning outcomes and used the criteria as the basis of her grading rubric.

After returning from lunch, we were a little tired as we directed our attention to a different batch of student evidence, copies of an exam given by Karl, a biologist in the group. We had been through our process for several copies of the exam. Some students had done fairly well, but several had not. Karl, who was a little irritated, kept expressing disappointment in his students' performance. "I know we covered these issues thoroughly in class, but looking at their exams I can't help feeling that most of the students didn't quite 'get it,'" he lamented. We all nodded in response, and I empathized with his irritation, thinking to myself, "I know the feeling exactly—not quite as bright as last year's class, and I wish they'd listened better and studied harder."

Amy responded to Karl, "I understand you are disappointed with their grades, but let's stay with our process here and try to be really neutral." After we had examined several students' exams, Sally pointed out, "This is interesting. The exam question asked students to list the points of an important plant ecology argument, but look at these two exams. It seems to me that the student who listed all the points of the argument got the B, but the student who *discussed* the argument got the A." You can imagine how the energy around the table was suddenly transformed, as when something startling comes into view after a long drive. Our tiredness gone, we were all looking carefully at what Sally had seen. It turned out that the pattern was consistent across the six exams that we had to examine. The issue was that Karl had actually wanted his students to discuss the argument—he just hadn't asked them to—and he graded the exam as though he had. The facts that the way he had graded the exam was not aligned with the exam question (that he had asked for one thing and graded for another) and that most of the students whose grades were affected had graduated several months earlier were deeply humbling and pretty embarrassing, even though we were all friends and had worked together for years. The rest of us, a little thankful that it had not been our assignment, were somewhat mortified by the fact that none of us had seen the disconnect between what was being asked and how it was graded, even though we'd been looking at the same two pieces of student work for half an hour. I think we all understood that any one of us could have easily made the same error.

Interviews: Inquiry, Motivation, Approach

Before detailing the method I used for the second interview study, and discussing what were for me very exciting results, I want to speak briefly on the potential of the collaborative review of student work as a powerful learning experience for faculty. More than anything else, excitement over my own learning experience is what propelled me into the second interview study.

Rationale for My Second Interview Study

I think many of you may find the previous story a little disturbing, much as I did. It was certainly a monumental experience for me and stimulated a great deal of thinking on the degree to which grading is subjective and influenced by much more than a student's performance. I will say that from my experience working with faculty at California State University Monterey Bay (CSUMB) and other campuses this kind of disconnect is not rare; most of us are not aware of issues such as this because few of us ever put ourselves or our students' work in a setting in which this kind of problem can be brought to our attention. I expect that most of you would experience what I did, and that almost all of you would learn much about your teaching and assessment by engaging in collegial, collaborative peer review of your students' work.

This kind of practice not only brings to our attention disconnects and deficits in our work; there are also wonderful opportunities for gratification, for sharing excellence with other faculty colleagues and being acknowledged for it. The *real* opportunity, however, the one that my interview subjects found productive and very gratifying, and the one that had a profound impact on faculty across campus, was that the process allowed faculty to look deeply into their teaching. It allowed them to study with multiple sets of eyes the evidence of student learning and their practice of teaching and assessment, as well as to use what they learned to improve their practice. Similar kinds of faculty experiences are addressed throughout the literature on the collaborative review of student work (Bella, 2004; Blythe, Allen, & Powell, 1999; Langer, Colton, & Goff, 2003).

Methods for the Interview Study

From the previous story, it may be obvious why I was compelled to conduct a second interview study. Similar to how developing criteria and standards for the science general education learning outcomes led to my excitement about my teaching, which inspired my first interview study (see chapter 6), the collaborative analysis of student work made me rethink my teaching in a whole new way. This work helped me to look into my course structure and shed light on my teaching, including disconnects similar to those in Karl's story, depicted earlier. With the positive feedback I'd received from my presentation at the CSU Assessment Conference, I was excited to develop a second interview study. This study would be much more robust and include a full third of the faculty who had participated in the collaborative review of student work. In this study, I delved much more deeply into my subjects' experience; asked more questions, more open-ended questions; and pursued unresolved issues with follow-up questions. Most of the interviews took more than an hour. I was amazed at the depth to which faculty members, most of whom I did not know prior to the interviews, allowed me into very personal and private aspects of their professional and personal lives. The intimacy and poignancy that transpired during many of these interviews was indicative of the profound professional and emotional impact that the collaborative review of student work had for many of my interview subjects. It is a pleasure to share their experiences with you here.

This research is best described as an ethnographic interview study, for I was a participant as well as an observer (Esterberg, 2002). Certainly my interpretation of the interview data was influenced by my experience as a participant. I selected interviews for data collection rather than surveys because I did not believe surveys would capture what I experienced as a participant. It was important to hear faculty voices and faculty thinking. Answering the research questions required in-depth exploration of faculty members' insights, perceptions, and evaluation of the assessment experiences. The interviews were semistructured (in-depth), thus allowing me to probe the meaning of my subjects' assessment experience.

I interviewed 17 of a total of 53 faculty members, and all of the general education faculty learning communities (FLCs) were represented in the study. Interviews were tape-recorded and recordings were transcribed. The interview subjects selected broadly represented the experience of general education FLCs. Interviews were conducted in person in subjects' offices and consisted of the following nine questions:

1. What was the purpose of the peer review of student work—what were you trying to achieve?
2. What did you learn about teaching and learning from this process?
3. What did you learn about assessment from this process?
4. What did it affirm or reinforce about your thinking or practice of teaching and learning?
5. Are there any changes you'll make in your work as a result of this process?
6. What did you learn about our general education outcomes, criteria, and standards?
7. Did this work affect or influence your thinking, or how you feel, about outcomes-based education?
8. Were you surprised about anything that came up during the process?
9. Is there anything else you'd like to add about the process?

In addition to the interviews, independent of this study, and as part of a recent program review of our general education program, learning community members wrote a brief summary and analysis of what they learned from the peer review of student work. I analyzed these summaries as well as transcripts of the interviews. I read the entire set of transcripts twice and then coded them to determine themes that arose in more than four interviews. I then read the transcripts a third time and scored them for the presence of the different themes and for the identification of examples (Esterberg, 2002; Johnson & Christensen, 2000).

We at CSUMB first implemented the collaborative review of student work in our general education FLCs. CSUMB has 13 FLCS, one for each general education area. These FLCs meet once a month and are charged with developing and maintaining the general education outcomes, criteria, and standards; developing and sharing effective pedagogies for teaching to the various general education learning outcomes; and reviewing courses that serve the specific general education area. Faculty members who teach general education courses participate in their area's FLC. Tenure-track faculty members attend general education FLC meetings as a function of their workload. Part-time faculty are expected to attend and are paid a stipend for their participation.

After the campus implemented the general education FLCs' work that developed examples of student evidence, criteria, and standards for the general education outcomes in courses over three semesters, Amy approached the members of these communities with another question. However, before doing so she acknowledged and praised what the faculty had accomplished, our work instituting examples of evidence, criteria, and standards across the GE system, and also acknowledged that they were now established in the support of successful student achievement of the learning outcomes. Then, once again she probed: "But how do we *know* that students are achieving the learning outcomes in general education courses and that courses/faculty are actually making good on their commitment to hold students to the learning outcomes?"

The Process of Analyzing Student Work

In response to Amy's question in the previous section, faculty who taught general education courses collected examples of student work, assignments designed to demonstrate student achievement of one or more general education outcomes. These examples consisted of work that was exemplary, work that was satisfactory, and work that did not meet the outcomes. We analyzed the student evidence through a three-step process similar to that used in qualitative research (the process summarized here is detailed in chapter 9). The analysis was done collaboratively in small groups of four to eight faculty members. Copies of identical pieces of evidence were given to each faculty member, and the whole group worked on only one piece of evidence at a time. Faculty read the same piece of student evidence three times focusing on a different purpose with each reading.

The purpose of the first reading was to develop a broad understanding of the student's work and to determine holistically whether the student had met the outcome. This was done to check reliability as well as provide a basis for the second reading. The purpose of the second reading was to check validity by studying and substantiating the evaluation made in the first reading. The purpose of the third reading was to allow faculty to study the work through the lens of the student's experience regarding the instructor and course materials. Now I'd like to shift to the results of the interview study and share what our campus learned from our collaborative review of student evidence.

Response Themes

Eight different themes emerged in the transcripts of interviews of what faculty learned from the collaborative review of student work. Several of these themes were identical to or overlapped considerably with themes from my first interview study presented in chapter 6.

1. Building consensus on what learning outcomes mean to faculty
2. Fear and vulnerability
3. Bias
4. Aligning teaching and assessment with learning outcomes, criteria, and standards
5. Changes in teaching, assessment, and reflection on pedagogy
6. Peer review and collaboration
7. The value of outcomes-based education (OBE)
8. Benefits and value

Building Consensus on What Learning Outcomes Mean to Faculty

In chapter 6, I spoke at length of how the process of developing examples of evidence, criteria, and standards required faculty to develop a shared understanding of their learning outcomes and forced many assumptions regarding language, philosophy, and academic discipline out in the open. All of my subjects in the first interview study indicated that although they had assumed a common understanding of the outcomes the process helped them to realize that different faculty members had very different interpretations of the learning outcomes. The same issue emerged in this interview study. Almost 60 percent of the subjects indicated that the discussion helped to build a common understanding of what the learning outcomes mean to the faculty, as illustrated by this comment by one of the interview subjects: "The outcomes may mean different things to different members of the committee. . . . It has led to subsequent discussions of 'what *do* we mean by . . . ?'" Other authors and faculty who have a great deal of experience with the collaborative analysis of student work make similar observations (Bella, 2004; Blythe et al., 1999; Langer et al., 2003; J. Abromeit, personal communication, June 26, 2006).

As an outcomes-based institution, this is a particularly important finding for CSUMB because it illustrates the importance of ongoing discussions of what our learning outcomes mean, and the importance of maintaining our FLCs or other venues to promote these discussions (Blythe et al., 1999; Maki, 2004). For individual faculty members, it is clear that you need to question and discuss outcomes with each other to fully understand how you may be using language differently. The experience of CSUMB faculty speaks to the importance of questioning a group's use of language and highlight the fact that it is probably safer to assume that you may be using key terms differently, especially when you are working across disciplines. Their experience reaffirmed that a common understanding of what outcomes mean comes through dialogue and discussion.

I would like to shift the focus of this theme from faculty back to students and learning. Students are likely to need the same kinds of support that faculty do, if not more so. Given the challenge that using language differently presents for faculty, I believe it is safe to assume that you will need to discuss your use of key terms in your learning outcomes with your students. You may find, as I do, that engaging your students in exercises that force them to come to grips with your learning outcomes is a very productive form of pedagogy.

Fear and Vulnerability

If most teaching, as Lee Shulman writes (1993), is done behind closed doors, then I warrant that much assessment is done under lock and key. Most of us know it as a very private endeavor, and the reasons for this privacy likely derive from a mixture of expediency and the fear of risk and exposure. The literature on the collaborative analysis of student work discusses faculty fear (Blythe et al, 1999; Langer et al., 2003). Eighty-three percent of my interview subjects whose students' work was reviewed experienced fear and described feeling vulnerable as well. My interviews were very poignant because in talking about their vulnerability my colleagues again made themselves vulnerable. Almost all of those who spoke of their discomfort also spoke of the benefit of their work being made public. Listen to how one of my colleagues described the experience of having other faculty members analyze her students' work: "I was actually fearful to have people from other departments listening in on my teaching process." She then explained how validating the experience was: "I really felt like part of the group after that happened. These were probably some of the best moments I've had with faculty across the campus."

You understand that the fear wasn't necessarily rational, however. One faculty member who said, "The level of vulnerability was stunning," also acknowledged that he was a tenured full professor with little or nothing to lose. It was more a matter of making public something that had been intensely personal and private, and in which he had invested a tremendous amount of himself. That particular faculty member went on to reflect, "I felt exposed—like if the other faculty didn't value my work it would feel like one of my kids returning after 30 years to detail the worst of my parenting."

Although it did not surface as a theme, several subjects spoke about the constant tension of not knowing how their evaluation of student work compared with that of other faculty members. Were they harder, or easier? Were they consistent? These subjects also spoke about the relief of seeing how, through collaborative analysis, other faculty members evaluated a particular piece of student work and finding that their evaluation was similar to their colleagues' evaluations. Their feelings are acknowledged in the literature as well (Blythe et al., 1999; Langer et al., 2003). I believe this kind of apprehension is common across academia. Johnstone, Ewell, and Paulson (2002) talk about this absence of both discussion and consensus when they acknowledge the lack of academic currency in higher education that we talked about in chapter 1. The collaborative review of student evidence served to decrease this kind of anxiety and to support students by building a consensus of expectations.

In spite of the fact that many interview subjects spoke of their fear, I believe one of the things that made these faculty development processes so successful is that faculty members were willing to take risks and this willingness actually derived from considerable trust among themselves. Angelo (1999) discusses developing shared trust as a precondition for FLCs, and it is certainly clear to me that collaborative analysis of student work cannot happen without shared trust. However, FLCs themselves seem to be an excellent venue for developing shared trust among faculty and administrators who focus on assessment, and I believe that that was the case at CSUMB. The substantial time that faculty spent together in their respective FLCs developing our general education program allowed them to build rapport and considerable shared trust, which led to the success of our assessment processes. In addition, the assessment processes deepened the trust within the FLCs. The assessment processes implemented here might have been valuable for faculty who were strangers; however, I believe that the familiarity and trust built in the FLCs paved the way for a deeper experience. I also believe that the results presented here speak strongly about the potential of using FLCs to support assessment activities on other campuses.

For those of you who wish to pursue assessment activities in which faculty share their assignments or students' work with their colleagues, it is important to recognize that fear of exposure is a given and, furthermore, that you need to anticipate it and develop ways of working with it. Assessment should be done to help improve student learning, programs, and so forth, rather than to target individuals. Make it clear to your colleagues that the results of your assessment work together will be kept anonymous, and that there are mechanisms in place to ensure that the results will not be made known to individuals. Along with a framework that protects, it is important for the participants of assessment activities to build rapport and trust with each other. You can do this through, for example, community/trust-building exercises and FLCs.

Bias

Three fourths of the interview subjects said that the collaborative review of student work revealed some aspect of their bias. Some faculty members whose students' work read very differently with their peers than when they evaluated it during the course attributed this difference to bias, and some were caught off guard by the experience. "I'm more biased than I thought, candidly," one faculty member said. Others saw how qualities of the student work other than the criteria being evaluated influenced their grading. Note the surprise expressed by my colleague as he explained how the quality of students' writing influenced his evaluation of their work—even though writing quality was not being assessed: "In some cases I was dazzled by excellent writing to the point that I actually *missed holes* in the evidence." The fact that this work surfaced so much bias brings to light the consistency, or lack thereof, regarding faculty judgment in evaluating student work. You can see how it highlights the need for very clear standards or grading rubrics and the value of this kind of collaboration among faculty members (Johnstone et al., 2002).

Aligning Teaching and Assessment With Learning Outcomes, Criteria, and Standards

One of the most valuable results of CSUMB's collaborative review of student work was that it illustrated disconnects among teaching, learning, assessment, and learning outcomes. My faculty interviews revealed three kinds of disconnects that faculty identified as a result of their work. The first was between what was being taught and the stated learning outcomes. For example, one faculty member stated, "I think we were all a little horrified at what came out—here it is, big as life, one of our outcomes and we're not even really addressing it in any significant way."

The second kind of disconnect, between assignments and learning outcomes, was discovered when some faculty members observed that students really had followed directions—and accomplished what they had been asked to; it was just that the faculty had really wanted something else. You can hear the chagrin in my subject's voice as she discovers that what her learning community wanted from students was not aligned with what the faculty members were asking for: "We really wanted them to do one thing, but we were asking them to do a different thing—and they gave us what we asked for . . . and, gee, what a revelation." The third kind of disconnect, asking for one thing and grading for another (no connection between an assignment and a grading rubric), is illustrated in the story at the beginning of the chapter, and the theme of that story repeated itself many times as the process revealed identical issues for other interview subjects.

The collaborative review of student work showed faculty that alignment among learning outcomes, learning activities, and assessment activities must be intentional and cannot be taken for granted. Several interview subjects echoed, "This process underscored how critical it is to align assessment standards and criteria with the resources and learning activities that are facilitated in the class." There were many more who noted how the process impressed upon them the importance of carefully crafting questions used in assessment.

Many of the changes that faculty made in their teaching and assessment as a result of this work were geared toward better alignment. Again and again, they indicated how the process facilitated a deep reflection on what was working and what was not. Overall, 82 percent of interview subjects indicated that the process revealed at least one of the preceding disconnects. The importance of this result is not so much the individual issues that were raised, but the fact that this collaborative review of student work gave faculty a tool, a lens, for looking into their teaching and assessment; for discovering and addressing teaching materials and strategies that did not work; and, in many instances, for celebrating the things that did.

The disconnects revealed in the interviews remind me of an important aspect of Barr and Tagg's (1995) model. In the learning-centered institution, student learning confirms what kinds of teaching activities work; lack of learning (poor performance) informs areas of instruction that need to be improved. In this model, faculty are accountable for, and therefore share the responsibility of, student learning with their students. If we neglect studying student work, we miss out on a valuable method for examining and improving instruction. Our faculty found that the collaborative review of student work provided a powerful, learning-centered method for doing just that.

Changes in Teaching, Assessment, and Reflection on Pedagogy

Along with using the review process as a lens for reflection on their practice, I think one of the most remarkable results of my study is that 88 percent of those interviewed said that they had made changes in their teaching. Many of these changes involved rewriting assignments to clarify language, and connecting them to learning outcomes better. Several faculty members indicated that they were building better scaffolding into their teaching to promote cumulative learning to reach the outcomes. Others noted that they would shift from assessment at the end of the semester to more regular and iterative assessment. My experiences in the collaborative review of student work have pushed me to change the way I look at my own assignments and assessments. When I begin to see consistently incorrect answers on my assessments, I begin to scrutinize my questions or the directions. I use the same kind of negative evidence to reflect on how well I have taught that piece of the curriculum, how much opportunity my students had to practice the skills, and how well I scaffolded my instruction.

Sixty-five percent of the faculty members interviewed indicated that the collaborative review process was useful as a tool for reflecting on pedagogy. Some appreciated the fact that the review forced them to look critically at their own pedagogy, while others who had been using assessment solely as an evaluation tool came to see assessment as a valuable teaching tool.

Peer Review and Collaboration

It has been said that university faculty are more likely to collaborate with colleagues across the globe than with those down the hall. One thing that stands out in my study is that the faculty interviewees really enjoyed and valued collaborating with colleagues down the hall. As you might imagine, there was a spectrum of comments regarding the value of collaboration. Similar to the first study (see chapter 6), some faculty members spoke effusively about how valuable and powerful it was to work with colleagues in this way, how we frequently get to collaborate with students like this but rarely with faculty colleagues. Overall, 82 percent of the subjects interviewed spoke positively about the collaborative aspect of the experience. The importance of faculty collaboration in the analysis of student work and in assessment in general is addressed repeatedly in the literature I've cited in this chapter and in chapter 9. Since collaboration is truly the hub in a collaborative peer review process, the number of subjects for whom it was important stands out as significant. As you look to develop assessment and the analysis of student work on your campus, one of the ways you can support this work is to create and maintain venues for faculty members to collaborate with each other on teaching, learning, and assessment.

The Value of OBE

The collaborative review of student work was interesting with respect to how this process influenced faculty perception of OBE. Twenty-nine percent of the faculty members interviewed indicated that the process reinforced (positively) their perception of OBE. For another 65 percent, the value of OBE increased as a result of the process. Some faculty members said that the process improved their ability to implement and to actually achieve OBE, and for others the process has allowed their teaching to become much more intentional. A few went so far as to say that it was the collaborative review of student work that has enabled us to actualize OBE at CSUMB. One faculty member said, "This helped us take OBE to a whole different level." The fact that the value of OBE increased for almost two thirds of the interview subjects as a result of these faculty development processes implies that the work had a profound impact on faculty attitudes toward OBE and probably on assessment.

The impact of the collaborative review of student work on faculty attitudes toward OBE for our campus are remarkable. CSUMB has made the claim of being an outcomes-based institution and, thus, it is reasonable to assume that an accreditation agency will be very interested in how we support that claim. This evidence goes well beyond documenting having developed learning outcomes (what we would have done without the interview studies) by illustrating that our faculty have actually taken ownership of OBE and are using it to develop more effective pedagogies.

I do not wish to oversimplify the implications of the study findings. OBE remains a complex issue at CSUMB, as I am sure it is on your campus. The first interview study revealed considerable nervousness and apprehension about OBE, and similar issues surfaced for three subjects in the second study. At least one subject, although thrilled about CSUMB's interpretation of OBE, associated OBE more broadly with oversimplified teaching and the pernicious and insidious form of high-stakes testing prevalent in K–12 education. Another subject who praised OBE for making her teaching more intentional still voiced major reservations about OBE because of its potential to promote learning outcomes that are overly simple and easy to assess. Still, the larger picture is that for the majority of my interview subjects, the value of OBE grew considerably as a result of our collaborative review of student work.

Benefits and Value

As with the interview study on what faculty learned from developing examples of evidence, criteria, and standards (see chapter 6), one of the most striking themes apparent in this second interview was how faculty perceived their experience especially in terms of its value to their assessment work. Eighty-eight percent of those interviewed indicated directly that they appreciated the work and routinely used words and phrases such as *excellent, great, fantastic, exciting, enjoyed, fascinating,* and *absolutely wonderful* in describing their experience. I am sure you can appreciate that these are not typical faculty responses to assessment work.

Several faculty members indicated that initially they were worried that the work would end up being just one more burden but came away from the work feeling very positive. In fact, not one subject spoke negatively about the process or product, and more than half of the subjects expressed gratitude to Amy for the opportunity to participate.

As in the first interview study, the power of the faculty members' experience and why they valued it varied considerably. Some faculty members, especially those whose students' work was reviewed, found it validating. Reflecting on the experience, one of the interviewees said: "It was very validating to hear my colleagues say, 'Oh, what a good idea. Now I know how to talk about what I do in my class.' I suddenly realized I was serving as a good role model. I hadn't expected that."

For other faculty members their excitement was driven by seeing how they could apply collaborative review of student work to other aspects of their teaching or programs. One said, "I got so excited about this that I wanted to extend it to the whole department so we could go through the same process for the major learning outcomes." Because our faculty found the process so valuable, you can imagine how interest in it spread from our general education areas across campus and in fact led several of our degree programs to begin collaborative review and analysis of student evidence.

Some faculty members told of how the process helped them to rethink their own practice. Listen to two of my colleagues as they describe the potency of this work in reflecting on their teaching and assessment:

> "The benefit of assessment is that you get to see where you went wrong. You see the mistakes. And if you don't take the time to reflect on them, then you'll never improve in those areas. I really can't overstate how valuable I found it."
> "I've been teaching 20 years and this is probably as deep as I've gone into my own thinking, evaluation, and rethinking of my teaching. And it's been the most meaningful time too."

In addition to appreciating and valuing the work, faculty said the work was important. Eighty-two percent of those interviewed said that the process should be repeated periodically, and many felt that the process was essential for the success of OBE on our campus. Subsequently, the general education learning communities voted unanimously to create policy to repeat the collaborative review of student work with the Center for Teaching, Learning, and Assessment every other year. These findings are critical in that they portray not the stereotypical resentment and resistance by faculty, but an appreciation and enthusiasm for these assessment processes because of their value and meaningful connection to teaching and learning.

Implications of the Collaborative Review Process for Individual Faculty Members, Faculty Development, and Institutions

During and after the interviews, I thought deeply on the attributes of the collaborative review of student work that made the work so successful and powerful for faculty, and I have continued this reflection during subsequent review sessions. The more I reflected on the assessment process, the more I realized that these attributes are the same as those I strive for in my best teaching and that this is hugely influential on the success of this process. The process was constructivist and faculty centered. It drew upon faculty expertise, and faculty were clearly aware that *they* were driving the process. Perhaps more than any other, this aspect of the work facilitated faculty ownership of the process as well as the results of the process.

Just like the development of examples of evidence, criteria, and standards, the collaborative review of student evidence was a process of inquiry and discovery. The question that drove the process—"How do we actually *know* that students are mastering the learning outcomes in general education courses, and if they are, can we point to the evidence in student work?"— was open ended and had no predetermined correct answer. The facilitator's role was to provide support in pursuing greater clarity and depth.

The assessment process was collaborative and clearly benefited from multiple perspectives. From faculty responses, it was clear that one of the things faculty liked best and valued most about the process was collaborating with colleagues on campus and learning about what was going on in the minds and classrooms of colleagues across campus.

The assessment process engaged faculty deeply on issues that they cared about and were relevant to their professional interests. Our general education learning areas at CSUMB derive from the university's vision statement, and the courses are understood to be where students get to become intimately familiar with different aspects of the vision. Thus, there was genuine passion for producing excellent work.

Finally, there was tension, risk taking, and excitement, and, ultimately, faculty had to confront their models with real-world observations—they had to grapple with "how they knew what they knew." This confrontation between what they thought was occurring and the data (in the form of student work) was a very rich experience for many faculty members—just as it is for our students when we contrive situations in which they are forced to confront their preconceived notions of what is true with hard, factual evidence.

While faculty as adult learners may be better able to garner knowledge from passive forms of instruction (i.e., typical faculty development) than many of our students, for learning that transforms, the excellent pedagogies of engagement that we (educators) have developed for our students have serious potential to transform faculty development processes that focus on assessment. For me it was interesting to read "Principles of Good Practice of Assessing Student Learning" (AAHE Assessment Forum, 1997, pp. 11–12) after conducting the interviews because I found that many of the interview subjects had discovered several of those nine principles for themselves—that many of those principles were made evident in the activities and work of the assessment processes. AAHE's principles are very well written and obviously valuable, yet I suspect that the results of my interviews would have changed substantially had I interviewed subjects after they had merely studied the principles, rather than going through the intense and engaging experiences facilitated by these assessment processes. Although other explanations for my data are possible, I believe that these assessment processes appealed to my subjects' affection for self-study, to their desire to find the answer to the question, "What is it that my students are learning and what is true about my teaching?" because they were deeply engaging activities whose processes and products shed light in areas in which they are passionate about—student learning.

With respect to institutional change and improvement, these are very important results. On many campuses, faculty development processes that decrease faculty resistance to assessment would be considered significant news. Although CSUMB engaged in the collaborative review of student evidence on a fairly large scale, I believe that faculty working in small groups, such as part of a teaching cooperative or a scholarship of teaching and learning work group, could benefit in all of the same ways that we did. No matter what scale, generalizing from our experience, I strongly urge those of you who wish to engage your colleagues in these kinds of activities to develop a supporting structure, faculty development, and process that are collaborative, inquiry based, question driven, and faculty centered, and to focus on issues about which faculty care deeply.

A Conversation With Amy

After reading about what my colleagues and I learned from our collaborative analysis of student work, you can see how the process has been a great help in our efforts to become more learning centered. As you plan similar kinds of activities for your campus, I think it will be very helpful to learn from the experience and perspective of our facilitator, Amy.

Amy, after the success of the campus's work developing examples of evidence, criteria, and standards, you must have been looking forward to the prospect of using the criteria and standards to review student work. What did you most want from the experience, and what did you think the campus would learn?

I must admit that some of the insights that emerged from the review/ analysis of student work were not anticipated.

You mean like the number of disconnects faculty found between their teaching/ assessment criteria/learning outcomes?

That, but also that faculty were so energized and enthusiastic about the process and the results of the work. I never dreamed that faculty would spend as long as they did on each piece of evidence and was stunned by the persistence at analyzing every last word of student papers or items on their posters for the value and lessons.

That illustrates how enthusiastically the faculty engaged in the process. What were your biggest concerns?

My first concern when I designed the process was to be able to say that students were meeting the outcomes—that accountability issue. It was important and we needed to attend to it. Then my second concern was to ensure that our outcomes, criteria, and standards were the right ones—a bit of validity. Were we looking for what we thought we were looking for? But then the teacher in me just had to investigate the pedagogical learning that was potentially within an examination of student work. So I added a third process, that last review to learn what we could about the teaching and learning. I did not anticipate that we would learn so much about teaching from the other two processes or steps, but I was thrilled and enthused right along with the first groups of faculty. I clearly became a learner with the groups of faculty.

That is pretty inspiring but I want be sure that we address the tougher issues in facilitating this kind of work. In subsequent work that you and I have done together, and from the interviews, it is clear that faculty who supply their students' work to the process have the deepest learning experience. Yet, sometimes faculty are defensive, and that defensiveness really undermines their experience and the progress of the group. For our readers who want to do this kind of work with faculty on their campus, give us some strategies for working with faculty who are defensive about their students' work.

Well, Swarup, I see the resistant or defensive faculty a bit differently. I think of them as vulnerable. It is such a new experience to have colleagues examine the work students create in your class. Parker Palmer talks about how private our teaching is and the tradition for that is long and entrenched, so it takes a lot of courage. I'm not sure that I would address an individual faculty member; instead, I would work consistently to build a community of trust and collaboration with lots of opportunity to reveal questions, and concerns. Faculty have had so little experience with discussing pedagogy throughout their professional lives that anything like that feels strange and probably threatening. In truth, what we found is that after several very experienced or secure faculty had volunteered to have their student work examined by peers there was little resistance. We actually had volunteers who asked to have their work studied so that they could learn from the process. And, as you know, some faculty insisted that we had to continue to do this work. There's another important message here: when you gather faculty for assessment work, you must make sure that it is time well spent and that they find value in the process. When that happens, it's not hard to get them to come back and it doesn't take much to get them to volunteer students' work.

You know, Amy, looking back on the interviews, and even on this conversation, four themes dominate: trust, ownership, empowerment, and a lens through which we can examine our teaching. They've become important reminders all through our chapters. If we take them to our classrooms and apply them to how we teach and guide our learners, we will probably achieve learner-centered education.

References

American Association for Higher Education Assessment Forum. (1997). Principles of good practice of assessing student learning. In L. F. Gardiner, C. Anderson, & B. L. Caimbridge (Eds.), *Learning through assessment: A resource guide for higher education* (pp. 11–12). Sterling, VA: Stylus.

Angelo, T. (1999). *Doing assessment as if learning matters most* [On-line]. Available: http://frontpage.uwsuper.edu/frc/Scholars/assess.pdf.

Barr, R. B., & Tagg, J. (1995). From teaching to learning—A new paradigm for undergraduate education, *Change, 12*(6), 13–25.

Bella, N. J. (2004). *Reflective analysis of student work: Improving teaching through collaboration.* Thousand Oaks, CA: Corwin Press.

Blythe, T., Allen, D., & Powell, B. S. (1999). *Looking together at student work.* New York: College Teachers Press.

Esterberg, K. (2002). *Qualitative methods in social research.* Boston: McGraw-Hill Higher Education.

Johnson, B., & Christensen, L. (2000). *Educational research: Quantitative and qualitative approaches.* Needham Heights, MA: Allyn & Bacon.

Johnstone, S. M., Ewell, P., & Paulson, K. (2002). *Student learning as academic currency.* ACE/Educause Series on Distributed Education: Challenges, Choices, and a New Environment. Washington, DC: American Council on Education.

Langer, G. M., Colton, A. B., & Goff, L. S. (2003). *Collaborative analysis of student work.* Alexandria, VA: Association for Supervision and Curriculum Development.

Maki, P. (2004). *Assessing for learning: Building a sustainable commitment across the institution.* Sterling, VA: Stylus.

Shulman, L. (1993). Teaching as community property—putting an end to pedagogical solitude. *Change, 25*(6), 6–7.

MOVING TO OUTCOMES-BASED ASSESSMENT AND LEARNER-CENTERED EDUCATION THROUGH THE SCHOLARSHIP OF TEACHING, LEARNING, AND ASSESSMENT

T his last chapter is different from the rest of the chapters. The first difference is its practicality, with lists of activities and exercises for you to use to maintain the momentum initiated in the other chapters. These activities and exercises are practical in that they are not overly time-consuming and are useful for your teaching. In keeping with this book, they are also learner centered so that they support your commitment to that quality in your work. Many are focused directly on your students as learners, and some are focused on you as a learner, because they are meant to be learning activities and exercises.

This chapter is also directed to the practicality of integrating the contents of this book with your scholarship of teaching. All of the ideas in our lists will give you ways to study your teaching. The scholarship of teaching has been defined as a process of inquiry and reflection into teaching in order to achieve new understandings, to raise new questions, and to ultimately improve teaching and learning. The idea of teaching and learning as subjects for scholarship came about when Boyer (1990) expanded the traditional notion of scholarship to include studies of pedagogy. Shulman (1993) extended the momentum of the new scholarship when he urged faculty to make teaching public or community property by studying classroom practices and sharing their insights and improvements in teaching. Most recently, Huber and Hutchings (2005) gave the definition of scholarship of teaching and learning useful form when they stated, "The scholarship of teaching and learning includes the kinds of inquiry and investigation that faculty are most likely to undertake when they examine and document teaching and learning in their classrooms in order to improve their practice and make it available to peers" (p. 4). They also articulated the defining features of the scholarship of teaching and learning. In their words, they described "what it looks like" or identified "what faculty actually do" when doing the scholarship of teaching and learning (p. 20). These descriptions include the following features:

- *Questioning*—not a new process for most faculty, but one that is not often pursued. The inquiry process in which faculty engage will direct them to questions and studies that they really care about and in which they are deeply interested.
- *Gathering and exploring evidence*—requires that faculty design a process to explore and respond to their questions, staying focused on teaching and learning, while producing credible and significant data or evidence.
- *Trying out and refining new insights*—the expectation that faculty will try out and use evidence for improvement, a nonlinear process that involves changing midstream, refining, and responding to new questions.
- *Going public*—takes this scholarship beyond individual improvement to "the production of knowledge that is available for others to use and build on" (p. 27).

Most of this chapter is devoted to the first three features, but we address the last one at the end of the chapter.

Banta (2002) has taken the scholarship of teaching and learning a bit further with the scholarship of assessment, which is absolutely appropriate for this book. She sees the scholarship of assessment as an attractive form of scholarship because "it has the potential to respond to many real, widespread needs in higher education" (p. 190), and we agree. Some faculty members have indeed engaged in the scholarship of assessment but have placed it in the category of the scholarship of discovery, thus aligning it with traditional forms of research. However, if your campus is not ready to expand to another form of scholarship, then the scholarship of teaching and learning provides an ideal context in which to demonstrate your scholarly work.

By now, you are probably wondering what is in those lists we mentioned. First, the lists are arranged in categories that correspond to most of our chapters. Within each subject category, the list contains a series of reflections, inquiries, and self-assessments that range from simple to complex. Second, most lists include a relevant reading to expand your understandings of the topic, clarify your remaining questions, or prompt new questions. Third, the lists contain ideas for action research projects related to each subject area or topic. Action research projects provide a study of our teaching on a very practical level. They respond to important questions about our teaching and guide us to data- or evidence-based answers about how our pedagogy supports or does not support student learning. Ideally, action research leads to action to improve teaching and learning. Our action research ideas are not fully developed because they need to be designed to fit your course and classroom context. They give you ideas to prompt interest and curiosity and, it is hoped, more questions.

A final reason for the uniqueness of this chapter is that there is an expectation of last chapters to be summaries, and neither Swarup nor I favor summaries. Ordinarily we would repeat the main ideas of the preceding chapters or provide some wisdom that synthesizes all the ideas that you have read. Instead, we put our heads together to think of a creative way to pull the information together, make it interesting again, and make outcomes-based assessment as useful as it could possibly be. We think that the pages you are about to read meet these criteria and may be the part of the book that you choose to return to as you teach students and collaborate with your colleagues. That is our intention.

Before we take you to our lists of activities and exercises, we have some suggestions for how to use these materials:

1. Use the ideas prompted by our lists for self-reflection and assessment as an individual faculty member, and record your responses, inquiries, and plans in a teaching journal or scholarly paper format. Plan to share your insights and innovations with colleagues.

2. Select a teaching partner, another faculty member with similar interests or curiosities who is willing to work through the lists and engage in critical analysis of the ideas and information that emerge from your activities. Often teaching partners observe each other's classes, provide feedback and questions based on observations, and collaborate to study ways to improve. Such a partnership is an ideal context in which to use this chapter.

3. Organize or join a teaching co-op, a group of teachers who commit on a weekly or biweekly basis to meet, study, and collaborate on the study of teaching. We sponsored a teaching co-op every year at California State University at Monterey Bay, each one focusing on a different pedagogical theme. Ten or twelve members is ideal for the kind of interaction and engagement that can yield insights about and changes in teaching and learning.

4. The work of this chapter is ideal for the kind of faculty learning communities (FLCs) that we described in chapter 2, if you have access to such communities or feel inclined to start one. For a new community, select the simpler activities and reflections in our lists to get started. If your community has been functioning for years, try the more complex activities. You will probably come up with your own action research projects as well.

The checklists that follow provide activities for you to engage in by yourself or with other faculty. They are intended to keep the momentum of your reading going, support your continued learning about the topic of outcomes-based assessment, and ensure your progress toward or enhancement of learner-centered education. The first list acts as a preparation phase to accelerate your thinking about outcomes-based assessment and prompt inquiry about your work.

Preparation Phase: Beginning to Think About Outcomes-Based Assessment (chapter 1)

____ Determine what you already know about outcomes-based education (OBE) and assessment (make lists of your information).

____ Talk with colleagues about their impression of OBE and assessment. What do they know? List their responses and compare them with yours.

_____ List your concerns and hopes and those of your colleagues (make a departmental or unit overview) about OBE and assessment.

_____ Assess what you know about learning, ask students what they know about learning, and ask colleagues what they know about learning. Then compare the ideas.

_____ Read the article by Halpern and Hakel (2003) found in the references in chapter 1. List the new understandings you gain about learning.

_____ Have a conversation with a colleague about the kind of learning that we expect from students, record the qualities you are looking for in student work, and share your satisfactions and dissatisfactions. What qualities are present and which ones are missing?

_____ Begin identifying the sources of support for making changes in your teaching. Who or what would help you?

_____ Consider your feelings about moving assessment from a private process to a public process. What fears, expectations, or concerns does it bring up?

_____ Reflect on assessment experiences you had as a student—positive ones and negative ones. What were they like and what made them different? How did they affect your learning?

_____ If you have enough colleagues who would like to begin some of the work we have described for outcomes-based assessment, begin looking for a facilitator to guide your efforts. What qualities will you look for in that individual?

Action Research Ideas

1. Once you have investigated what you and your colleagues know about learning and have read Halpern and Hakel's article, translate one of the ideas into your teaching to see if it makes a difference. For example, if the authors were to recommend that learning takes place most effectively when students understand the rationale for the activities in which they are engaged, you would begin to describe why you do all of the activities you do in class and provide rationales for assignments. You might say, "Today we're going to role play the varied individuals in an ethical dilemma so that you can gain a deeper understanding of what the impact is like for different individuals or groups," or, "When you complete that analysis assignment, you will

have a clearer sense of the different possibilities for solving the problem." To find out what difference it makes when you provide students with the rationale, ask them at the end of the course, "When you knew the reason for your assignments, how did that affect your work?" Or, give two similar assignments and provide a rationale for one but not the other. Compare students' work when they have a reason for doing it and for when they do not.

2. Ask your students what helps them learn or supports their learning. Select two or three of the most common responses of "supports," and ask students how their course with you could be revised to use those "supports" or be more helpful for their learning. Use their ideas to make realistic revisions of the course, and at the end of the course, ask students about the changes and whether they made any difference in their learning. Urge them to be specific. Be sure to reflect on whether the changes made a difference for your teaching.

Examining Your Work Culture (chapter 2)

_____ Assess the professional context in which you work by listing the qualities that would describe it. Categorize those qualities that support your learning and those that do not.

_____ Assess your department or unit for the qualities of FLCs listed in chapter 2. How does your department rate as a "learning community"? How could it be improved?

_____ Pose questions about student learning and assessment in which you are genuinely interested. Gather questions from colleagues.

_____ Read some of the chapters or all of Cox and Richlin's (2004) *Building Faculty Learning Communities* (see the reference section in chapter 2 of this book). List three useful ideas for creating your own formal or informal learning community, or for assessing and improving your existing learning community.

_____ Review purposes of assessment for your work, your department, and your college or university. Ask students to describe their perceptions of the purposes of assessment. Consider the implications of their perceptions for your courses.

_____ Develop a mission statement for assessment with a list of purposes. Ask your students what they think about it.

_____ Reflect on your experiences with collaboration—why they worked or did not work. What would you do differently?

_____ Use Kezar's (2005) list of organizational features (see the references in chapter 2) to assess your department or institutional readiness for collaboration. Make recommendations based on that assessment.

Action Research Ideas

1. Ask students in a particular class what they think assessment does for their class with you—its purposes. Then ask what they would like assessment to achieve for them if they were to design it. Redesign the assessment of your course to achieve some of the students' desired purposes. At the end of the course, reflect on the course effectiveness, student learning, student motivation and satisfaction, and your own satisfaction. Ask students to describe the effects of the changes.

Shifting to Outcomes (chapter 3)

_____ Read Ray Gonzales's story from chapter 3 to one of your classes and listen to student responses. What do those responses tell you about your own teaching?

_____ Assess whether you could meet the outcomes at the beginning of chapter 3 when you finished the chapter.

_____ Write an outcome for each of the dimensions—knowledge, skills, attitudes and values, behavior—for one of your courses.

_____ Check your professional disciplinary association for outcomes. If they exist, are the outcomes helpful and relevant for your teaching? Can you or have you integrated them into your courses?

_____ Assess your own skills using Bloom's taxonomy. Where are your strengths? Where are your limitations?

_____ Study the taxonomy and think about where your students' work is placed. Rate the assignments and assessments of your course for their level on the taxonomy. Is that what you intended for your course? Do changes need to be made?

_____ Find out if there is a mission statement for your department or unit. If there is one, are expectations embedded in it? How do your courses align with the mission?

____ Try the exercise we describe in chapter 3 under "Using Learning Outcomes as a Centerpiece" with a group of colleagues or on your own to experiment with creating curriculum and pedagogy from learning outcomes.

Action Research Ideas

1. Introduce Bloom's taxonomy to your students in one of your courses. Discuss how the levels of the taxonomy move from simple to more complex thinking. Provide and elicit many examples of each level to promote student understanding of and comfort with the taxonomy. Then each time students complete an independent assignment or participate in a classroom learning activity ask them to indicate the taxonomy level that they are demonstrating. Once they are accurate about the levels, engage them in redesigning assignments or learning activities that expect higher-level processes. For example, if an assignment has asked for a definition and description of a process of communication, redesign the assignment to require analysis or comparison. At the end of the course, reflect on whether and how student thinking changed. Ask students to assess the effect of their redesign work.

Getting Beyond Final Exams (chapter 4)

____ Return to the memories of assessment that you experienced. Think of examples that inspired you, taught you, and helped your understanding.

____ Discuss with a colleague the differences between the learning of today's students and your learning experiences.

____ Read about Gardner's multiple intelligences and/or Kolb's learning styles. Keep notes of insights that will be useful for your teaching and learning activities.

____ Analyze your own intelligence and learning style. How is it connected with your teaching approaches and style?

____ After identifying your learning preferences, analyze whether they influence your courses, planning, and teaching.

____ Discuss fair and unfair assessment practices with students and colleagues.

____ Attend an assessment conference (e.g., the annual assessment conference sponsored by Indiana University–Purdue University at Indianapolis every October).

____ Review your directions for assignments and assessments. Also ask a colleague to review them, and ask students to critique them. What kind of changes need to be made?

Action Research Ideas

1. For an entire course, have students explain each assignment and assessment, including the directions, purposes, and expectations, before beginning their work. At the end of the course, ask students to reflect on the impact of the clarification processes. Ask about motivation, confidence, effort, and satisfaction with their work in those reflections.

2. Take one of your large summative assessments and break it into formative tasks that students can do in an ongoing manner during your course. For example, if you require a substantive project, break it into small tasks from start to finish (e.g., project purpose, goals and objectives, preparation, resources, and schedule) and have students turn in small sections one at a time for feedback and guidance. Look at Dan Shapiro's strategy for handling large research papers in his course in chapter 4. At the end of the course, have your students write reflective assessments of the quality of the work and how the ongoing assessment influenced the final assessment. Do this yourself as well.

Pulling Those Expectations Out and Public for Students (chapter 5)

____ Think about the criteria or qualities you set for yourself in terms of your teaching, your research, your participation in committees, and your engagement with community. Make lists of those criteria or qualities and reflect on them.

____ Put yourself in your students' shoes as you read your descriptions of assignments and assessments. What questions would you have?

____ When students' work disappoints you, what's missing? How could the work be improved? What could you do differently in the course? When students' work excites you, what's present? What can you do in your course to encourage that quality?

____ Lead a discussion with your students about what they think faculty look for in their work. What qualities do they think are important for their work?

Ask them how you and other faculty could provide help so that they could produce work with those qualities.

____ Connect with a colleague who teaches similar content and develop a list of qualities that you both would like to see in your students' work. Discuss and plan how to encourage students to display those qualities.

____ Develop a checklist with your students of those qualities or features that you have listed to use in the review of students' work. Encourage students to use the checklist when they prepare assignments.

Action Research Ideas

1. After listing and describing how students' work disappoints you and how it excites you, share the information with your students. Ask them what you could provide in class to support more "exciting" work and less disappointing work. Use one or more of those ideas in your teaching, in learning activities, or in designing assignments so that you can check whether the change or changes make a difference in the quality of the work. Have your students reflect on the impact of the change or changes. Reflect on that impact yourself as well.

Designing a Syllabus That Informs, Supports, and Is Aligned with Learning Outcomes (chapters 7 and 8)

____ Engage with a colleague or two in reviews of syllabi—strengths, usefulness, messages, innovative approaches, need for clarity, too much or too little information, and so forth. Use the feedback to revise your syllabus, and prepare a before-and-after display for your colleagues.

____ Ask students to critique your syllabus using some of the same prompts used with colleagues. Record their ideas and revise accordingly. Distribute the revised syllabus in the following class and ask for feedback again. Have students reflect on the process.

____ Have students rate the sections of your syllabus as "most helpful," "helpful," and "not helpful." Once you have analyzed the data, ask students how the "not helpful" sections could be revised to be helpful.

____ Ask students to produce a web of the learning outcomes in your syllabus (see chapter 7). Hold a class discussion of the rationales for their webbings.

____ Read Judith Grunert's (1997) *The Course Syllabus: A Learning-Centered Approach* (see reference list in chapter 7) in its entirety (it's short and it's worth it), and make a list of revisions that you will make in your syllabus and of its strengths in its current form.

Action Research Ideas

1. Try the research project in which Professor Guidry and her colleagues engaged in chapter 8 with a little variation. Select a course that does not feel as effective as it could be, or a course for which you have questions about student learning. On your syllabus, rate how well you think your pedagogy helps students to achieve each of the outcomes for each of your class sessions using "most effective," "effective," and "least effective," or a corresponding number rating. Then complete the grid described in chapter 8 using your syllabus and the directions in the chapter. On a weekly basis, have students record what outcome(s) they experienced in each class session using the form in chapter 8. When reviewing the student data, determine which outcomes had the most agreement and which the least agreement. Compare these with the ratings of your effectiveness for each outcome and see if there is a relationship. Then check for a relationship between your rating of a class session and students' agreement with your outcome. The analysis should reveal the areas in which you need to focus your improvement efforts. Once you have redesigned the course, you might wish to repeat the study.

Learning About Teaching From Students' Work (chapter 9)

_____ Brainstorm what collaborative review of student work would do for your teaching and for your institution.

_____ Determine whether review of student work is already occurring on your campus, and, if so, investigate its effectiveness for improving student learning.

_____ How would you rate yourself, your unit or department, and your campus with respect to developing learning outcomes, examples of evidence, criteria, and standards?

_____ If your campus has developed learning outcomes, criteria, and standards, what activities have you engaged in to ensure that you and your colleagues have a common understanding of them?

_____ Have there been successful projects on your campus in which faculty have benefited from collaborating with each other? If so, how can you use these projects to showcase the benefits of collaboration when encouraging your colleagues to "buy in" to the review and analysis of student work?

_____ What would you worry about if colleagues were to examine and analyze the student work from your class? What could you learn from this analysis?

_____ Make a list of the circumstances under which you usually review student work—setting, feelings, pressures, quantity of work, insights about teaching. Now contrast those circumstances with the description of analyzing student work in chapter 9.

_____ When you begin to develop your method for the collaborative review of student work, be sure to read Blythe, Allen, and Powell's (1999) *Looking Together at Student Work* (see the references section in chapter 9). Their work focuses on primary and secondary school educators, but it has huge implications for those of us in higher education and informs many of the issues that you will need to consider.

_____ How could the review/analysis of student work be used for your own scholarship?

Action Research Ideas

1. Provide students with a set of criteria and standards for an assignment in your course. First, ask students to write a description of what they think the criteria mean and how they would use them to prepare for and do the work of their assignment. Next, you have the following two options for your study:
   • Option A: Collect and evaluate the students' understanding of the criteria. What did you learn from their descriptions? Did their understanding concur with yours—would they have been able to use the criteria to do the work, to self-evaluate the work, to improve it and really address what you wanted in their work? Or, for your students to effectively use your criteria would you have had to teach them what the criteria mean and how they could/would be used to evaluate the assignment? Document how you modify your instruction in response to their reflections.
   • Option B: Have a discussion with students about the meaning of the criteria and standards. Describe how you will use them. Then

distribute several examples of student work that represent different levels of expertise. Have students use the criteria to critique these examples of student work. Have them discuss their evaluations in groups, and then have the groups present their findings to the class. After this class session, have students use the criteria and standards to modify their own assignment—one that they had earlier turned in electronically—as well as write a reflection that illustrates why they made each of the changes and how the criteria informed the changes (or not). Then evaluate both the modified assignment and the reflection so that your students can see how you used the criteria as well as the progress that they made on their own work using the criteria. Document the improvement in the modified assignment and what your students reveal in their reflections. This will inform you about your teaching and your use of criteria and standards as a result of the changes that the students made.

Summary

Do you remember that fourth feature of the scholarship of teaching and learning that Huber and Hutchings (2005) described for us? They called it "going public," and we are ending this chapter by encouraging you to share what you learn about teaching and learning when you engage in the reflective activities of this chapter and when you conduct action research. You may not know this, but there are many faculty members, at your own institution and in higher-education in general, who will be interested in and committed to the same questions and improvements that you have explored throughout this book. Once you offer to share your work—be it a "brown-bag" seminar in your department or on campus, a round-table session at regional and national conferences on higher education, a poster for new faculty or for a series sponsored by your center for teaching and learning, or a paper at your disciplinary meeting—you will be pleasantly surprised by the response you will get from "going public," and you will have the opportunity to make connections with colleagues who are engaged in the scholarship of teaching and learning. Together you can make a difference as you pursue outcomes-based assessment to achieve learner-centered education. We support you.

References

Banta, T. W. (2002). *Building a scholarship of assessment.* San Francisco: Jossey-Bass.

Boyer, E. L. (1990). *Scholarship reconsidered: Priorities of the professoriate.* Princeton, NJ: Carnegie Foundation for the Advancement of Teaching.

Huber, M. T., & Hutchings, P. (2005). *The advancement of learning: Building the teaching commons.* San Francisco: Jossey-Bass.

Shulman, L. S. (1993). Teaching as community property: Putting an end to pedagogical solitude. *Change, 25*(6), 6–7.

FACULTY TEACHING VIGNETTE ONE

Connection, Reflection, and Assessment: Assessing Learning Outcomes in a Multicultural Conflict Resolution Course

David A. Reichard

As a faculty member in the Division of Humanities and Communication (HCOM) at California State University Monterey Bay, I teach courses in history, politics, and law in society. One of my favorite courses is Multicultural Conflict Resolution, which highlights theories and methods of conflict resolution. The curriculum is interdisciplinary, drawing on U.S. and world history, law and society, politics, communication studies, ethics, theater, literature, and film. In addition to readings, hands-on workshops, structured role plays, question-and-answer sessions with visiting experts, and student-directed group projects help students develop concrete skills. Teaching the course was an exciting and complex undertaking.

Multicultural Conflict Resolution meets learning outcomes for "Relational Communication," a requirement for the HCOM major.[1] These outcomes were originally designed to enhance the "development of the knowledge, skills, values, abilities, and understandings that today's graduates would need in order to live meaningful and successful lives in the 21st century," as one faculty member instrumental in developing them recalls (J. Makau, personal communication, May 20, 2003). Specifically, by taking this course, students were expected to develop the knowledge, skills, and abilities described in the following outcomes:

- Identify and describe complex issues or problems requiring a decision-making process.
- Describe the impact of interpersonal, intercultural, small group, and/or institutional communication dynamics on the decision-making process.
- Analyze complex issues or problems from the perspective of the impact of communication dynamics.
- Identify and describe one's own relevant beliefs, attitudes, and values in their sociohistorical context without imposing them onto others.
- Identify and describe other decision-makers' relevant beliefs, attitudes, and values in their sociohistorical context without judging them.
- Use a cooperative deliberation practice to identify, understand, and assess the range of options available.
- Anticipate consequences of each option, carefully considered from the viewpoints of all those affected.
- Employ a win-win ethic in the decision-making process.
- Consider a means of accountability for decision-makers' processes.[2]

Teaching to these outcomes provides a concrete focus for my choice of issues covered, course materials, and hands-on learning experiences. For students, they provide a map indicating what students should expect to work on during the semester and how they are going to do so. Yet, I have struggled over the years as I have taught this course with how to assess student learning. How would I know whether students can describe complex problems, consider how decisions are made, identify their own and other people's values, and anticipate the consequences of decisions? Several semesters of "trial and error" or "experimentation and reflection" led me to an experience that begins to answer my questions. Looking at one semester's experience illustrates.

In fall 2003, I asked students to complete short weekly papers in which they made connections among course readings, class discussions, workshops, and their personal experiences. Students also completed two formal assessment essays—one at midterm and one at the end of the course. These essays directly asked students to provide a road map for whether, how, and why they have met the learning outcomes. I asked students to demonstrate specifically how particular readings, workshops, and other learning experiences shaped their learning progress in achieving the outcomes.

One student's final paper illustrates what I learned from my students. "Donna" structured her paper around each element of the Relational Communication outcomes. She points to specific course materials, discussions, or workshops as evidence of her progress, explaining and evaluating their meaning for her learning. One portion of the paper is especially instructive. She initially points to our stated outcome of describing the impact of interpersonal, intercultural, small-group, and/or institutional communication dynamics on the decision-making process. After highlighting various texts that we read, she specifically credits the play *My Children, My Africa* by Athol Fugard as an especially important example of how her understanding of the outcome deepened. She writes:

> Fugard's show of communication dynamics presents the reader with a challenge to be told and discover[ed] at the same time, how racial conflicts greatly influence the way of life in Africa. In addition to reading, the acting/reading of the scenes were [was] absolutely wonderful to help drive the differing points of view home. I say this because, even though we know the faces of our classmates, it was nice to be able to put ANY kind of face to the characters, and to hear the speech out loud with (mostly) portrayed emotions of the characters. This was a very powerful activity in the realization of the different thinking of different cultures if nothing else.

Here, Donna is engaging in a complex reflection about the content of the course as well as her own learning. She not only uses the text to illustrate progress toward the learning outcome itself, but does so by distinguishing content from process. She reveals how the text itself was useful and how performing scenes out loud became especially meaningful for her understanding. Such close self-reflection is possible for two main reasons, I would argue. First, Donna uses concrete learning outcomes against which to measure her understanding. A play about cross-cultural conflict allowed her to see what the consequences of interpersonal communication dynamics meant in a concrete case. Second, Donna uses her own self-generated raw materials to develop her analysis—her weekly connection papers—to facilitate her ability to pinpoint how and where her learning occurred. "The only real way to hold us accountable and ask us to validate our newfound skills," she notes later in the final assessment paper, "is/was through the weekly connection papers. Our connection papers forced me to think about how I felt and why I felt that certain way. I was required to provide accountability for my thoughts and actions based on what was studied, taught and learned in the context of the class." Thus, while providing students with learning outcomes is essential, we must ask them to look carefully at their progress along the way and to engage in self-assessment. Integrating assessment within the course, providing students with frequent opportunities to make connections, and asking them to provide evidence of their learning allow them to draw linkages between learning outcomes and actual learning. Donna's case nicely illustrates what that might look like for students.

The learning outcomes of our course helped me to structure the connections, reflections, and assessment for the students. In some ways, those outcomes were also outcomes that I needed to meet. As students prepared evidence of meeting the outcomes, I was forced to assess myself and be accountable for the same learning. As I wrote this vignette, the realization of the impact of learning outcomes on my role as teacher was an unintended insight that emerged from my own reflection.

Notes

1. The Human Communication major is interdisciplinary—bridging multiple disciplines in the humanities, communication, and ethics. HCOM 412: Multicultural Conflict Resolution meets major learning outcomes in MLO 3 (Relational Communication) as well as two concentrations: Pre-Law and Practical & Professional Ethics. Students have multiple opportunities to meet these outcomes through various learning experiences. Thus, whereas the content of MLO 3 courses may vary, the learning outcomes do not.

2. Division of Humanities and Communication (2006). Major Learning Outcomes, MLO 3; Relational Communication Skills [On-line]. Available: http://hcom .csumb.edu/site/x4169.xm/

FACULTY TEACHING VIGNETTE TWO

Graphic Organizers Guide Students to Achieve Multiple Learning Outcomes: Constructing Meaning in a Community-Based Watershed Restoration Course

Laura Lee Lienk

S tudents at California State University Monterey Bay (CSUMB) hail from traditionally underserved communities, and more than 30 percent are the first in their families to attend college. Like most students nationwide, students at CSUMB have grown up in a culture that depends equally on visual and auditory transmissions of knowledge and on that of the written word. CSUMB has chosen to bring together the diverse learning styles and experiences of our students, the rich learning opportunities offered by relevant community service, and the dictate of academic excellence by requiring that all courses be outcomes based. Thus, as faculty, we are challenged to create rich learning experiences that meet multiple objectives. I have chosen to employ "graphic organizers" as the threads to help students weave meaning from the multiple learning opportunities in which they participate over the course of a semester.

Introducing the Course

Community-Based Watershed Restoration Service Learning, "ESSP 369S," is an ever-evolving course that I have taught every spring semester since 1995. Through participation in the course, students receive required graduation credits toward upper-division service learning, toward a culture and equity requirement for general education, and toward science major learning outcomes. As such, the course has nine learning outcomes that require students to integrate a myriad of service, classroom, reading, and writing experiences as they address the course's "metaquestion": "How can environmental restoration and community restoration be linked to address issues of social and environmental injustice?" As in all upper-division service learning classes at CSUMB, the course metaquestion necessitates the examination of both disciplinary and service learning themes, in this case linking social change and social justice.

Course Pedagogy

My teaching approach is to offer students a broad array of opportunities to experience, read about, and reflect upon the emerging community-based restoration movement. Besides their required 30 + hours of community service with hands-on community-based restoration and education programs, students experience a semester's worth of activities—over 30 distinct learning activities (readings, field trips, group projects, and reflections)—aimed at addressing the course's metaquestion. The challenge is to empower the students, and indeed myself, to "construct" our own knowledge from the experiences. Together we pull meaning from the activities and co-construct knowledge as described by Resnick (1996). The environmental science student emerges with a greatly expanded view of the roles of scientists as agents of social change, while for me the intense student/teacher dialogue engendered each semester fosters continual rethinking and enriching of the course. As such, the course has evolved from a traditional teacher-centered course to an entirely student-centered learning community offered as a guided seminar.

The course/seminar is held together by *graphic organizers*. These "help the students organize their thinking, organize new information, and organize connections between previously learned ideas and new ones being taught. . . . Graphic Organizers are visual representations of information, concepts, relationship or processes" (Freiberg & Driscoll, 2006). These organizers allow students with varying learning styles to visualize, connect, and synthesize the many diverse and yet relevant parts of the class. Even though the graphic organizers that I present and the course outcomes are the same for each student, how each student assembles or constructs his or her learning is entirely student specific.

Learning Outcomes Paired with Graphic Organizers

For the purpose of this vignette, two of the course's learning outcomes are paired with graphic organizers designed to help students assemble information and ideas to meet those outcomes. Ultimately, a "supersized" final essay graphic organizer incorporates insights from the first two graphic organizer examples. Now, let's take a look at these organizers.

Section I. CSUMB Culture and Equity ULR—Learning Outcomes: "Students analyze historical and contemporary cross-cultural scenarios of discrimination, inequity, and social injustice in the United States and other societies."[1] This outcome asks students to rethink previously learned U.S. history in light of social justice issues. In this course we use two texts: *Natives and Strangers: A Multicultural Story of Americans* (Dinnerstein, Nichols, & Reimers, 2003) and *The Japanese in the Monterey Bay* (Lydon, 1997). The former is designed to give a broad cultural overview of U.S. history, the latter to present a more local and watershed-based picture of immigration, cultural shifting, and citizen relationships to the environment using the experiences of one ethnic group (the Japanese) as the example. Field trips, invited speakers, and classroom discussions are scheduled to parallel the readings. It has been extremely challenging to get the students to read the texts, so I have had great success using the following graphic organizer to encourage students to synthesize, or pull together, the various experiences and to have new and frequently individual meaning for themselves.

> Graphic Organizer #1. "Timeline." One week before the Timeline is to be constructed, the class is divided into groups of 5–6 students per group. Each member of the group is assigned 2–3 chapters from each of the two texts for which they are to become the team expert. As individuals, they are instructed to carefully build a chronological outline of their assigned chapters.
>
> Constructing group Timelines in class: I have allotted two class periods for this activity. Each group is given a 15-foot roll of construction paper and markers. Immediately the physical space of the classroom becomes rearranged! The simple assignment is that each group is to construct one chronological timeline of the cultural history of the US using the information from the two texts—the national level from Dinnerstein and the local from Lydon. I have chosen to have this assignment done in class because of the rich interplay that takes place between group members and across

groups as these science students realize how little they know of the cultural history of our nation and region. As the work progresses, students are instructed to add elements of their own family history onto the Timeline. (Note: personal/family cultural vignettes are shared earlier in the semester.) They also add perspectives from their community service site garnered from interviews with and shadowing of their community partners. Also added to the Timelines are references from other assigned readings in the class. Each group's Timeline is different—and they can start to become "messy"—which is good. Each group is then instructed to find "hotspots" of social and environmental injustice on their Timeline. It is the reporting out between groups of these "hotspots" that really empowers the students to develop individual insights and achieve the outcomes in different ways. Students can be seen pulling out their "Gem Cards" (see below) as they hear others from the class putting stories from their service placements and from their own families into both national and regional contexts. Thus, students create or synthesize for themselves a pattern or structure not clearly seen before. Complex learning is the result (Bloom, Engelhart, Furst, Hill, & Krathwohl, 1956).

Student Scott Norris reflects on the timeline experience and the visit of a member of the Japanese American community to class. "My biggest 'Aha!' with respect to culture and identity was during Larry Oda's talk. Larry mentioned that as the Japanese came to America they created their own culture. This complemented our timeline representation showing the immigrants becoming their own subset of people, partially Japanese, partially American. As they remained in America they created their own cultural identity, and became a unique group. Separated from the Japanese mainland and segregated by the American public, old traditions and new practices merged to create an identity that was not Japanese or American. This process is not unique to Japanese Americans but takes place in each of us. This hybridization portrays culture as an infinite conglomeration of micro and macro institutions that combine to create one's distinctive cultural and personal identity. "[2]

When I viewed the timeline that was created in class, it was clear that factors including the desire and/or need for cheap labor was a major pull factor for immigrants to come to the United States throughout the history of the nation. Labor is still a huge pull for immigrants both legal and illegal to come to the United States. I have heard it be said that you can tell a lot about a society by the way it treats its children I think this also can apply to the way a society treats its poorest, weakest members.[3]

Section II. A Course Specific Service Learning Outcome: "Students will be able to articulate how community based habitat restoration projects address, or don't address, issues of social and environmental injustice. Students will examine the nexus between the social problem and local environmental work" (ESSP 369S, Spring 2005).

This learning outcome, which closely parallels the course's metaquestion, is addressed by many aspects of the course and, as such, challenges students to capture the course "gems" as they synthesize their own meaning.

> Graphic Organizer #2: "Gem Cards". On the first day of class, each student is given a starter set of about 25 pieces (5.5" x 4" size or index card size) of neon bright colored paper—their own supply of "Gem" Cards. They are instructed to keep these cards tucked in their class journal, to bring them to class with them every day, and to keep them nearby when they are completing reading assignments outside of class. On the cards they are to record (and annotate the source) "gems" from the class. The gems can be poignant quotes from discussions with other classmates, particularly profound concepts from a journal reading, and most importantly vignettes and quotes from their community service placements. They also copy each of their personal gems into their own personal class journals where they form the basis of weekly written reflections.

Each day in class, gem cards are brought out and are the basis of guided class discussions in which the cards serve as notes for the students to lead them into sharing their ideas. Then, the colorful gem cards are collected and placed in the "gem bag," held by me, the instructor. There, the gem cards accumulate until the end of the class, when the final course-assessing paper assigned. The following are anonymous student gem cards:

> *The reason why the environmental injustice and social injustice exist is people have lost connection to each other. Everyone eats food that farm workers produce but many do not know and care about who grows and harvests the food. I was one of the people who did not care who produces my food, but the community service showed me a part of farm workers life and their families. It helped me make a connection between myself and my food. I now would be very happy to pay an extra 50 cents to improve farm workers health care. I now feel somewhat responsible as an adult for providing kids with adequate education and a safe childhood.* (Anonymous student, 2006)

Restoration allows us to work on the solution to the issue instead of giving us guilt about the environmental problems we are causing. . . . I have a responsibility and a need to give back to my community, to repay the privileges I have been afforded. . . . Through my service I validate the privileges I have been given, I recognize and embrace them. I do not feel guilty for what I have been blessed with because I use them to strengthen those around me and create the same opportunities for others. (Anonymous student, 2006)

Connecting people of all ages with their environment is the best way to increase the preservation of our environment. (Anonymous student, 2006)

Section III. Synthesizing the Learning Outcomes—A Final Organizer. A heavily weighted final paper is the assessment for this logistically challenging yet rich course in which students engage in community-based environmental and watershed service, community members come to class, the class visits with schoolchildren at diverse places such as restoration planting sites and a newly emerging community/homeless garden, in-class book clubs discuss readings, weekly reflective journals provide a personal dialogue between the instructor and the students, 15-foot Timelines are constructed, colorful gem cards capture shining moments, and each student's constructed learning is unique. The paper, introduced by another graphic organizer, assesses the course metaquestion: "How can environmental restoration and community restoration be linked to address issues of social and environmental injustice?" The paper also enables students to demonstrate the many course outcomes.

Graphic Organizer #3: The Watershed Graphic. Four weeks prior to the end of the semester, students are assigned their final course essay, a 15–20 page paper where they are challenged to construct their own learning around the course's meta-question and the many outcomes. For this synthetic assignment, I help the students assemble the pieces of the course using both a "super sized" graphic organizer in the form of a Watershed sketch, and the graphic organizers previously mentioned:

A. The Watershed Graphic Organizer: I distribute to each student a large sketch of a watershed—with three mountains each representing and labeled with the course's service learning, the culture and equity, and the science themes with the individual outcomes represented on three streams each flowing from a different mountain—and converging into a "bay of understanding" representing the meta-question. This graphic organizer can be either on paper or digitally with an idea organization program such as Adobe Inspiration. (See Figure 1).

B. The Gem Bag, now bulging with course gems is brought out and all the gems are shuffled and placed face down on a table. Students then randomly and equally draw all the gem cards until they are all distributed. Students can trade or copy each other's gems. Each student thus receives a sampling of quotes and ideas compiled by various class members which will enrich his/her own thinking and writing.

C. Then, looking at the outcomes listed on the Watershed Graphic Organizer the students sort the Gems according to the outcomes to which they relate. Students note on the Watershed Graphic how each gem supports a particular outcome. Students do the same with each of the class activities, as well as, vignettes and insights from their service experiences. The Watershed Graphic becomes a pictorial outline for the final essay.

D. For the next two weeks students work on drafts of their essays, using the graphic organizers covered in this article, the Watershed organizer, the Gems organizer, the Timeline organizer, and their own personal journals to coalesce their ideas. At the end of this second week students bring printed drafts to class where in pairs they review, critique and borrow from each other's papers.

E. Two weeks later I receive their final papers. Each paper is unique, each is rich, and each represents how that particular student assembled his/her own thinking to address the meta-question of the class. For example one student wrote:

"Consumer based culture continues to distance peoples from the traditions and actions that preserve their way of life and cultural identities. The act (or art) of service and restoration embraces these differences. It respects that which makes us unique and unlike. Service and restoration capitalize on the special abilities and talents of diverse populations to create a better world for everyone. Service and restoration seek to preserve diversity in order to generate an equitable and sustainable environment for all."[4]

In reality, with this organizer, I find that they are chronicling their personal social and environmental justice history, while charting their own route toward being more socially responsible and engaged scientists and citizens. Here is one student's response to this organizer:

"This class has become an examination of how I view life and others around me. I have learned that there is no one culture that any person belongs to, but

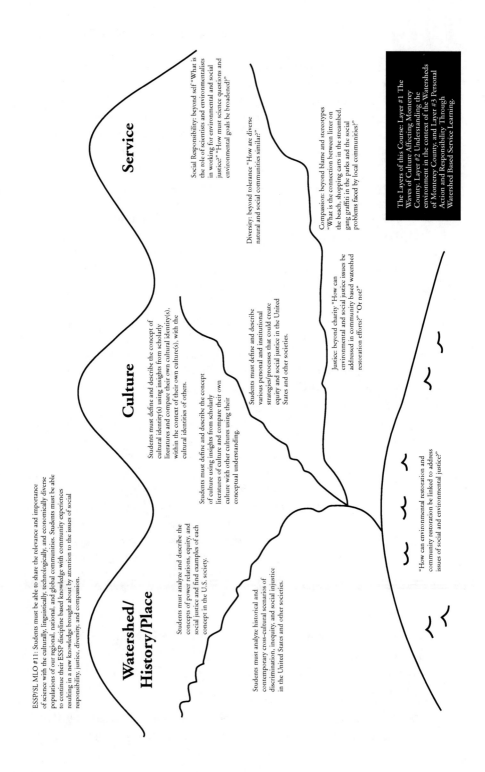

ESSP/SL MLO #11: Students must be able to share the relevance and importance of science with the culturally, linguistically, technologically, and economically diverse populations of our regional, national, and global communities. Students must be able to continue their ESSP discipline based knowledge with community experiences resulting in a new knowledge brought about by attention to the issues of social responsibility, justice, diversity, and compassion.

Watershed/ History/Place

Students must analyze and describe the concepts of power relations, equity, and social justice and find examples of each concept in the U.S. society.

Students must analyze historical and contemporary cross-cultural scenarios of discrimination, inequity, and social injustice in the United States and other societies.

Culture

Students must define and describe the concept of cultural identity(s) using insights from scholarly literatures and compare their own cultural identity(s), within the context of their own culture(s), with the cultural identities of others.

Students must define and describe the concept of culture using insights from scholarly literatures of culture and compare their own culture with other cultures using their conceptual understanding.

Students must define and describe various personal and institutional strategies/processes that could create equity and social justice in the United States and other societies.

Service

Social Responsibility: beyond self "What is the role of scientists and environmentalists in working for environmental and social justice?" "How must science questions and environmental goals be broadened?"

Diversity: beyond tolerance "How are diverse natural and social communities similar?"

Compassion: beyond blame and stereotypes "What is the connection between litter on the beach, shopping carts in the streambed, gang graffiti in the parks and the social problems faced by local communities?"

Justice: beyond charity "How can environmental and social justice issues be addressed in community based watershed restoration efforts?" "Or not?"

"How can environmental restoration and community restoration be linked to address issues of social and environmental justice?"

The Layers of this Course: Layer #1 The Waves of Culture Affecting Monterey County, Layer #2 Understanding the environment in the context of the Watersheds of Monterey County, and Layer #3 Personal Action and Responsibility Through Watershed Based Service Learning;

a web of cultures that each individual weaves throughout their life. . . . I came into this class thinking that I would be serving my community from which I take so much. But I have learned over the semester that this class was about affecting the way in which I view service, about impassioning me to be the change in which we seek to see. . . . Restoration allows us to work on the solution to the issue instead of giving us guilt about the environmental problems we are causing."[5]

Summary

I believe that the use of graphic organizers caters to the diverse learning styles of my students. Each of my three graphic organizers goes beyond their visual pedagogy in supporting student learning. The first organizer uses physical and social learning, an integration of student lives with historical texts, and a concrete production of connected learning. The second organizer empowers and honors students as individual sources of insights and uses social learning in the process. The third organizer accesses both verbal and written learning with symbols, graphic representation, and words. It provides a true synthesizing experience in a collaborative context. In chapter 4 of this book, the authors describe the importance of designing evidence of student learning that provides opportunities for diverse learning styles and multiple intelligences to emerge. The diversity of my graphic organizers matched to the course's learning outcomes supports success for all students in my course.

References

Bloom, B., Engelhart, M., Furst, E., Hill, W., & Krathwohl, D. (1956). *Taxonomy of educational objectives: The classification of educational goals Handbook I, Cognitive domain.* New York: McKay.

Dinnerstein, L., Nichols, R., & Reimers, D. (2003). *Natives and strangers: A multicultural story of Americans,* 4th ed. New York: Oxford University Press.

Freiberg, J., & Driscoll, A. (2006). *Universal teaching strategies.* Boston: Allyn & Bacon.

Lydon, S. (1997). *The Japanese in the Monterey Bay.* Capitola, CA: Capitola Bay Press.

Resnick, M. (1996). Distributed constructionism. In *The proceedings of the international conference on learning sciences.* Association for the Advancement of Computing in Education, Northwestern University, Chicago.

Notes

1. See the CSUMB Web site at http://csumb.edu/site/x4357.xml.

2. Norris, S. (2005). Used with permission from Final Paper in ESSP 369S course, Spring 2005.

3. Phipps-Craig, D. (2006). Used with permission from Gem Cards in CSUMB ESSP 369S course, Spring 2006.

4. Norris, S. (2005). Used with permission from Final Paper in ESSP 369S course, Spring 2005.

5. Cowan, R. (2005). Used with permission from Final Paper in ESSP 369S course, Spring 2005.

FACULTY TEACHING VIGNETTE THREE

First Year Seminar: Orienting Students to Outcomes-Based Education

Natasha Oehlman

T he First Year Seminar Program supports students' transition to university life and preparation for academic success. It engages students as learners, citizens, and community members in the context of multiculturalism, academic rigor, critical thinking, and college-level reading and writing. As the program introduces students to California State University Monterey Bay's (CSUMB's) core values, the pedagogy inspires and guides the development of intellectual and diverse communities for student engagement and commitment.

Introduction

Students are introduced to outcomes-based learning the minute they step foot on to the CSUMB campus. The first course that all new freshmen take, aptly titled First-Year Seminar 100 (FYS 100), begins to familiarize first-year students with outcomes-based learning; with thinking, being, and responding on a college campus; and with what it means to be an educated person.

The first-year program is not new to many colleges and universities; well-established, flourishing programs aimed at acquainting students to university life are often already in place. Our campus is unique, with its university vision statement and mission, and outcomes-based learning. The major focus of cultural diversity prompts the recruitment of and invitation to students from underrepresented groups to attend the university. Thus, our campus finds it especially necessary for students entering the university structure to become aware of how the higher-education academy has its own discourse community and what is involved in becoming a CSUMB student.

In working with outcomes-based education (OBE), I have realized that students can best be supported to achieve learning outcomes with active and tactile hands-on learning approaches. Here, I reflect on a series of such learning activities to engage students in learning around our set of outcomes. What follows is a description of activities created to meet the course outcomes, as well as student feedback around certain activities. Ultimately, I illustrate that using an outcomes-based teaching approach demands an orientation to outcomes and the OBE approach to help students be successful in such an educational environment.

My Teaching Philosophy and Approach

As much as possible, I encourage students to become active learners. I try to design activities that involve collaboration, group or pair sharing—all within the framework of encouraging inquiry toward student learning. I want to see students grapple with concepts and share ideas in the class. I want them to each take a certain amount of ownership of the class, and I find that this works best when I act as facilitator of the course, helping students make connections and learn together, rather than dictating to them what they need to learn.

About the Course

Twenty-two students from diverse backgrounds typically meet for the first time in my four-unit academic course. The course, as created, is divided into three major sections: Orientation to the Academic Community, Exploring Fields of Study, and Diversity and Community. For the purposes of this vignette, I focus on the outcomes of the orientation section. A look at the entire orientation section will put that outcome in context for understanding my approaches.

Section One: Orientation to the Academic Community

1. **Exploring our identities as new members of an academic community— Learning Outcomes:**
   a) Students explain the concept of academic community and compare it to other communities
   b) Students use CSUMB's Vision and core values to define what is unique about the CSUMB academic community
   c) Students identify the type of classroom activities, experiences, and environments that best supports their learning, development, and participation in an academic community
   d) Students explain their roles and responsibilities as students in an academic community

2. **Understanding and articulating outcomes-based education—Learning Outcome:**
   a) Students explain outcomes-based education and describe how outcomes support their learning.

Part I of the Course

Community and Outcomes-Based Learning

Curriculum Focus
- Exploring our identities as new members of an academic community—Learning Outcomes a.–d.
- Understanding and articulating Outcomes-Based Education— Learning Outcome a.

Community

Community is really the crux of my first-year seminar program. To help new students to begin feeling like part of the academic community, I engage students in ways that begin to invite new students to envision themselves as members of this new and specific community.

For the first couple weeks of the semester, I plan several different types of community-building activities to allow students to meet and get to know one another and work toward building a classroom community, within the larger framework of the campus academic community. For example, on the first day of class I ask students to engage in an interactive activity called Trading Places (Silberman, 1999). This activity asks students to trade and exchange notes based on new ideas, values, opinions, or solutions to problems written on different-colored Post-its. Students trade their own values and opinions, experiences or ideas with other students who wish to possess or learn about that particular trade. This activity has been quite successful in encouraging students to engage with their classmates and form the foundation of a classroom community. During this activity, students begin to develop bonds and learn from one another. Out of this 20-minute activity comes a discussion around community and its place in the academy. Specifically I ask: What defines community? Why place any value or importance on community? We also explore their different communities and how membership in each is defined.

With the students I have worked with in the past, the first set of outcomes (I. a.–d.) had the potential to be both informative and enlightening as they began to survey their place in the academic community. Several core assignments to meet this outcome throughout the semester include reading, thinking, discussing, and writing about the university vision statement followed by class discussion on the value of the words, and examining case studies of college students, specifically ethical dilemmas that most college students might face. The final, three-part collaborative project, called Campus Life: In Search of Community, is one in which students work in pairs to investigate campus resources that make up the community; interview current students around their views on campus community and areas of importance in the CSUMB community; and, finally, observe one place on campus and report back to the class about how this place can foster the CSUMB community.

In my experience, students find the college student case studies relevant and meaningful, and they generally get involved in learning problem-solving strategies and analyzing the ethics that surround the different decisions being made. During the semester, we explore topics such as academic integrity, grading, cheating, tolerance, diversity, hate speech, loyalty, friendship, community, drinking, and religion. All of these topics are contextualized in the framework of understanding and living in a community. Students also enjoy activities that get them out of the classroom and exploring their new college campus. The campus life project resonates with them because they are able to experience firsthand the various resources on campus and places to go that make up and contribute to their community.

At the quarter-semester evaluation, I ask all students to fill out an anonymous minicourse evaluation that will help me gauge how they are feeling about the course. I inquire about certain outcomes that we have covered and ask for their specific understanding, probe what activities have helped them understand the outcomes, and explore future concepts that they may look forward to studying. From the discussions around community specifically connected to the first learning outcome, students have made these comments:

> "My new community doesn't involve my parents, so I have to be extra aware of my behavior and know that I have to motivate myself to come to class and be part of this community."
>
> "I do not see much of a community at all outside of class. My identity in this community has not yet been defined. I understand that when moving onto a college campus it should be like joining an academic community, but I have yet to feel that way."
>
> "I am getting more out of my classes because I'm a lot more engaged as a member of the community, and recognizing what I can contribute to this community."
>
> "Everyone here plays an essential role in our academic community."
>
> "I have discovered my identity as a new member of this academic community through teachers, and classes and my acceptance in them. I feel that I am an active member in this academic community because I participate and learn in class."

Students also spoke to specific activities that helped them understand the first learning outcome:

- Reviewing the case studies about academic dishonesty and engaging in discussions about academic community
- Presenting and researching the campus life project and the different resources and places to go on campus
- Participating in class discussions
- Becoming involved in different events

Outcomes-Based Education

In my experience, one of the most difficult concepts for new students to understand is OBE. Once freshman are introduced to this assessment approach, they struggle to comprehend outcomes, but eventually they do get it. FYS 100 aims at introducing freshmen to the OBE concept using a variety of activities for students to begin to understand the campus's outcomes-based approach.

For one such activity that I use (a modified activity from FYS 100 training with Amy Driscoll), I ask students to write down their goals as part of a journal entry. Then I ask them to think about the word *outcome* as a single term and how this term applies to the FYS 100 course. Having explored the term, they come to the next class with a definition to share. Students form five small groups and discuss and collect their definitions on large pieces of butcher paper. Each group presents its small-group discussion on the term *outcome* to the whole class, and I take notes on a white board to gather the students' ideas into one large, collective definition. I appreciate activities such as this one because it works directly from the students' prior knowledge and ideas. After the small group discussion, and all the definitions are on the board, we then turn to a larger discussion around outcomes and I fill in any missing pieces—or include ideas that I want them to think about.

For the next part of this activity, I ask students to remain in their small groups and to take out the course syllabus, if they haven't already done so. I assign each of the five groups to one of the outcomes. In their small groups, the students are to

- Read and comprehend the outcome to the best of their ability.
- Summarize the outcome and its specific parts in their own words.
- Discuss the outcome's importance and relevance to them as university students. In other words, why is the outcome valuable, or not?
- Ask questions about the outcome, particularly if a word or concept is unclear or difficult to comprehend.
- Tell the group what parts of the outcome sound intriguing and/or exciting.

The groups then explain their outcome to the entire class, highlighting their questions and related parts of the course. The groups often rewrite the outcome. I instruct the students listening to each group presentation to take notes on the outcome and to record any new rewritten version of the outcome, because their notes will help with a future homework assignment. Later, I ask them to write a journal entry about what they learned about OBE and what they think each outcome means to them—in addition to what parts are confusing and what parts they find exciting. Finally, I ask them to consider how this new information about the course outcomes fits with their course goals previously written for a journal entry.

Once the groups have presented, I ask each individual student in the groups to go back to the outcomes and using two different colored highlighters to mark in one color anything that sounds confusing, difficult, or unclear, and in the other color, anything that sounds exciting or a concept that they look forward to learning about; these notes will be the start of their journal entry for homework. As an instructor, I walk around and help facilitate the students' progress.

I find this activity to be extremely stimulating and an excellent way for students to try to unpack the OBE terminology and understand the course outcomes within the larger context of OBE. I enjoy watching students decode and deconstruct academic language together as they grapple with terminology and bring their prior knowledge to the activity. They are intensely engaged as they try to figure out what the terms mean and how these terms when put together will help them achieve the course goals and outcomes. Students are active and learning together, from one another, and this type of synergy not only fosters increased community building, but also creates a learner-centered environment where students know and feel that their ideas are valued and respected.

These activities engage students in actual outcomes as well as promote increased understanding and ownership of the outcomes. Later, in reflection papers, I ask students to identify which class activities or resources helped them achieve the outcomes. From there, the course turns to topics that appear to be much more interesting to students: exploring major programs of study, analyzing social and cultural identities, and forming a concept of what it means to be an educated person. As students reflect on their learning at the end of the course, the outcome language appears again when they struggle to describe an educated person, as illustrated by this student's comment: "When I wrote about what it means to be an educated person, I began to understand what outcomes were about, and I could explain myself pretty well." By the end of the course, students have integrated the OBE concept and understandings into their learning plans, their review of major programs of study (which all articulate learning outcomes), and their own approaches to their education.

Reflection from Teaching First-Year Students

I cannot imagine expecting our students to be successful in our OBE environment without a meaningful orientation to the approach. The meaning of outcomes alone is essential to their pursuit of learning within the CSUMB curricular context. Once they understand the meaning and purpose of outcomes, many of the students are able to apply them to their studies. In a short time, our students expect the clarity of intentions that they gain from outcomes and are articulate about those expectations. As faculty, we have a responsibility to ensure that OBE will be provided consistently and in meaningful approaches.

Reference

Silberman, M. (1999). *Active learning: 101 strategies.* Upper Saddle River, NJ: Pearson Education.

COMMENCEMENT SPEECH

Megan Jager

Good morning parents, family, friends, administrators, faculty, staff, and my fellow CSUMB graduates . . . WE DID IT!

It is with great pleasure that I have the opportunity to speak on behalf of the CSUMB graduating class of 2004. Although I gladly accepted this opportunity, I found myself wondering what profound statement I could make for all of us here today and what lasting remarks I could leave with my fellow graduates as we enter the world.

I realized after reflecting on my experiences here at CSUMB that I do not have one profound statement to make, but rather, to acknowledge that the experience and learning provided here at this educational institution is inspiring within itself and will continue into the future.

When I first arrived on this campus four years ago, like many of you, my classmates, I questioned the unique paradoxes of this institution. I was going to get a degree but it was going to be "outcomes based." What the heck is that? Not only was ice plant spread all across the campus and the school mascot, an otter of all things, but my professors explained in their syllabi and in classes that we had to meet outcomes in order to pass our courses. All over campus, the phrase "outcomes-based education" could be heard, and I was completely unsure of what that meant and how it would affect *my outcome* to receive a degree.

My parents kept asking "and what kind of *job* does an outcomes-based education get you?" All I knew at that time was that I wanted to get a degree and it did not matter to me how I learned the information to obtain that goal.

Now, as I stand here today, I realize we are some of the luckiest students in the country because we attended and are receiving a degree from an outcomes-based institution where true learning is at the forefront of this University's goals. This extraordinary learning environment, CSUMB, is one of the most unique educational institutions in the country because our learning is not measured through a single test or exam, but rather through the insights and critical analysis that we demonstrated through verbal presentations, written work, collaborative projects, reflections, and service learning experiences. We all leave this learning arena prepared to go into a world as citizens who value the setting and achievement of outcomes within our careers and our personal lives, and with a commitment to serve our community and the world at large. We are entering an international community, where it is imperative to serve our fellow men and women and strive for a peaceful world.

High aspirations indeed, but I believe CSUMB, this university of the future, has helped us attain that lofty goal. We, the graduating class, have already seen what our small efforts can do through service learning and activism in our small community.

I am proud to come from a University that took action, where the outcome was the development of the Proclamation naming CSUMB *a hate free zone.*

I am proud to be a part of a university that puts resources into the outcomes of acknowledging and *celebrating* cultural, gender and political differences every day!

These are but a few outcomes that we have achieved through our learning and they far surpass the outcome of obtaining just a degree.

Just think what outcomes we can create in the real world.

You see, four years ago, I figured the outcome of going to a four-year college would be a degree and as my parents hoped, some gainful employment!

But, we leave with much more. We leave here as products of a brilliantly crafted Vision statement that is not just words, but a daily, living document of the CSUMB culture. It is a document that has been translated into learning outcomes for our education.

We will live up to this Vision statement by continuing to do what CSUMB has taught us during our travels down its educational paths. We have learned to be question askers, to question information, to question our own belief systems, and when we think we have discovered an answer, to question even more in order to work towards social change and be the productive citizens that our Vision statement has intended us to become. Our Capstone journeys are evidence of the questioning that we have all experienced. During the past week of Capstone demonstrations and presentations, Human Communication graduates have questioned the ways we teach high school students about the power of language through critical literacy and how to be aware of persuasive language in the media, about stereotypes associated with females and tattoos, and the ideas of cultural citizenship and redemption in the Rastafarian culture. Questioning continued as a Teledramatic Arts student with his documentary posed questions about the use of police dogs in the field. Earth Systems and Science Policy students continued the campus-wide inquiry with questions about cancer and clinical trials. Our University enabled and supported us to design and produce Capstones in which we raised and responded to expert questions about issues important for us. We had the opportunity to become knowledgeable researchers on issues with potential for social change. Our Capstones were the culmination of the questioning that we have been trained to do. Now we must take those skills of questioning issues and addressing controversies and the inclination to do so into our lives and become and remain active citizens.

And we will!

Indeed these are impressive outcomes. And as we gaze to the future, we stand high on the shoulders of those who brought us to this day. The pedagogy of outcomes-based education could not occur without the commitment of the faculty on this campus. The professors at this University are the most dedicated, supportive and inspiring group of educators. They have spent hours teaching and challenging us to become critical thinkers, while being of great support and carefully guiding our journey. Every single one of us has a handful of professors from this campus that have not only challenged us to become lifelong learners, but have acted as mentors and inspired us to reach our goals. Four years ago, I thought a professor was simply a person who would put knowledge into my brain, but I was wrong. Here at CSUMB, our

professors have helped us work on our run-on sentences and solve the difficult math equations, but they have truly challenged us to find our own
knowledge through collaboration and analysis of our individual roles in society. While this is a day of great achievement for we graduates, it is also a day
of great achievement for our faculty members, for we now represent their
vision and their dreams. We shall not disappoint them!

At this time, I ask that we show our appreciation for all of their work and
for enabling us to reach our goals and find our own outcomes. You, the faculty, are amazing people and will leave lasting impressions on all of us as we
continue into our futures.

Finally, to the graduates of CSUMB. While graduation today is a great ac-
complishment for all of us, it is also a commencement day, a day to begin
and accept a new challenge. Throughout my four years of study at this educational institution, I have realized the impact of education and the importance of becoming active in my community. CSUMB has instilled in all of
us the inclination and desire to forever be lifelong learners and to dedicate
our lives to facilitating positive change within our communities. I leave you
with a challenge today.

Your challenge is to follow the vision and goals of CSUMB's outcomes-based
education by using your degrees to create change for the benefit of all people
in our society. CSUMB has instilled within us the idea that it is not simply
enough to have a degree, but rather that the choices we make as we use our
degrees will be the true outcome.

Those aspiring to be teachers can use your degrees to obtain your teaching
position, but the real outcome lies with how you create change and improve
the educational system.

Those on their way into the medical field may use your degrees to work in
hospitals to help others remain healthy, but the real outcome is how you use
your degree to work toward health opportunities and equality for all people
in need of medical attention, thus fulfilling a much desired outcome for all.

Those of you aspiring to be writers or published authors may use your degree
as an entry to publication, but the challenge is *to speak truths and break si-
lences* in your writing to obtain a true beneficial outcome for our world.

CSUMB has taught us that education is not just about a degree or even about achieving learning outcomes, but rather about how we use our learning to create change within communities as the real outcomes. I challenge you all to accept your degrees with pride and as evidence of the hours and years of hard work you committed in order to be here today. I also challenge you to accept your degrees with the acknowledgement that another significant challenge awaits us.

The world needs enthusiastic, civic-minded individuals. It needs controversy, creativity and collaboration to address our troubled times. The world needs people who are knowledgeable and skilled in achieving positive OUT-COMES. The world needs us!

Congratulations to you all for all your hard work and accomplishments. Remember that today signifies not only a graduation, but more importantly our commencement into a world that awaits eager people willing to create beneficial outcomes for all. It is now our responsibility and I know I speak for all of you when I say that we accept that responsibility, and WE ARE READY!

Good luck to all of you and once again, congratulations to the 2004 graduating class of California State University, Monterey Bay!

ASSESSMENT WEB SITE RESOURCE LIST

American Council on Education
www.acenet.edu

American Library Association
www.ala.org/ala/acrl/acrlstandards/standardsguidelines.htm
www.ala.org/ala/acrl/acrlstandards/informationliteracycompetency.htm

Arizona Western College
www.azwestern.edu/assessment

Association of American Colleges and Universities (Greater Expectations
    National Panel)
http://greaterexpectations.org

Bowling Green State University
www.bgsu.edu/offices/assessment

California State University, Bakersfield
www.csub.edu/AssessmentCenter

California State University Monterey Bay
http://csumb.edu

Council of Writing Program Administrators
www.wpacouncil.org/positions/outcomes.html

Eastern New Mexico University
www.enmu.edu/academics/excellence/assessment/index.shtml

Indiana University–Purdue University Indianapolis
www.eport.iu.edu/about_the_project_frameset.htm

Johnson County Community College
www.jccc.net/home/depts/S00015/site

Mesa Community College
www.mc.maricopa.edu/about/orp/assessment

Portland State University
http://portfolio.pdx.edu/Portfolio/Institutional_Effectiveness/Assessment_
    Student_Learning

Rose-Hulman Institute of Technology
www.rose-hulman.edu/IRPA/assessment/index.html

Washington State University
www.wsu.edu/gened/curric-outcomes/goalsoutcomes-index.html

Alignment A process of connecting significant elements of a program or course—originating from mission and goals; translated into learning outcomes, pedagogy, and curriculum; and ensured through assessment—with the ultimate intent of maximizing learning.

Assessment A process of gathering information or data or evidence of learning. The process begins with the articulation of learning outcomes in order to determine what kind of evidence to gather.

Criteria The qualities that faculty expect in student work to demonstrate achievement of a learning outcome. Those qualities enhance faculty decisions about whether students have met the outcomes.

Curriculum The content of what is taught to learners—it provides context for the pedagogy, describes the information or concepts to be understood and used by learners, and sequences and connects the content in ways that support learning.

Evaluation A process of making decisions or judgments based on assessment information. Judgments may focus on determination of whether learning has occurred, and decisions may focus on how to support and improve learning.

Goals Broad and long-term descriptions of learning expectations.

Learning outcomes Specific descriptions of expectations that contain the behaviors and skills, knowledge and understandings, and attitudes and appreciations that learners can demonstrate when they complete a course, program, or baccalaureate degree.

Pedagogy Encompasses the broad range of teaching and learning activities that are directed to student learning in courses and programs.

Rubrics Scoring guides containing subtasks or components of a work assignment along with criteria used to guide and evaluate student work. Ideally, rubrics also contain standards for rating how well the criteria are met.

Standards Descriptions of levels of achievement related to the criteria expected in student work. Standards describe and define the criteria and are helpful to both faculty and learners.

ANNOTATED BIBLIOGRAPHY

Although the references that follow are not necessarily the most recent publications on assessment, they represent the resources from which we learned and developed our thinking and practices for assessing student learning.

Allen, M. J. (2004). *Assessing academic programs in higher education*. Bolton, MA: Anker.

After years of leading assessment workshops that guided thousands of faculty, staff, and administrators, Mary Allen integrated the interactions and insights of those workshops with her "handbook of materials" into a helpful and pragmatic book. Allen takes her readers through all of the steps of the assessment process, provides a wide range of strategies, and makes meaningful connections among assessment and teaching and learning. The book's guidance is threaded with illustrative examples and cases and communicates in user-friendly language. The assessment glossary at the end is a rich resource for assessment work.

Banta, T. W., & Associates. (2002). *Building a scholarship of assessment*. San Francisco: Jossey-Bass.

In this book, Trudy Banta is joined by leading experts in the field of assessment—Angelo, Mentkowski, Kuh, Ewell, Palomba, and others—to describe the developments in assessment leading to our current state of practice. She introduces the concept of scholarship as a central theme of the book to communicate the strength of the assessment movement and its potential, and to encourage faculty, staff, and administrators to pursue assessment as a scholarly practice. She urges those who are engaged in assessment to do so as an inquiry process, as a field of study, with the end result being scholarly assessment. This book represents the hope of many in higher education that significant faculty work such as teaching and assessment will be recognized, honored, and rewarded as scholarship.

Huba, M. E., & Freed, J. E. (2000). *Learner-centered assessment on college campuses: Shifting the focus from teaching to learning*. Boston: Allyn & Bacon.

The authors stay consistently learner centered throughout their very practical guidebook to assessment. The approaches of the book are grounded in the principles of constructivist theory and are aimed at moving faculty from the teacher-centered paradigm to the learner-centered paradigm, a shift that higher education is currently embracing. The assessment approaches of this book are connected to the hallmarks of high-quality undergraduate education, principles of good practice in assessment, and best practices in teaching and learning. The book's impact goes beyond assessment to supportive relationships with students, course planning, and designing of pedagogy. The chapters on critical thinking and problem solving are rich resources for any institution. This is an introductory text for individual faculty as well as a resource for institutional change.

Maki, P. L. (2004). *Assessing for learning: Building a sustainable commitment across the institution.* Sterling, VA: Stylus.

The title of this book describes well the author's intention of providing a framework, processes, strategies, and structures that "build sustainable commitment across the institution" for assessment of learning. Maki describes assessment as "a systematic and systemic process of inquiry" and takes her readers through such a process, chapter by chapter. The book is a comprehensive guide for faculty, staff, and administrators. In addition to the "nested sets of decisions, tasks, and interdependent kinds of discourse" that progress from an overview to a commitment, there are institutional examples, and meta-sites for larger sets of resources, worksheets, guides, and exercises.

Suskie, L. (2004). *Assessing student learning: A common sense guide.* Bolton, MA: Anker.

As a "common sense guide," this book is replete with practical advice grounded in current thinking and practices of assessment. The strength of this book is Suskie's in-depth descriptions of a wide range of tools for assessing student learning. She follows that information with guidance for summarizing, analyzing, and communicating assessment results and using them effectively and appropriately, something that is often neglected or done poorly. The organization and language of this book are enhanced by the emphasis on student learning embedded in examples, questions, advice, and resources. Suskie's writing will encourage hesitant faculty, ease their fears of assessment, and support their development of understanding and skills that can be adapted to their institutional circumstances.

INDEX*

Italicized entries indicate graphic matter.